A Practical
Way to
Get Rich . . .
and Die
Trying

A Practical
Way to
Get Rich . . .
and Die
Trying

A MEMOIR ABOUT
RISKING IT ALL

John Roa

VIKING

VIKING
An imprint of Penguin Random House LLC
penguinrandomhouse.com

LIBRARY OF CONGRESS CATALOGING-IN-PUBLICATION DATA

Names: Roa, John, author.
Title: A practical way to get rich . . . and die trying : a memoir about risking it all / John Roa.
Description: New York : Viking, 2020. |
Identifiers: LCCN 2020020015 (print) | LCCN 2020020016 (ebook) |
ISBN 9781984881229 (hardcover) | ISBN 9781984881236 (ebook)
Subjects: LCSH: New business enterprises. | Entrepreneurship—Psychological aspects. |
Success in business.
Classification: LCC HD62.5 .R583 2020 (print) | LCC HD62.5 (ebook) |
DDC 338/.04092 [B] —dc23
LC record available at https://lccn.loc.gov/2020020015
LC ebook record available at https://lccn.loc.gov/2020020016

Printed in the United States of America
10 9 8 7 6 5 4 3 2 1

DESIGNED BY LUCIA BERNARD

Some names and identifying characteristics have been changed to protect the privacy of the
individuals involved.

For my parents. None of this was your fault. You did great! ☆

Contents

PART TWO: THE TURN

PART THREE: THE PRESTIGE

Introduction

I'm excited to share this story with you. I'm also quite petrified, as I'm about to tell strangers all about my crazy life, wildest proclivities, and darkest secrets.

Well, too late now. So much for being a private person.

At the age of twenty-six, I was dead broke and ready to give up on my life goal of being an entrepreneur. At twenty-nine, I was a millionaire and running one of the fastest-growing companies in America. Two years later, I sold my company and my mind was ruined.

To you, my story may be entertaining, motivational, demotivational, funny, unbelievable, familiar, sad, or absurd. That depends on your perspective. All I can promise you is that it's honest: a true account of how one young man navigated his way through the painful yet powerful lessons of success. It's the type of story I wish I could have read half a lifetime ago as I prepared for my own entrepreneurial journey, rather than yet another whitewashed, bullshit memoir about what reaching the top in business supposedly looks like.

I've always thought of myself as a pretty normal guy. I grew up in the Midwest with three siblings and a loving family. We didn't have a ton of money, but we did have a golden retriever and presents under the Christmas tree. Having my life defined by high-stakes entrepreneurship wasn't exactly my plan. I had never met another entrepreneur in my youth, and, frankly, didn't even know there was a term for people like me, who love hustling, doing deals, solving problems, and taking risks. I dove down that rabbit hole, and what happened next was anything but normal.

For better or worse, society today is defined by tech entrepreneurship. Technology has changed how we communicate, find love, travel down the street, stay in touch with friends, and battle disease. No other industry produces more billionaires and billion-dollar returns. It's virtually the only industry in which anyone with a good idea can go on to change the fabric of the world in a matter of years and become incomprehensibly wealthy.

It's the modern-day gold rush—except that the prospectors of the 1850s knew that when they went west, they likely weren't coming back, at least not with their physical and emotional health intact. Today, we prefer to keep that possibility a secret. No one wants to talk about the price we entrepreneurs pay in the pursuit.

Entrepreneurship is a wide-ranging topic. God bless the ambitious individuals who set up a hot dog stand or take over a small family business, but that's not who I'm talking about in this memoir. My subject is those who go for glory, and are willing to leave limbs on the field in their pursuit. The maniacs who trade safety, sanity, and sensibilities for a shot at becoming rich and even famous. Or, for a chance to permanently change the world.

That's the lens that formed the foundation for this book, that made me ask: What really makes an entrepreneur? What separates us from normal people? Are we really as crazy as we seem? Or is it the current culture of entrepreneurship that forces us to do crazy things to succeed? And finally, what did I really learn from the journey?

This is a raw, behind-the-scenes look at my path to prosperity at a tender age, with *all* of its flaws and absurdity. Other successful entrepreneurs' stories will differ from mine, but based on numerous private conversations with my self-starting brethren, the core themes of what I experienced are far more common than you may think.

Winning in this game isn't necessarily clean, dignified, or healthy, and that must be accepted and acknowledged. My biggest issue with the narrative of success today is that in business, we are pressured to always look strong and godly, even during difficult periods. This quickly becomes a toxic model that aspiring entrepreneurs are forced to emulate, and then when they struggle, which is inevitable, they are led to believe they are the only ones doing so, or that they are somehow doing it wrong because everyone else makes it look so easy and graceful. In every single business memoir I've read, the author somehow makes even the worst aspects of the job sound aspirational.

I believe we could benefit from illuminating the realities of this closely guarded world. Rather than the never-ending books and films that have been carefully manipulated to perpetuate dangerous myths about business and success, I think there should be a candid discussion of some hard truths. Let's talk about why entrepreneurs have 60 percent more mental health issues than the general public, or why the suicide rate among youth in Silicon Valley is four times the national average. Let's talk about the culture that encourages us to risk *everything* in the pursuit of success, and whether that is the right attitude.

The predominant culture in startups today doesn't even try to disguise itself. "Move fast and break things" is the mantra of the startup founder. "Fake it 'til you make it" is our rallying cry. "Do whatever it takes to succeed" is the unspoken golden rule. "No pain, no gain" is motivating only until you consider how toxic that guidance is. Entrepreneurs are incentivized to put personal wellness aside, manipulate the truth, take outsized risk, and cheat where necessary in order to win.

The worst part of this mindset is we also lie to ourselves. We become so accustomed to our perceived worlds that they can become a new reality. We end up believing our own bullshit, further blurring the lines between what is real and not. We exist in a perpetual reality distortion field. This delusion makes us isolate ourselves, ignore warning signs, build on artificial confidence, and push ourselves and the people around us too far. And if things go bad, we are suddenly confronted with the mountain of decisions we shouldn't have made and lies we must face, and only then do we become aware of the consequences.

Imagine being told there is a pot of gold atop a huge mountain in front of you. Even though you can't see the summit, you think to yourself, *I bet I can climb that.* You take no consideration of safety or risk. No gear. No net. Just start climbing. That is entrepreneurship in a nutshell.

This mentality defined my rise to the top and fall to the bottom. While I'm ultimately proud of what I accomplished, there is also a lot to be said about what I learned, the downsides of my lifestyle, and what I would have done differently. Until recently, I never allowed myself to be honest about those things, because I felt an obligation to play the part and not show vulnerability publicly. When asked about my experiences in an interview or onstage at a conference, I would perpetuate the same heroic narratives that everyone else does in business. Often I'd be speaking to young, impressionable people, and I believed this made me sound smart and strong.

I would play the role of the impervious young CEO they all wanted to see. I would hide my humanity and struggles. I refused to show any sign of what I perceived as weakness. I wanted people to aspire to be me. I suppose I still do, but for different reasons. I've chosen to no longer perpetuate the superhero myths of entrepreneurship.

Instead, I now want to embark on a campaign of vulnerability and honesty, in an industry that currently lacks both. What you're about to read is the beginning of that journey, and I hope it makes this book feel a little bit more approachable than others in the genre. I didn't create a well-known, billion-dollar company. I am not famous. I didn't have anyone backing me. I'm just a guy from a suburb in Detroit who fell upward through the world of startups.

The idea of baring my soul to the world is, I admit, unnerving. I worry about the damage it could do to my reputation and relationships—at least from anyone who wants to judge me for my behavior when I was making too much money at too young an age. Or for what it feels like to have a drug- and sex-fueled bender you almost don't wake up from. Or for some of the vile ways mental illness takes hold of your mind as you try to handle the stress and pressure of running a tech company with lightning-fast growth. There were many times I almost buried this book in the ground, but I stopped myself from doing so because of the important discourse I hope it can foster. In order to facilitate those discussions, I've chosen to lead by example. That is why you're now reading this.

This is a true story based on my best recollections over three decades of my life. In some instances, I had to compress or rearrange events to facilitate the narrative. Because hundreds of people involved in my story were innocent bystanders, I've taken certain liberties by changing some names and recreated dialogue to protect their privacy. Others don't deserve that courtesy.

Enjoy.

A Practical
Way to
Get Rich . . .
and Die
Trying

1 | VEGAS (2014)

The maid at the door looked horrified.

I could think of three potential reasons as to why: First, I probably looked like a strung out pirate, staring at her through one twitching, deeply bloodshot eye, the light from the hallway making it far too hard to open the other.

Second, it could have been the smear of dried blood across my stomach. Seemingly, I hoped, from the blistered, fresh tattoo on my forearm, which I had just now noticed.

Third, and most likely, was that I had answered the door stark naked. Despite her best effort, she stared down at my old boy with a sickened look, as if there were a crocodile attached to it, and then probably reconsidered her choice of employment.

This is Vegas. She's seen worse, I thought.

Our eyes remained locked for a few more moments before I shut the door without a word. I felt my way to the Wynn's plush curtains and ripped them open, which sent the midday light flooding into the room. The sun was a knife to the center of my brain, amplifying the pounding in my temples and the toxic feeling in my chest. My mouth tasted evil.

I pondered this bizarre wasteland that had become my all-too-frequent playground of choice. My detachment. I then noticed what looked like the frosted ghost of someone's ass on the window. The two girls in the bed behind me explained that. I suddenly had a flashback to the prior night's hedonistic chaos, to our bodies smashing against that window—the only thing between us and a five-hundred-foot drop—thinking to myself, *I wonder how strong this glass is?* and not being terribly concerned with the answer. There were worse ways to go, I figured.

They lay snoring in a naked tangle on top of the covers, a mess of hair, tattoos, and dried sweat. I couldn't tell you a single thing about them. If I was supposed to feel anything at that moment, I didn't.

I considered the mayhem of the room and then saw the bedside clock, which revealed that I was dangerously close to missing my flight—for the third day in a row. Through fogged vision, I threw my clothes haphazardly into an expensive leather bag, rubbing a tiny pile of cocaine that was left on the table across my gums. As it turned out, I accidentally took one of the girls' dresses with me. I also left behind an $18,000 watch and three shoes.

Back to Chicago. Back to work. Back to my life of organized chaos overlaid with a thick patina of professionalism. Back to my throne as the thirty-year-old CEO of one of the fastest-growing companies in America.

Twelve hours later I was in the back of an ambulance. I knew I was dying.

PART ONE

The Pledge

2 | MOTOR CITY

When I was three years old, my preschool teacher described me to my mother as "mature"—certainly an odd descriptor for a toddler.

As it turns out, she had picked up on my most distinguishable skill, even at that age: my gift of gab. I've always been able to get a quick emotional read on anyone to whom I'm speaking and deliver my message with a ferocious confidence. This skill exists on a scale ranging from charm to manipulation. Even as a child, I would speak to adults as their equal, and pick them apart in the process. I would change my tune for each to get exactly what I wanted.

My mom, for example, would begin reprimanding me for doing something wrong, and only minutes later would be rewarding me, without ever realizing I had orchestrated the entire transition.

I grew up in a suburb of Detroit, Michigan, during the last decade of its glory days. Like all children, I wasn't introspective enough to realize how great my parents were when I was young, which feels like a shame. My mother—what a wonderful woman. She is the living embodiment of all the positive characteristics the world is losing too quickly: a generous heart, unbreakable optimism, and a truly commendable naïveté fostered from her midwestern Americana upbringing. She has red hair, freckles, and blue eyes, all of which give her the appearance, at times, of a Disney character.

My father's from Venezuela, where he worked as an engineer in the oil fields before emigrating north and meeting my mother—his polar opposite—in college. I am convinced that it was my mom's flower-powered, subversive-hippie mindset that drove her toward my dad so that she could bring a dark guy back to her überconservative parents and watch them squirm. My father often told us stories about how during the 1970s he would repeatedly get pulled over in the suburbs of Detroit because he was an immigrant driving a shitty car.

Dad sought to live the American Dream, starting as a union assembly line worker at Chrysler during Detroit's heyday. He spent the next twenty-five years there, working his way up the corporate ladder, until the city burned down. It was easy to admire my dad's work ethic. Out at the crack of dawn, back for dinner. He was learning English at the same time as his kids. Always studying. Always professional. Always on time. If his emotional range was limited to that of a typical Latin American patriarch, my mom more than made up for that.

My older sister, Isabel, represented my first real challenge in life—one of survival. She was seemingly quite content with being the only child, so she spent our first years together trying to dispose of me and return to the status quo. The stories of her attempts are funny but tragic: my being pushed down a flight of metal stairs while still inside a baby walker, being shoved over briefly after taking my first steps. I had to be held down, kicking and screaming, while my MD grandfather stitched my scalp shut after another assassination attempt.

This is the same sister who at twenty years old beat late-stage cancer through a sheer will for life that few could demonstrate. Years later, despite doctors saying it was probably impossible, she had my niece, Margaux, whom I adore with all my life. My sister ultimately became one of my best friends and was the source of many lessons on both life and death.

Our childhood, along with that of our two younger siblings, was a reasonably classic midwestern one. Isabel was popular and ambitious. Andy was the lovable comedian. Maggie, the youngest, was introspective and intelligent. Dad worked, Mom took care of the kids. We went to a good public school and played sports afterward. Pretty normal, pretty boring.

Up until just after my first decade, I was the angel: a teacher's pet, highly advanced in math and science, always well-behaved and "mature," respectful and diligent. When a teacher would phone our home, it was invariably to laud me for some positive behavior she would just "never expect!" from a kid my age.

However, that all came to an end for me around the age of thirteen. A series of events occurred then that would forever shape my attitude, character, and career, spearheaded by two very different friends, Doug and Vince.

3 | DOUG AND THE GUITAR

Doug was the epitome of cool in middle school: good-looking, long blond hair, already wearing ripped jeans and carrying a skateboard around. And of course, showing rapid promise on the guitar, which even at that age attracted the attention of the most popular girls.

This was in fairly stark contrast to myself: tall, lanky, big metal braces on my teeth, and still very much into math. My early growth spurt made me a candidate for sports. I excelled at baseball and ended up in a travel league with a bunch of guys who went on to play in college and the pros. I then discovered lacrosse and became a brutal enforcer in that game until I became too injured to play.

My only other nonnerdy outlet was my love for music, which led to begging Mom for a drum set and lessons. In retrospect, I really should have picked up an instrument you can actually play without a band and doesn't disrupt an entire city block. I would go down to the basement of our house, put a giant amplified speaker next to me, and bang my brains out to Pearl Jam or the Smashing Pumpkins.

This is how I met Doug. He and a few more cool kids were looking to start a band, and because I was the only guy who had drums, a space to practice in, and parents who would put up with that headache, I won a spot in the group by default.

As with most things at that point in my life, I found myself out of my element. Not with the music—there I excelled. Rather, with the social dynamics of my bandmates and their friends. They seemed to share a language I didn't understand. They were *smoking cigarettes*, which to me was just obscene. The boys and girls had figured out what to do with one another, and it was an epidemic. They were stealing forty-ounce bottles of beer from gas stations and hanging out in Detroit's deserted parks.

Detroit in the mid-'90s was as dire a city as America had to offer. The downtown area was virtually lawless, and avoided. A few landmark downtown streets were looked after, but past that, it was one dangerous, run-down cesspool. The aforementioned parks were the hub of gang activity—the makeshift headquarters of the city's degenerates. On a regular day, there would be open drug dealing and drug dealing gone wrong. I saw my first dead body there.

And yes, this is where we yuppie white kids were hanging out, so it isn't a stretch to imagine what came next for me. I tried one of those cigarettes. I drank one of those beers. I took a fancy to one of those girls.

This was the turning point of my adolescence. Dead was the innocent boy, born was the young man, a bit too early. Within a year of meeting Doug, my entire suite of interests changed. Gone was the teacher's pet, the math whiz. Gone was the straitlaced kid with the world on a string.

Phone calls from teachers were now a nightmare for my parents.

"John hasn't been in class in days."

"He failed his last test."

"He isn't going to pass."

Fuck it, I thought. *Why should I go to school? Who are my parents to tell me what to do?*

I went from being considered for advanced placement in college math classes to arriving at my first day of high school tripping on acid. The only real memory I have of that day is my history teacher's skin melting off like a candle as my fingertips grew little flowers.

My parents couldn't understand it. What happened to their perfect son?

Looking back, I know two things to be true.

First, it was ridiculous what we were doing at that age. I owe my parents a serious apology. The fact that we survived is a miracle.

Second, this period of my life did far more good than harm. It unlocked a substantial characteristic that no one had known I possessed: a deep, natural subversiveness. I began to question every standard and norm suburban society shoved down my throat. At this point in time, it made me insufferable to those in authoritative positions, but in years to come, it would be one of my most vital strengths.

At that point another friend, the polar opposite of Doug, entered my life and completed my 180-degree turn. Without knowing it then, he set up what would be my life-or-death journey two decades later.

4 | VINCE AND THE COMPUTER

Dumpy, unpopular, and a bit creepy, Vince was an asshole at the core, though I didn't know it then.

His character wasn't necessarily his fault—he learned much of his behavior from his parents. His mom was a nasty woman who was also a sitting judge for the city of Detroit. His dad was a chain-smoking, beer-bellied deadbeat with a law degree who made his money ambulance chasing, probably off the confidential details from his wife's court cases. Every third word out of both of their mouths was either a racial slur or a swear word, and every other action was physical violence against each other.

Vince pretended he was a natural-born white-collar criminal. He told people he was Italian, because that's what his dad had told him, and it made him sound harder. But he was in fact about as Italian as fucking Olive Garden.

Given his personality, had he been born a century earlier, Vince would have run alcohol and women during Prohibition. A few decades later, he would have been a member of the Vegas mafia. And decades after that, a coked-out stockbroker during Wall Street's prime. Unfortunately for him, he was born in the early '80s in a suburb of Detroit, so he made do with what he had in front of him.

His mindset was that money was more exciting to make when it wasn't completely aboveboard. When we became friends, I am pretty sure his entire income history had been sketchy—from selling mass-produced pirated CDs to off-loading stolen merchandise at pawnshops to participating in shady multilevel marketing schemes. Even though I didn't realize it then, I, too, loved the thrill of pushing the boundaries of the law—albeit not as much as he did. It was intoxicating to try to subvert the institutions that ruled the world.

Vince was also a precocious technology buff. While everyone else was trying to figure out how to turn a Walkman on, he was already building computers, coding, and finding ways for those skills to make him money, on either side of the law.

That's where I came in. It was in these pivotal years that I discovered my own knack for computers. I just seemed to naturally understand them.

I'll never forget when my dad brought home our first family PC, which was given to him at work. Here was this ugly beige tower that weighed about a million pounds, with an equally dumpy monitor, unceremoniously set up in the corner of our living room.

The first thing I did was tear it apart. I was fascinated with being able to see each component of the machine and trying to figure out what function each performed. My method wasn't wholly scientific: I would pull a component out and see what error the computer screamed at me.

ERROR: RAM NOT FOUND.

Ah, so that's the RAM . . .

ERROR: CPU FAN NOT INSTALLED. PROCESSOR IS AT RISK OF OVER-HEATING.

Aha, so *that's* where the CPU is . . .

This went on for months and months. I would dig into system files to understand how the operating system worked. I bought a book on C programming to learn how to write my own applications. I got all the new computer games and played them until I fell asleep on the keyboard. I was addicted.

The computer "broke" an uncountable number of times in my fooling around with it. Generally, I would be able to find a fix. But at some point, my luck ran out, and it just quit turning on. I was dismayed—as was my father. For my strapped-for-cash family, this wasn't great news.

"Broken? What is John doing all day on that stupid computer?" my dad yelled from the couch. "He should be watching TV!"

Mom helped me disassemble the whole apparatus and pack it into the car. The boxes of hardware, wires, keyboard, mouse, and monitor took up the larger part of the trunk and almost threw out our backs getting them there.

We drove to our local computer repair shop, complete with a nicotine-stained drop ceiling and the exact type of individual you'd expect to be working at such a place: a big fat guy with a ridiculous little beard and a God complex, because he could fix computers.

I walked each piece in, one by one, and laid them on his operating table as if I were delivering a sick puppy to the vet. I remember it being freezing cold and thinking how absurd it was that it took all of this to fix something as simple as . . . whatever it was that I broke. Likely the power supply was fried. I just needed him to pop a new one in.

"What seems to be the problem?" God asked.

"My computer won't turn on," I said.

"Okay," he muttered as he started to label each piece with a sticky note and load it on a large metal shelf.

I was dumbfounded. Why wasn't he trying to fix it?

"Sir . . ." I said in my adult voice. "How long is this going to take?"

"We are pretty backed up right now. You'll get a call in two or three weeks."

Two or three weeks? Are you fucking kidding me?

"Sir . . ." I started again, voice shaking. I was trying not to think about what I would do during this eternity if this wasn't a sick joke. "How could this possibly take that long to fix? I'm sure it is a simple problem."

"That's not the point, kid. We are very busy. See all of these machines?" he said as he swung his arm behind him to what looked like an electronics graveyard. "They are all in line to be fixed before yours."

It hit me over the head like a bat: My first trigger. A problem that I couldn't accept, and one that I felt compelled to fix myself.

Years later, I would identify this incident as when I realized I was an entrepreneur.

5 | ONSITE OPERATIONS

On the way home from the computer repair shop, I was having some kind of meltdown. I was going to be without my beloved computer for weeks, and had no ability to get another one. Aside from band practice a few times a week and skipping school to smoke weed, I had nothing else going on in my life. This was tragic.

I can vividly recall peppering Mom with questions in the car on the way home to try to understand this travesty.

"Why is it going to take so long?"

"I don't know," she said.

"Why couldn't he just fix it right then and there?" I shrieked.

"Because other people were in line before us," she explained.

"I don't *care*. I am sure it will take him a few *minutes* to fix. Couldn't we have paid more for it to be quicker? Couldn't someone have just come to our house to do it?"

And there it was. My little mind started whirring. I thought about the stacks and stacks of sad computers waiting to be serviced. The inefficiency of the system upset me. Even with my basic knowledge at that point, I knew that most "repairs" involved either curing a simple virus, replacing one of the commonly malfunctioning pieces of hardware, reinstalling an operating system, or just showing a clueless user how to do something.

Shit, I thought. *I can do that. And I don't need a dirty shop to do it in. I'll just walk into their home and solve their problem without them having to go through all the fuss.*

Just like that, my first company, Onsite Operations, was born.

I didn't waste a second. With fifty dollars that I begged my father for, I got to work. First, I went to the electronics store to get a pager on a prepaid plan. At the office supply shop I ordered the cheapest flyers they offered with the tagline "Computer Repair—We Come to YOU!," my pager number, and a website address. I hadn't ever made a website, but I reckoned I could get one up and running before any customer would go to it. These were the early days of the internet, after all.

I then tasked my little brother with walking up and down every street in our neighborhood, slipping flyers into mailboxes for hours and hours until they were gone. He must have hit three hundred houses. A fair trade for his using my paintball gun, even if he was unwittingly breaking the law.

The very next day my pager danced on the table with my first prospective customer. I went down to the basement where it was quiet, prepared my big-boy voice, and called back.

"This is Onsite Operations," I said. "How can I help you?"

My heart was hammering. The rush of the moment was so strong I realized I wasn't listening to the woman's response.

"Sorry, bad connection," I said. "Can you repeat that?"

"My kids have been using our computer, and suddenly we can't access the internet," she said. "It just pops up all this crap and won't let us surf to any websites. It was a miracle we got your flyer!"

A miracle, indeed. This was simple—just removing some basic spyware.

"No problem, ma'am. We can take care of this for you. I can be there in less than thirty minutes. Our fee is fifty dollars," I said, with a huge smile on my face. It couldn't be *this* easy.

"Fifty dollars? Okay, that's fine. We are on Berkshire in the Park," the wealthy woman said.

This was my big moment, and I had prepared for it. While I was getting my flyers made, I had also purchased an official-looking metal binder, like the ones cable repair guys carried. I also bought generic three-ply receipts with carbon copy centers.

I put them in my book bag along with a few floppy disks containing debugging software, a screwdriver, and a magnifying glass, though the final item was just for show. I was coming off my teenage growth spurt, and conveniently fit into my father's clothing, or so I thought. I borrowed a pair of loose khakis, an overstarched white button-down shirt, and was ready to roll. My confidence couldn't have been higher. *I got this.*

I headed east, toward the large, perfectly manicured homes of Grosse Pointe Park. I knocked on the door, metal binder in hand, and firmly shook the hand of the middle-aged woman who answered.

She considered me quizzically, apparently trying to gauge if I was actually a kid or just looked like one. Here I was, clearly dressed in someone else's clothing, with a baby face, metal braces, and a book bag. But I exuded professionalism. She was in good hands.

I was out in less than thirty minutes, with one highly satisfied customer and a check for fifty dollars, made out to Onsite Operations. Aside from employing my younger siblings at a lemonade stand when they were toddlers or getting paid to do errands for my dad, I had never made money before. Especially not *real* money like this. I had struck gold.

I immediately walked to the local bank where I'd watched my parents deposit checks and strode to the teller's window. I slid the check across the counter with a smirk that announced I had figured something out the whole world would love to know.

The teller looked at the check and asked a question I didn't expect, "Who is Onsite Operations?"

"Onsite Operations is *my* company," I told him with great satisfaction.

"Does your company have a bank account?" he asked.

That one stumped me. A bank account?

". . . no," I said, still trying to act cool. Maybe this was a test. "I just want my fifty dollars."

"Sorry, *sir*," he said, amused. "This check is made out to a business, so that business must have an account in order to cash this check. And you must be eighteen years old to do that. I am sorry. Maybe ask your parents."

I was dismayed. But not deterred. I just had to make one change to my business: Onsite Operations was from then on a cash-only business. Screw these banks.

6 | ASCENSION

As I began to grow my business, I was also getting high and playing music with Doug and hanging out with Vince, honing my technical skills. His basement became our makeshift headquarters. We set up an array of computers and servers and would spend countless hours down there seeing what the capabilities of these machines were.

I couldn't tell you exactly where the money for this setup came from, but there were all sorts of things that made the basement unique for the times. A dedicated T1 line routed straight to the basement, providing lightning-fast internet. A half dozen phone lines enabled us to connect modem-to-modem. And there was as much soda and pizza as we could hope for.

The power we had from this command center felt limitless.

We excelled at computer games because no one could match our hardware.

We had half the town's computers hacked because we thought we were smarter than everyone else.

We took advantage of the internet's infancy with clever tricks that paid some serious dividends.

One of our most memorable creations was a virus that was coded into a simple game of *Pong* we would send to our friends. They thought they were playing a cheeky little game we had created. What we were actually doing was installing a powerful backdoor into their operating system without their knowledge, one that would give us root access to their system. This meant that anything they did sitting in front of their computer, we could see from our own secret lair. We could watch what they typed; we could type for them. This led to some quite funny times, like when we kept injecting *fart* into a friend's midterm paper while he was writing it, and having him call us in a panic to help fix the problem. It also led to some quite unfunny times, like when we found out a friend's father was trafficking drugs out of his garage for a cartel, or that another friend's brother had an affinity for child porn. I didn't say I was proud of this.

I'll never forget our first real scam. Microsoft had recently introduced software licensing and cloud-based digital rights management, making it much more difficult to share software among peers. But we hackers fundamentally refused to pay for software, and a massive, worldwide pirating industry emerged. Software was originally traded on FTP servers housed at large corporations. (This was what that dork in IT whose job it was to fix your office telephone would do in the basement when no one was looking.) The brokering of these files was conducted on the world's largest multiplayer chat room, called Internet Relay Chat or IRC. This became our home.

Our IRC personas were famous—we had built bots that acted as brokers for pirated software, and the servers on which we transacted were only for the elite. Our counterparts were the world's most well-respected hackers from distant lands like Sweden and Iran. If you knew what you were doing, you could find virtually anything on these servers, from expensive software to unreleased music albums to porn to bomb-making recipes. I didn't say I was proud of this, either.

As the capitalists we were, our goal wasn't to simply trade and "free the internet" like our libertarian cohorts. Instead, we wanted to make money, and make lots of it.

A new type of marketing had become popular online at this time—affiliate marketing. Companies interested in generating leads for their products or services would award serious sums of money to people who could get others to fill out a form or buy a product. All I had to do, for example, was send someone a link with my unique code; they would fill out a form with their name, email, address, et cetera, and I would be paid. Simple, and highly exploitable.

Our first plan to exploit this method was a bit too simplistic. We figured we could use our network of hacked computers to produce fake leads by logging into them, remotely filling out the forms, and getting rewarded. The problem here was the "payout" system: it was programmed to flag leads all coming from a particular geographic area (e.g., our town) and would not qualify most of them. However, we did receive a check for about one hundred dollars. So, we knew the system worked.

Then we got cunning. We had thousands of people per day from around the world downloading illegal software from our army of FTP servers. We figured there must be a way to get these guys to fill out the form in exchange for their downloads.

It was ingenious, really. We locked our files so they couldn't be used until the affiliate form was filled out.

The next day, we woke up to $4,000 in authorized leads in our payment account—in ten hours. This was working a little *too* well.

Despite our shrewd plan on the front end, we hadn't fully thought through the back end. The account we had registered with as an affiliate contained real information: name, address, Social Security number. If they caught on to our scam, it would take a fraction of a second to have us in handcuffs.

As it turned out, Mr. Piece of Shit was just upstairs, taking a break from doing nothing, and had some sound guidance for us: Register a post office box with false information at a downtown bank and use that as the mailing address. Sign up for a new affiliate account with the matching false information (remarkably, they didn't verify anything) and keep a low profile when picking up checks. If anyone cared enough to look into this, it would take them a long time to put a case together. We easily had months to run this scam.

And run it we did. We dialed down the distribution network so as to not bankrupt these companies paying us our commissions or to sound any alarms. Our accounts grew, and as if we were playing out a scene from a heist movie, Vince's father would drive us to the bank, where we would go pick up our monthly check wearing hoodies and deposit it for cash at another bank down the street. We suddenly had cash to not only continue funding our little operation but also to spend on anything we wanted. The freedom that cash provided was intoxicating. Vince bought a gold watch. I opted for another paintball gun, a hip new color-screen cell phone, and the fastest gaming computer money could buy.

We ran this scam for a handful of months, and in the grand scheme of things, it didn't make us a ton of money, especially after splitting it three ways. But it set the stage for far more ambitious ploys.

Unlike my coconspirators, I had an equal appreciation for legitimate business as for illegitimate. This respect was heightened after I returned home from school one day to find three federal law enforcement agents in suits sitting at the kitchen table with my parents, waiting to "have a quick chat" with me about some suspicious activity from my home IP address. They were here, it turned out, because I had accidentally hacked into a bank months prior during one of my phishing expeditions. They weren't even aware of the scam that had netted me and Vince all this money.

I was scared; visions of steel bars and prison tattoos flashed through my brain. I clenched my jaw and tried to persuade everyone in the room that I didn't know I had done anything wrong, I was just a kid experimenting with the new internet!

My parents were dismayed. This is what their little boy had become—straight outlaw. Can you imagine thinking your teenage kid is on prison's doorstep? My shame matched my fear. However much I denied any knowledge of the accusations, they knew better. They still vigorously defended their son, though. My mom was on the verge of tears. My dad was giving me that Homer Simpson look, as if he were going to strangle me as soon as our visitors left the room.

Mercifully, the "investigation" didn't extend past this encounter. But I was scared fucking straight, and my parents knew it, which was enough penance. Time to go legit—mostly. I was sixteen years old.

7 | EXPANSION

As I worked my way through early high school at Grosse Pointe South High, I became fully focused on running Onsite Operations. The school had a reputation for pumping out star athletes and academics alike, and even for being the setting for the eponymous John Cusack movie. Its campus looked more like that of an Ivy League college than of a high school.

I was continuing to barely pass classes and to get into all sorts of trouble. We tried to steal expensive wireless microphones from our auditorium and pawn them off so we could buy weed. We got caught and suspended from school. We shoveled huge mounds of snow into the principal's office as an end-of-year prank. I took the fall for that one, knowing I would be the best at getting out of it, which I did.

I hated school so much that I wheeled and dealed with my teachers to just get through it. I had no idea that dropping out was really an option, or I would have done so. Instead, I figured out various loopholes to diminish school's interference with my business.

The first was a little-known program that permitted students with part-time jobs to substitute their employment for two classes' worth of credit per semester. Basically, you could work half the day, and go to class half the day. This program was designed for students who had the burden of helping to support their families. It certainly wasn't intended for the purposes for which I planned to use it, but I exploited it anyway. My employer, Onsite Operations, produced very official-looking time card reports of the hours I was putting in.

This freed up time to really focus on the business, which was thriving. I had far more work than I could handle, and I was filling up entire weeks' worth of appointments. I was still being a malcontent with Vince and playing in the band with Doug, but I quit drinking and drugs.

This, ironically, led to my second school-thwarting scheme. I found out through my guidance counselor that a number of elective after-school programs counted toward class credit. Especially if you had a higher position in the organization, you could offset up to two classes per semester. Shortly after learning this, I became the president of Students Against Drunk Driving.

I had now systematically eliminated two-thirds of my class load, while still receiving full credit. I strategically booked my other classes so I would need to make it to campus only for the first half of two days per week—the equivalent of one full school day.

Nothing could stop me now. This hustle was intoxicating.

My parents kept an eye on me, uncertain whether to be proud or worried. I was running my own business, making respectable money, and seemed to have found something that I loved. On the other hand, I had effectively dropped out of high school and was addicted to computers. This was before young entrepreneurship and technology were in vogue. It must have been hard for them to try to give me the space I needed, while worrying that I was getting lost.

I was very good at making the business look much larger than a one-man band. The website looked like that of a large corporation—pretty much because I had ripped off the design of dell.com, which was the gold standard at the time. I now had advertisements in the local Yellow Pages and even a billboard hanging up on the busiest street in town.

I had also gotten around that pesky bank issue. A marvelous mechanism called a DBA, or Doing Business As, allowed me to function with a business name, without needing to actually have an incorporated legal entity. And the best part of all was that I didn't have to be eighteen to set one up. Now I could deposit checks made out to Onsite Operations into my personal checking account. Done and dusted.

With all the interest in my services, I realized my only limiting factor was that I was doing this alone. I needed help operating the business, answering phones, and scheduling appointments.

I had to find a place to accommodate my new employees, so I set out to find some office space. I walked into a real estate brokerage in town and boldly declared that I needed an office—*stat!* I can only imagine what those old brokers must have thought when they saw a sixteen-year-old in a shitty car with an ONSITE OPERATIONS magnet stuck to the side pull up and ask to be shown furnished office space. But I didn't care. I knew what I was doing.

Within a few days, I found a little space above a coffee shop in our local downtown, conveniently across the street from my bank. They had a few desks left behind by a past tenant that were perfect for me. I asked if I could pay the first year's rent up front, in cash. They had absolutely no problem with that and even allowed me to sign the lease personally.

Now I just had to find someone to help me. The obvious choice was Vince, given that he was the only person I knew who could match my knowledge of computers. He had had a front-row seat to my little business venture since day one, and had nudged me a few times to ask how he could get involved. Even though he was a friend, I didn't wholly trust him, because I had watched him skim and scam hundreds of people by that point. But I didn't really have another option, and what was the worst that could happen?

He jumped aboard, and our productivity went through the roof. His skills were on the marketing and operations side—helping to keep business coming in the door, which allowed me more time at the customers' homes. He helped hire a secretary to answer the phones and also helped with the more difficult repairs that came back to the office. We split the profits. For a moment everything was wonderful.

A few months later I had a conversation with a business-minded family friend, which seemed innocuous at the time, but in fact, changed everything.

"John," he said to me. "Your parents told me about your success. Very impressive." He then asked, "Have you incorporated this business?"

"Thank you," I answered, surprised that my parents were this tuned into my little venture. "And no. I can't incorporate until I'm eighteen. So, I plan to then," I said confidently.

He looked at me a bit skeptically and asked, "Are you paying taxes on your income?"

Taxes? I had obviously heard of them. And until then, would have classified them as one of those unpleasant things you have to deal with when you're old, like back pain.

"No . . ."

"Oh, John," he said, stopping me. "This isn't good."

I then got a crash course on how taxes work. Who knew!

He told me that I was probably safe, because the IRS doesn't generally audit teenagers, but I had better get this thing buttoned up and prepare to file the following year. Doing so was a simple process, he explained: Just pop down to the county clerk's office with my mom, have her register the business, get myself an Employer Identification Number, and at the end of the year, find a good accountant to help me file and write off expenses.

I took *almost* all that advice, bar one important piece: Rather than bringing my mom with me, who I figured would complicate the process somehow, I asked Vince, who at eighteen was a year older than me, to register the business. We were partners, after all.

8 | CONNIVANCE

Some months had gone by when I arrived at the office as if it were any other day. The only person there was Vince, who had a sheepish look on his face. This wasn't unusual—he almost always looked somewhere between nervous and constipated. But I could sense something was wrong.

"Hey, John," he said, quietly. "I have to talk to you about something."

"What's going on, Vince?" I asked apprehensively.

"Yeah, um, well, I've been talking to my dad. He doesn't think you are doing a very good job at running this company," he said. "He thinks we will be better off doing it on our own."

What was he talking about? Doing *what* on their own?

"I'm not sure what you mean," I said, trying to keep my voice steady. "This is *my* company. You work for *me*."

And then it hit me.

"No . . . actually it's *my* company. I registered it, remember?" he said, feebly.

I did remember. This couldn't be.

"I am sorry," he said. His voice was part defiance, part shame. "We're going to take it from here. This is your half of the money," he said, handing me a thin white envelope.

Another reality hit me. When we had incorporated, I rolled everything from my personal bank account into the business bank account. Everything I had made running Onsite Operations was in that account. While I didn't know exactly what that kind of money would look like in cash, I knew it had to be quite a bit larger than the envelope that he handed me.

I sat in my car and cried, and cried some more. I called my mom, who did her best to comfort me, bless her, but it was no use. There was nothing anyone could have said then to make me feel better. I had just been betrayed by my best friend. My company had been stolen from me, along with all my money. This wasn't just a matter of losing a business. It was losing a piece of my very soul, ripped out of me.

Even though it hardly mattered, I opened the envelope, and then it hit me harder. As I suspected, he had given me a tiny fraction of what I estimated was in the bank account.

My little heart was broken. I considered throwing the envelope out the window, out of spite. But I had worked too hard for that money. I felt a dark, stirring energy welling up inside me that I had never felt before. I sat there until the emotion drained out of me and I felt numb.

9 | HUSTLE

My oath to never start another business lasted a month. During yet another after-school detention, I overheard my chemistry teacher venting to a colleague that they had lost the DJ for the junior prom, which was in a week. Despite their ludicrously high offer of $2,000 for providing only a few hours of music, they didn't have any takers.

"Mr. McGuire—I'll do it!" I said as soon as he hung up the phone, almost knocking over my chair in my rush to talk to him.

He looked at me quizzically. "Do what?"

"DJ prom," I said, smiling wide.

"You're a DJ?" he asked, with appropriate skepticism. He had more than enough reasons not to trust me.

"Yes," I said. "Well, no, not technically. But I'm sure we can do it. Doug and I. We have almost all the equipment we need from our band. And we will rent what we don't have. I assure you, we'll do a great job. Two thousand dollars. Do we have a deal?" I asked, holding out my hand.

He hesitated and then shook it with a very odd expression on his face. These are the exchanges I look back on and wonder, *What the fuck were they thinking?* Who would hire an inexperienced trou-blemaker to DJ the school prom and pay him thousands of dollars to do so? How did I get people to agree to this stuff?

I rehearsed the speech in my head as I drove to Doug's house. Over a cigarette, I would confidently declare we were now DJs. SouthSide DJ, more specifically, a name I believe I pulled from a Santana song I was listening to on the drive.

Doug's pragmatic brain immediately went to the details and al-most made me question what I had agreed to: We didn't have most of the gear we would need. We needed lights and a way to control them. We had absolutely no idea what kind of music to play . . . and where would we even get it? Was it legal to play burned CDs?

"You're fucking insane . . ." he said.

I heard only surmountable problems, aside from that whole in-sanity bit. He went on and on but in the end, agreed. We did DJ our own junior prom. And a hundred other gigs after that, including Mr. McGuire's own wedding.

From then on, I found myself *always* hustling some new idea. Re-selling paintball guns. Installing car audio systems. Designing web-sites. If I could trade it, arbitrage it, service it, refer it, or distribute it, I was interested.

Entrepreneurship is a strong drug, and I was clearly a junkie. If I'm honest, perhaps some of the hustle was to wash away the pain from what Vince had done to me.

I did end up hearing he ran my little business for years after he took it from me. He also emailed me a decade and a half later to apologize and admit how bad of an influence his father was in his life. I still haven't quite reconciled with myself whether that makes me feel better or worse about the whole incident.

JOHN ROA

10 | HEADING WEST

Remarkably, I graduated from high school (with a 2.1 GPA) and enrolled in college, primarily for my parents' benefit. As any children of immigrants can attest, formal education is a nonnegotiable, as it is considered the only path toward career success. Despite knowing in my heart that college wasn't for me, I simply couldn't disappoint my father.

I figured I should put those years in front of a computer screen to good use, so I applied to the computer science program at Lawrence Technological University, a private school you wouldn't have heard of unless you paid a lot of attention to advertisements on the sides of buses in Detroit. I got in immediately, which should tell you a lot.

The fallout with Vince had taken a lot of wind out of my sails. It also led to my first noted bout of depression, which was instantly met with prescription medication being hurled at me by the family doctor. Even at that age, I didn't like the idea of taking pills, so I stored them away, hoping I'd never feel that sad again.

I had also lost some of my love for computers, except for one strange outlet I had found to consume my nerdy mind: competitive video gaming. By then computers had become powerful enough and games sophisticated enough that they had become tests of true skill, rather than just an endurance test of who could sit in front of a screen the longest. They drew upon the same natural advantages used in athletic sports: reflexes, motor skills, communication, teamwork, strategy, mental toughness.

After MTV aired a documentary about the first kid to make a million dollars by winning gaming tournaments, the world woke up to the industry, and it made its way to the mainstream. Nerds would show up at "LAN Centers"—vacated retail spaces in strip malls with tables, high-speed internet connections, and lots of caffeinated beverages—to game against other nerds for hours on end, or create teams to game on larger stages. As the industry matured, these teams were outfitted with coaches, practice routines, custom hardware, logos, sponsors, and celebrityism. Fans followed their every move and stood in line for autographs. I'll never forget when Subway started pasting their logo on these kids' shirts as if they were NASCAR drivers.

During the countless hours of gaming, friendships were formed with other faceless gamers, whom you spent more time talking to than your own friends and family. One such relationship I formed was with a Los Angeles–based kid named Ryan. In the virtual world, he was a bit of a star: an accomplished professional gamer and leader of a respectable team. Plus, he was from LA, a place the movies had carefully crafted for me as the modern Sodom and Gomorrah, which in my mind made him extra cool.

Ryan and I would discuss gaming and business in our free time, and a few months later he invited me to come to LA to attend E3, the Electronic Entertainment Expo, the world's largest and most provocative gaming conference. Basically the Super Bowl for dorks. These were either very different times, or my parents had by now simply given up on me. Today the notion of a nineteen-year-old traveling across the country to meet up with someone he met on the internet has all of the makings of a *20/20* investigative special. But I did it. And it changed everything.

E3 was a bizarre playground of supernerds and ~~strippers~~ models paid to fulfill our deepest teenage cosplay fantasies. *Is that Zelda with huge boobs?! Is that Princess Peach with huge boobs?!* These women were known as "Booth Babes" and were a staple of E3, until they were finally banned years later. They stood in front of the booths luring the gawking crowds toward new game releases, hardware, and contests. They were there to separate us from our money. Lucky for me, I didn't have any to give them.

What I did have was a new friend in Ryan, who turned out to be my double. He had an entrepreneurial brain that matched my own, a love for gaming, and an uncanny ability to get people to listen to him. We were even the same age. I had never met anyone so like me before. For the first time, I felt accepted, and perhaps even *cool.*

Over a round of overpriced energy drinks outside the Staples Center, we talked about competitive gaming and where we saw an opportunity. That conversation kicked off what would become the most important pivot of my life.

11 | ISAAC THE DESIGNER

Ryan liked me because I had a lot more technical knowledge than him and shared his vision for the future of competitive gaming. Our idea was to create a professional gaming, or eSports, media brand, to try to take advantage of what was clearly going to be a global phenomenon. We called it WiredLabs.

I returned to Michigan all fired up about this new opportunity, only to be reminded that I had in fact enrolled in college and classes were starting the following week. As I had in high school, I figured I could find loopholes to complete my courses with the least amount of effort possible. These were computer classes, after all.

For the most part the computer science department at Lawrence Tech became a comfortable place to work on WiredLabs. Class grades were based entirely on the final exam, which I expected I could get at least a passing C on without having to study or prepare. Ignoring the lecturer at the front of the room, I would bury my head in my laptop and work remotely with Ryan, who had pulled together a bunch of other gamer kids with complementary skills to complete our squad.

This virtual dream team would come together at all hours of the day and night, between college courses and full-time jobs, to craft what we believed was our meal ticket to fame and fortune. I had maneuvered my way to the number two spot in the group, behind CEO Ryan, as Executive Vice President Johnny. This title was wholly meaningless, as we didn't have a president to be "vice" of, nor any direct reports to be an executive over, but it was what we thought the next role behind CEO should be.

I also decided to go by Johnny, because John was just so not edgy, and certainly didn't match my newly donned ripped jeans and frost-tipped hair.

Our goal was to launch our flagship product, the *Amped News Network*. This was to be a full-blown online media outlet, covering the happening world of eSports as if we were ESPN. We "hired" writers and editors to create content. We "hired" artists and developers to put our platform together. By "hired" I mean we didn't pay anyone a dime, didn't have any paperwork, and had a loose mutual understanding of potential future shared success, if we ever got there.

My role in the group was to manage the designers and developers building the platform. The developers were simple enough to handle: I could speak their language, review their code, and even jump in and write a few lines where need be.

The designers were another story. I didn't have any artistic sense whatsoever and no appreciation for anyone who did. I got that they could make my code look pretty, but I wasn't sure how important that really was, especially when weighed against their missed deadlines and prima donna attitudes.

Then, a guy named Isaac came along and changed my life forever.

Isaac was an odd kid from Alaska. His last name was Wooten, which was kind of perfect. Sir Isaac Wooten.

Online, his nickname was Levid; he was a highly regarded professional gamer who had made a reputation for himself designing websites for all the best teams. As part of our little cohort, he was tasked with leading the design of *Amped*.

To say I didn't initially value his skill would be an understatement. This was around 2003 when the only people who used Macs were hipsters, and tech-focused Microsoft ruled the world. I thought of design as an artsy-fartsy discipline that was just putting pretty colors on top of the real work, the engineering and programming. This was also during the second generation of the internet, after the dot-com era had solidified its existence but when websites were still solely created to show that a company was legitimate. Pure function, no form.

Enter Isaac, and the neurotic weirdos like him. These guys were seeing the future in real time. They were following a process of product development completely foreign to us techies: design first, code later. They advocated that the experience of using a website should be thoughtful, beautiful, and pleasant. And therefore, it should be built completely around the human beings for whom we wanted to create that experience. They were thinking of issues like workflows, customer personas, and analyzing color psychology. I didn't understand any of it, and while I had a natural resistance to it, given how much time it added to the process, I could instinctively feel there was something very special happening here.

We finally got around to launching *Amped*, months behind schedule, to incredible fanfare. We instantly became the gold standard in our industry and stood out among our competitors. There weren't substantial material differences between us and the other guys. Our content was good; so was theirs. Our stats were accurate; so were theirs. Our media was timely; so was theirs. But I had a true epiphany: users were choosing *Amped* because they *loved the experience*. It was *enjoyable* to use our site, unlike those of our competitors. It took seeing high-quality user-experience design in the wild to fully understand it, but once I did, I was hooked. A switch had flipped in my mind, permanently. Design ruled the world—not technology. My focus now became not *how*, but *why*. I spent my free time studying the design-first mentality, from legendary industrial designers like Dieter Rams and Charles and Ray Eames to agencies like IDEO and innovative companies like Apple, who were just then bringing design to the mainstream. The key was getting inside the brains of the customer. We had to figure out what they wanted, even if they didn't know it, by digging down into their psyches and sussing out their innate desires, unmet needs, and motivations.

While undergoing this spiritual transformation, I was also approaching finals time at school. It only dawned on me as I was preparing to head to campus for the test that I had not paid any attention whatsoever the entire semester. I hadn't done homework. I hadn't listened to the lectures. I hadn't even gotten around to buying the textbook. All I really knew was that the test was going to be about advanced system design, because that was the name of the class.

It goes without saying, I failed, bad. I wasn't invited to return to that school.

My father was mortified. Not pursuing higher education was a mortal sin in his eyes. Trying to run some little gaming company was not a valid excuse. After a brief negotiation, I enrolled at Wayne State University in Detroit and signed up for the most basic courses with the lowest class load permitted. Conveniently, Doug was also going to that school, so I had someone to cheat off.

As poorly as my educational journey was going, the business was growing fast. The (still unpaid) team had expanded to over fifty people, all working remotely around the country. We even had our own booth at E3 the following year.

12 | WIREDLABS

With Doug's help, I passed my first college semester. I didn't really care, but it did make me feel better to know there could be an end to it all. I fucking hated school. I can remember sitting in a giant lecture hall, literally holding my eyes open, as a professor eight hundred yards away droned on about thermodynamics or the Italian Renaissance or something equally mind-numbing. After a while my vision would start to wobble and I had no choice but to take a catnap on the desk.

After the rapid ascent of WiredLabs in its first year, things naturally slowed down, but we still made impressive progress, especially given that we were a large group of volunteers. My role had shifted to primarily overseeing the designers even more than the developers to expand our offerings. I also began working with Ryan on the advertising sales, which is where I felt most at home.

Nothing has ever come so naturally to me as business sales. It was just so *easy* for me to persuade someone they wanted what I was selling—and while it helped that we had a great product to sell, in the end, it didn't really matter.

Mere seconds after walking into a room or getting on a conference call, I could write a dissertation on my opponent, and know what it would take to win. Once you knew that, how could you lose?

I found the process to be a game of psychological chess, and most opponents didn't know the rules.

Yeah, I said "opponents." And I said "win," and "lose." Don't let anyone fool you. Business is one big game.

And *fuck* was I good at it. It became a bit addictive to close deals, and the anonymity of our virtual company gave me an advantage. On the phone, I took advantage of my deep voice, strong command of the business vernacular, and ability to deliver my pitch with the conviction of Churchill. Virtually, at least, WiredLabs appeared to be an exclusive, growing enterprise with which the other side should be honored to be doing business.

In person . . . it was a bit harder. While I felt like an adult, and had certainly had some experiences that made me grow up quickly, I simply couldn't hide a young face. When I met someone with whom I had previously done business via email or phone in person, I could tell they felt slighted.

This is who I let beat me up on that deal? He's just a kid! I could see them thinking. It didn't matter. I may not have looked the part yet, but I knew this was my calling. Doing deals. Building businesses. Dreaming big.

Running WiredLabs exposed me to an entirely new side of the world. We hosted events in major cities around the country, including Las Vegas, Austin, New York, and Dallas. We helped manufacture products and white-labeled gear. I learned about supply chains and manufacturing.

Ryan had brought in a guy named Stuart to our team, because he had a rich dad who was willing to invest in our little venture, so we could afford to fly to conferences and pay for web hosting. This was the first time I saw how ugly it can be having investors. Not that any of the money was flowing to me. I was still effectively a volunteer, living on student loans. We had small bits of advertising revenue coming in, but it was being funneled straight back in to run servers and cover expenses.

Friends and family didn't understand exactly what I was doing, and I was perfectly fine with that. But this made real life, like college, that much more painful. Every moment I forced myself to listen to another professor ramble on about algebraic functions or chemical nomenclature, was another moment I couldn't do what I loved.

13 | KALAMAZOO

In retrospect, it's easy to say I just should have dropped out of college, but there was still no proof I wouldn't have to fall back on my education if I ultimately failed as an entrepreneur, and I still wanted to do right by my parents.

After a very painful two semesters at Wayne State, though, I knew I had to make a change. I was now twenty years old, with only one year of college under my belt, and aside from the satisfaction I got from WiredLabs, I felt as if the rest of life were passing me by. My friends were all studying abroad, throwing crazy frat parties, and experimenting with different lifestyles. I was living in the attic of an ugly house in Detroit, speaking on headphones to colleagues thousands of miles away, watching my waistline expand, and ultimately questioning my decisions more and more.

I started looking at options for a different school, which were few, given that I had to stay in-state to avoid more overly expensive tuition, and my academic record of having failed out of one school and fumbled through another wasn't exactly Ivy League–worthy.

I settled on Western Michigan University in Kalamazoo. Given the economic turmoil at that time and the university's local competition, it would be an understatement to say WMU had lax entry requirements. It seemed to specialize in the most boring business programs they could conjure up, like Supply Chain Logistics or Business Management. But amazingly they offered a bachelor's degree in Sales. Who knew?

I was accepted for the upcoming fall program, and my excitement grew as I began planning my transition. I visited the campus and looked for housing. Through a friend in Detroit, I had one contact at the school—an accomplished athlete named Josh, who lived with a few other guys in what I considered to be a luxury townhouse near campus. In a stroke of fortuitous timing, one of the guys was moving out, so I quickly snapped up the room.

I made the move a month before the semester started, so I could get a feel for campus life. Productivity on WiredLabs waned a *bit* as I began learning the fine art of the beer bong and dressing up in drag for a frat party. It felt good. I had to admit there was more to life than just business, and that there was a way to enjoy it all.

As it turned out, and contrary to its admission requirements, WMU took its business program *seriously*. And had packed it with wildly smart professors and students. On the first day of classes I strolled in hungover and casual and encountered a group of well-dressed, eager students. That guy I saw vomiting in the bushes over the weekend was now in a blazer, talking about his summer internship at Goldman. The girl who I'm sure I was doing body shots off two nights prior was in heels and reading glasses, head down with another student planning out their study sessions.

Holy shit.

The professor walked in and the room went silent, aside from the sound of books opening and syllabi being fanned out.

Where on earth did they get those?

The next three months were a master class in humility. I was way behind my peers in terms of formal business training, and my entrepreneurial intelligence helped little in this setting. Not least, my struggles to learn in a traditional academic setting continued. Unlike at my two previous schools, though, I was determined to apply myself and succeed. And doing so ended up becoming one of my greatest life challenges thus far.

Each class piled on the workload and demanded excellence. Professors with blindingly impressive histories blasted through all my bullshit and held my feet to the fire, even more than they did the other students. My tricks and charm were worthless here. Despite the difficulties, I inched my way through it all, if always with barely passing grades. I had won the favor of a few professors, mostly due to my entrepreneurial story. They occasionally showed leniency if I had to take a test remotely or missed class due to being in Los Angeles with WiredLabs.

And, for the first time since middle school, I was actually learning something. There was no way I could be taught the foundational skills of sales—those were baked deep in my psyche. But some of the lessons about negotiation, presenting, and presence were valuable, even if I was somewhat of a mockery to the educational system.

14 | DOWN AGAIN

Meanwhile, two things were happening at WiredLabs that began to concern me.

First, I found myself far less connected to the project than I had been during the first couple of years. It just felt as if I were drifting away. I wasn't driven like I had been, putting every waking moment into it. I'd settle in for a night of work, and then an invitation to a party or a text message from a girl was all it would take to divert me.

Second, I had a sinking feeling that Ryan, my business partner, was also drifting away from me. For almost two years we hadn't gone more than a day without talking and brainstorming and pushing the business forward. For much of this time, he was unquestionably the person to whom I was closest. I'd stay in the attic of his mother's house whenever I was in Los Angeles. We were brothers.

I couldn't tell if it happened quickly or slowly, but I came to realize that days and days would go by without a chat. I discovered that he told other people on our team about important meetings that he never informed me of. He would ask me strange questions or for access to certain files or emails so he could "consolidate" everything. He would randomly make trips to New York or San Francisco.

I don't know why this didn't trigger every warning signal in my brain, given how well I had done thus far when I mixed friends and business, but one day I got a text from one of the guys asking, "Have you heard?! Ryan sold WiredLabs! Someone in New York City bought us!"

All I could think about at that moment, lying on my bed and staring at the ceiling, was how I had no paperwork with Ryan, or Wired-Labs. He had told me since we started that we would "get there" once the time was right, and it was too expensive to go through all that legal work when there was no way we would sell the company or make any real money for a while. He assured me that I was an owner, a partner. That I owned a "big piece" of WiredLabs.

Tears slowly ran down my face. I knew in my heart that I didn't own a thing.

I was angry at myself. Ashamed that I let it happen again. I grabbed on to the hollow feeling in my stomach and didn't let it go. *Aren't people supposed to be good? Or am I stupid and naïve for believing that?*

I lay there for what felt like days, pondering my situation.

From a worst-case-scenario-in-life standpoint, it wasn't all that bad. I had lost a couple of friends, a bunch of money, and the first two companies I had created. I was healthy and young. But I still probably had grounds to give the world of entrepreneurship a big fat middle finger and move on with, well, any life but this. Only I couldn't, which made me feel crazy.

While many studies detail how many psychopathic, masochistic, or delusional characteristics we entrepreneurs and business leaders may have, my gut instinct is to say that such characterizations must be misleading. We aren't *actually* crazy. One of the defining characteristics of a psychopath is a lack of empathy and emotion. We entrepreneurs are generally the opposite—wildly sensitive and introspective. We need a high level of emotional intelligence to even begin to make it in this game.

But we are compelled to create artificial personas that pretend everything is fine when we are struggling, that succumb to compounding levels of lies, and that gleefully take high-risk bets with the odds stacked against us. We do this all willingly, over and over and over again, but also clearly have some attraction to the pain it is going to cause, either by way of others' accounts or having already gone through it ourselves. Some serial entrepreneurs do so dozens of times in their lives, and I can assure you, while there may be different flavors of pain and sacrifice, they never go away.

It's no surprise, then, that a huge number of entrepreneurs have issues with mental health (about 60 percent more than the general public, according to the few studies that have been done on the topic), ranging from garden-variety depression and anxiety to debilitating personality disorders. Some argue it is precisely these ailments that drive us to be entrepreneurs. Perhaps the chaos of doing business offsets our own emotional swings. Perhaps our imbalance embraces the risk.

Then there is the nature versus nurture debate. Are entrepreneurs born or made?

Eighty percent of what it takes to win the entrepreneurial lottery is ingrained deep inside one's mind and cannot be taught or learned. The remaining 20 percent comes from starting, trying, failing, and getting your teeth kicked in until you have a chance to do better the next go-round. And even then, it requires powering through hundreds of losing moments before you see real success.

Harvard Business School professor Shikhar Ghosh has done studies to identify why 96 percent of businesses fail within ten years. The main reasons relate to non-entrepreneurs trying to be entrepreneurs. The remaining just have a lack of experience.

I completely agree with that assessment. To me, it's all nature. In my own experience, and from my interactions with many other entrepreneurs, I've found that there is no question that we are simply made differently. You can track almost every successful entrepreneur's journey back to examples of their mindset in their earliest years. We were the ones profiting on lemonade stands at age five, selling burned CDs out of a backpack at fifteen, and already had an impressive list of failures at twenty-five.

This pattern of behavior isn't dissimilar from that of "superhero" professions like musicians and actors who are part of the .001 percent who succeed at a very high level. There is a reason why every rock star documentary in history features the inevitable photo of its subject playing piano before they could walk or an account of their dropping out of school to pursue music. These artists had no other path.

But what about the career of someone like Leonard Cohen, who didn't become a famous singer until age fifty? His biography might argue for nurture's ability to lead to success. But the reality is, Cohen studied music as a child, learned guitar at the same time, and had deeply musically inclined parents. He was a musician at the core; he just didn't find public success until he was older.

Today, success as an entrepreneur is perceived as being obtainable by almost anyone who studiously applies themselves to the task. Now that famous startup CEOs have become (depressingly) my generation's rock stars, what they have accomplished has oddly enough come to be perceived as something that is easily "accessible." If you were to ask a thirty-four-year-old forensic accountant if he could win an Academy Award for Best Actor, he would probably look at you strangely and give the fairly obvious response, "No . . . I'm not an actor." However, it seems that half the population regards themselves as entrepreneurs and has the next billion-dollar app idea just ready to launch.

Nature's lottery is a deeply upsetting concept to many people, especially those who believe you can be anything you set your mind to when you grow up.

For those of us who are born entrepreneurs, it can be difficult to come to terms with the implications and understand what to do with our "gift." Especially when we are fed so many fallacies about entrepreneurship at a young age.

For me, it was simply a path I had to pursue. It might not ultimately have worked out for me, but it was still my calling, so I had to keep at it until I was forced to quit. My mind could justify the risk. My heart could take the pain. At least I convinced myself of that.

15 | END OF ACADEMIA

My financial situation was really starting to worry me. I was over fifty thousand dollars in debt, with no sign of the losses slowing. All my "volunteer" time with WiredLabs had added to that considerably, by not allowing any time for a part-time job. My grandfather, who passed away when I was twelve, had left a small amount of money in a trust, which covered a bit of college, but that had been burned up years prior. And around this time, after decades at Chrysler, my father lost his job, going down with just about everyone else in Detroit. This was devastating news, as he was our only source of income, and my two younger siblings were still in high school. My mom began taking night classes to train as a nurse to make ends meet.

I felt guilty not being able to help support my family. I had to figure out how to make some money, and quickly.

I dug deep into the archive, dusted off the magnifying glass, and started driving around to computer repair shops to see if anyone would give me a job. After a few quick rejections, I only had one place left on my list, and I couldn't find it on a map. Even when I did, I figured it *had* to be some sort of joke. It was a tiny converted house, literally in the middle of the woods, with run-down cars out front and a hand-painted sign that read COMPUTER REPAIR.

At first glance there were no humans inside. Just a graveyard of computer parts, discarded fast-food wrappers, and the unmistakable smell of mold and cigarette smoke wafting through the open window.

If the boys from *Deliverance* had decided to get into the computer repair business, this would have been their headquarters.

I was desperate, but not this desperate.

As I turned to leave, a haggard woman emerged, smoking a cigarette, and loudly asked if she could help me. She wore an off-white, stained nightgown, flip-flops, and thick glasses.

This was a moment of truth. Did I *really* need to make money? Perhaps being broke and homeless wouldn't be *that* bad? Flexible living and all.

"Hi," I said, uncertainly. "I'm looking for a job. I know how to fix computers."

She stared at me blankly. At first I thought she was deeply considering my request, but after a few seconds I realized that something wasn't right with her. She was looking straight through me. She had short-circuited.

I was now thoroughly creeped out and made the decision that being a vagrant would be just fine. I turned and began heading for my car when I heard the door of the shop fly open. I rushed to get in my car, now truly believing I was in a survival situation. I looked over my shoulder to see a tall, squirrelly kid jogging out, waving at me. He wasn't carrying a shotgun, so I stopped to hear him out.

"Hey! Sorry," he explained. "I was in the bathroom when you walked up, but I heard you speaking to Betty. We need help here. Are you looking for a job?" he asked, a bit too eagerly.

Absolutely nothing about this situation felt encouraging, or even safe. But I started working that afternoon. Desperation is a funny thing. As it turned out, Betty was the wife of the owner of the establishment, whom I had yet to meet, and had a "bad back," so she popped OxyContin like Skittles, leaving her in a perpetual zombie state. And this was before opioids were in style. I consider Betty a trendsetter. The job itself wasn't the worst thing I've ever done. There was a steady stream of computers to be fixed, and I was paid a fair wage, and I also began to fix computers on campus for some extra cash.

In class, things were rough. I would hold my head up to try to absorb anything that was said, barely pass a test, kick ass at the in-person sales exercises, and move on to the next day. I so desperately wanted to finish. I would look around the classroom at these stiff-backed kids listening intently and taking notes, wondering, *Who are you people, and how do you do this?*

Years later I would be a prized alumnus of this institution and make my way back to campus to deliver inspirational speeches to students. The irony is not lost on me. During one such speech the director of the program introduced me with "John was a . . . different kind of student. Always working on something. Even though laptops were not allowed during lectures, he always had his out. I would see what I could say that would be interesting enough to get him to peer at me from over the screen, before going back to whatever he was doing."

Against all odds, I plowed through my final courses and could see graduation just ahead. Aside from an awkward encounter when I went to quit the computer repair shop, where Betty cornered me, asking if I would marry her daughter or if I wanted to buy some of her pills, I was free.

My father came out to help me pack up my apartment and enjoy the last few days of my academic career. No matter what happened in my life, I knew I would never sit in another classroom.

But because the universe has a tendency to fuck with me, it had one last send-off.

During a game of softball, I was running toward home plate to field a bunt. The batter pulled back, swung with all his might, connected perfectly, and sent the ball into my face at about a hundred miles an hour. Dad would later describe the event as "a cloud of blood came out of his face like a guy getting shot in a World War II film." I fell to my knees, and everything went dark.

Not since the interfamilial assassination attempts of the mid-'80s had I experienced my insides leaking out of my body. All my other injuries had been good old hidden injuries like broken ribs and concussions.

I woke up to incredible pressure on the right side of my face, everything feeling very hot. It was clear I was seeing the world through one very blurry left eye only. I hoped that was due to the bandages covering the right side of my face, but I had no way to be sure. I attempted to do a little forensic search with my tongue to determine the state of my teeth, but everything was so numb it was impossible to tell.

My dad was talking to the doctors, and I patiently waited for an update.

As it turns out, I had a pretty good-sized hole in my face. Amazingly, not from the impact of the softball (what a *stupid* name, by the way), but rather, from the pressure that rapidly built from the impact, which was technically at the bridge of my nose. Yes, you read that right. My cheek blew out from the inside, like an "overripe tomato," per the doctor.

Apart from the crater, my nose was broken, I had another concussion, and my eyeball was lacerated.

This wasn't the college send-off I had hoped for. But I would make do. It was also a painful, poetic representation of the last decade of my life. I had taken some serious hits. I had endured a lot of pain. I had thought I was doing the right thing and got screwed over, again and again. But I had hardened and learned many lessons. I felt oddly capable. I would never again be caught off guard. I would never be naïve.

Thankfully, my eye fought hard and won. My face healed, and apart from some light plastic surgery, I recovered over the winter and blossomed in spring.

School was over. I had a degree. I had survived another assassination attempt. My parents were incredibly proud—and surprised—that I graduated. It felt great. There hadn't been many opportunities to impress my parents since I started down this path a decade earlier.

So, there I was. Degree in hand. Broke, but free. Time to finally give up on all this silly entrepreneurial stuff and get a real job.

Or, not.

16 | EUROPE

I wasn't quite ready to enter the real world, so I instead persuaded my cousin Joel to join me on an adventure—backpacking through Europe. I was set on doing this right. Open-ended flight, unlimited train ticket, and few other plans. Move with the wind, chase around European girls, party, drink, smoke, enjoy life. Be free. I knew this would suit me well. For no logical reason, I just *felt* European. These were my people.

My parents did everything in their power to make me reconsider this trip, which I love them for. They told me it was irresponsible financially, which I knew. They told me it might not be safe, which I was okay with. They told me I should think about my future, which I was, just in my own way. But I also believe they knew there was no stopping me. I was growing up fast, and all they could do was hope their values and lessons would get me through.

I was so tired from the last decade—a cemetery of failed ideas, academic struggles, and other assorted heartaches. I deserved the chance to act like a kid for once, be an idiot, and see the world.

And that's exactly what happened.

We arrived at our first hostel in London and we were instantly hooked. It was a playground for people like us—carefree vagabonds from all over the world. We threw our bags down on one of the eight bunk beds in the room and went down to the hostel bar, which was packed with young travelers playing games, telling stories, drinking, and smoking.

We went to Paris, where I saw my first cabaret. We sat on the bridges of the Seine, getting drunk on cheap wine and eating baguettes. For someone who had never passed a history or geography test, I became fascinated by both. It finally made *sense*.

We went to the South of France, where we slept on the beach because we couldn't afford any other lodging.

We got lost in Venice. I looked at all the rich people drinking coffee outside their five-star hotels and riding teak powerboats. I wanted to be them.

We held full-stein drinking contests in Munich, resulting in me awakening from a drunken sleep in the middle of Englischer Garten hours later.

We partied in Berlin's underground dance-sex clubs until the wee hours of the morning.

We slept on the floors of train cars and park benches, with little care for cleanliness or safety.

On and on we went. Crossing thousands of miles by train and absorbing everything.

I was hooked. This trip revealed *me*. The freedom. The adventure. This was the life I desired. I so wanted to grab ahold of it and never let go.

17 | THE BIG BREAK

Returning to America was brutal and depressing. Reality is a cruel thing. I was now so broke there was no next credit card, no possible support from the parents, no emergency stash of cash. I was at financial rock bottom.

There was no way I was moving back full-time to the ravaged Detroit area, so I considered my options. I had to be in a big city to increase my chances of anyone hiring me. I figured there were three places that would fit that bill: New York, San Francisco, and Chicago.

I sat in my parents' attic, crafting a résumé, trying to make my professional experience look less ridiculous than it actually was. I figured my career to date at *least* showed some grit and determination, and that *someone* would have to see that. This résumé made its way to every tech company I could find that was hiring sales people, and in those days, there were a lot of them.

Unfortunately for me, this was 2007, the middle of the second tech boom, just before the global crash. The blue-chip companies had their pick of candidates, most of whom were exponentially more credentialed than I, at least on paper. Plus, tech had by now become an academic fraternity. Google would only look at you if you'd gone to Stanford or Harvard. Microsoft wanted to see a master's degree. Omniture was just an extension of the Brigham Young Marriott School of Business.

I started with those companies, but knew they were a long shot. Even when I did get a phone interview with Google, which I crushed, I knew it wouldn't go anywhere. I wasn't their pedigree. I never got a call back.

I then started going down the proverbial list, first applying to companies I had heard of but didn't know a lot about: Salesforce. Oracle. Adobe. Edelman. Bloomberg. E*Trade. Yelp. Again, not even a damned interview. Next I blindly applied to every company with available positions. I got responses, but it was clear I had hit the bottom of the barrel, as they were either hiring "commission-only" (a.k.a. work for free) or were multilevel marketing scams and pyramid schemes.

What the hell was I going to do?

Then an email appeared that I almost overlooked. It was from Steven Levin, the CEO of Varsoft Technologies in Chicago, a "leading, award-winning web design firm." He was *very* interested in discussing the role with me. When could I meet with him?

A day later, I was on a five-hour drive to Chicago. I had found a friend's couch to sleep on for the night. The interview was the following morning. I was high with excitement. I needed this to be my big break.

I had one decent suit, which had been required for the sales program in school. I did my best to get the wrinkles out and look professional. I walked through the Loop, Chicago's downtown, taking in the big city's energy. There were important-looking businesspeople everywhere. Doing deals. Having fancy lunches. Riding around in black cars, looking busy.

That was about to be me.

I arrived at 234 South Wabash, and my heart stopped. I had to be in the wrong place. There were no office buildings in the area, let alone high-rises. I had only minutes until the meeting was scheduled to start. I could feel the sweat start to roll down my brow.

I snapped around, saw a taxi, and ran to it.

"I need you to take me to 234 South Wabash, *now*," I screamed at the driver.

He didn't share my urgency. He slowly looked around.

"You're standing in front of it, retard." He then drove off.

I turned around again to consider the building. Between a dirty bodega and a greasy Italian beef sandwich shop stood a grimy glass door with the address "234" clearly at its center.

I slowly walked to the door and peeked inside. There was no signage of any kind, no attendant, no lobby—just a narrow, dank hallway with a small elevator at its end. I looked at the email I had printed with the confirmation, and noticed "Floor 6" after the address. Here goes nothing. I walked onto the elevator and hit "6."

When the elevator door opened I found myself gazing into an office that had apparently been frozen in time. It looked like a break room from *Glengarry Glen Ross*. Stained drop ceilings. Old, tattered carpet. Ancient off-white office furniture. Cubed desks to the side. The only somewhat modern-looking thing in sight was the die-cut metal VARSOFT TECHNOLOGIES sign on the wall. Behind the empty reception desk was a hall with an office, its door closed, and a small conference room.

I checked the clock above the reception desk, wondering if it actually worked. It read 11:00 a.m., on the dot. At least I was on time. I didn't know what to do, so I just stood in the lobby. Five minutes passed. Ten. Fifteen.

This felt ridiculous. Was I doing something wrong? Was this a test?

Finally, the door to the office swung open and I heard the sounds of an argument. A cute young woman emerged, responding to a man inside, who was *screaming* back at her. She saw me, smiled, shut the door, walked over to the reception area, and asked how she could help me.

When I told her that I was here for an interview, she looked at her computer for longer than it should have taken, and finally said, calmly, "Of course. Mr. Levin will be right with you. Please wait in here." She guided me to the small conference room and shut the door behind her.

Five minutes passed. Ten. Twenty.

I considered walking out then and there. But I needed this job so bad I had no choice but to wait.

A full forty minutes after I had been seated in the room, the door opened, and two men entered.

The first was a large, powerful-looking figure. He stood at least four inches over my six-foot frame, in a well-tailored suit and a ridiculous little mustache. He had a deep voice and a charming smile and introduced himself as Steven Levin, CEO. He apologized for the delay. Only months later would I realize that he had kept me waiting—as he did to both candidates and clients alike—as a power play, to show everyone that we were on *his* schedule.

The second was a strange, gaunt man with a heavy French accent; flowing, oversized casual clothing; and a tiny poof of hair on his head. He introduced himself as Henri, director of client services.

Despite the awkwardness of how the meeting came together, they began to ask me questions. I could sell. I could code. I could talk tech. I looked good in a suit. Steven stared at me as if he wanted to eat me. Aside from a few curveball questions, I was nailing it. And then Steven asked what my income expectations were.

"Sixty thousand," I boldly declared. I actually hadn't thought this through so just threw out as big a number as I could say with a straight face.

The room fell silent. The two men eyed each other, deciding who was going to reply. "This role . . . is new," Henri finally explained. "Steven does all our sales now. There is a lot of commission opportunity . . . but we don't plan on paying a base."

"I understand," I lied. I knew what they were doing. And I knew how long commission could take to earn, even if I was great at the job. Without a paycheck, I was dead in the water. I had to gamble and told them, "I require a salary in addition to commission. If you aren't able to offer that, I won't waste any more of your time."

"Wait," Steven said as I got up to leave. "We can work something out."

That evening I received my first offer letter ever: $35,000 salary, plus commission. I signed that son of a bitch without a second thought. I had hit the big time.

18 | VARSOFT TECHNOLOGIES

My older sister, Isabel, was living in Chicago at the time, so I went to the nightclub she managed to celebrate. I had never been to a nightclub before. I cringe at just how awkward and out of place I must have looked. It was also a harsh reminder of just how broke I was. As I was drunk and slurring by the end of the night, my sister guided me to the taxi line, put a twenty-dollar bill in the front pocket of my jacket, and told the cabbie to get me home safe. I remember thinking, *Wow, my sister must really be rich! Throwing twenty-dollar bills around like that.*

I moved what few possessions I had from Michigan to Chicago, settling into a tiny rented room in a larger apartment in Wrigleyville, with three random roommates, and got to work.

Varsoft wasn't quite as dire an operation as it had appeared during my interview. The core business was a standard-issue web design and development shop. A couple dozen people worked there, spread out across two floors. Everyone was young, talented, and underpaid, but excited to be doing something.

Steven was a consummate salesman, always hustling, and I became his right hand. He started bringing me around to meet our clients, showing me off like a new puppy. As it turned out, nearly every one of those clients was unhappy, and my role quickly became apparent: get close with them, use my technical knowledge to solve their problems, and find more ways to part them from their money.

What wasn't immediately apparent was *why* virtually our entire client list was unhappy. After going to a few new business development pitches with Steven, however, it all became clear: he was completely, utterly full of shit. He would say anything to a client to win a deal. Bald-faced lies about past projects, capabilities, number of employees—it didn't matter. Every case study we showed was a crock of shit, ranging from a total fabrication of someone else's work to false success metrics. The Varsoft website was equally as fake.

Right out in the open. He had absolutely no limits. It seemed a wildly unsustainable model, but I realized it had been working for him forever, and he somehow kept the racket going. This made fulfilling his promises almost impossible.

Steven was gay and an outright atheist. But even those were up for grabs to win a sale. I will never forget pitching a large church on designing their new website; during the pitch Steven excitedly talked about his wife, kid, and Christian upbringing, and even made a subtle, off-color gay joke.

Despite his outrageousness, I learned a lot from Steven. He was the greatest salesman I had ever come across. I would watch him work a room like an orchestra conductor, delivering the perfect blend of charm, confidence, and empathy. He could sell evil to the devil. He also dressed better than anyone I had ever met. He had a tailor who would come into the office twice a year and make suits right on his shoulders. He completed his outfits with custom cuff links, matching pocket squares, perfectly shined shoes, and a tie bar. At first, I found this a ridiculous affectation. We were in tech, and customers expected us to be in jeans and T-shirts. But that's exactly why Steven's method worked. A power business suit immediately commands respect the same way a police uniform does, especially when weighed against your underdressed competitors.

Steven was also a true entrepreneur, the first, other than Ryan, I had ever really been close to. If he could make money at it, he didn't care what the business was. This was exemplified by the other "division" of Varsoft. Through a strange set of circumstances having to do with his dad, who was a city manager, and some bizarre lawsuit, Steven had found a loophole in the Illinois Municipal Utility Tax Code, allowing municipalities to levy huge fines on utility companies that mischarged for services and consumption. Somehow, Steven had written software that automated an auditing process to ferret out these cases on behalf of various municipalities—and built an entire company around it, Varsoft Audit Solutions. This small team of lawyers and techies were hidden on a dark, cavernous floor of the building, crunching numbers and reaping huge rewards, oblivious to their sister company. It was in a strange little boiler room on that floor that I would eventually meet one of the most important players in my entrepreneurial story, Kevin Lerash. We will get back to him soon.

I quickly excelled in my role. I didn't need to bullshit *quite* as much as Steven to win a sale, but I did stay in line with the general company tone. No one questioned it. I was closing deals, becoming a rock star internally, and taking in the commission checks. I also began to look like Steven's stunt double. I dressed like him, talked like him, and would march around the office like I owned the place. I caught the eye of my female coworkers.

In my first year at Varsoft I cleared $30,000 in commission. By then I had rented my own tiny studio apartment on the north side of Chicago, so I was still at a barely livable income level. I hadn't yet touched my huge pile of debt, but at least I wasn't adding to it. I was moving in the right direction. Life was pretty good.

But by my second year at the company, I began to get restless. Every day I would mentally fume about having a boss. Some people clearly thrived in a hierarchy, under management and mentorship. I despised it. Steven and I would clash on almost a daily basis. I resented him having power over me, and he hated having someone as capable as I was showing him up. He would ask me to stay late into the evening, just because he could. I would talk over him at a pitch meeting, just because I could. However good I was at this job, being the best salesman at this hackshop was like being the best gymnast at a nursing home.

I had to get back to being an entrepreneur. I had to try my hand again.

Aside from my rapid departure from the computer repair shop in college, I hadn't ever really quit a job. To be honest, I wasn't even sure how to do it. Was there some form I was supposed to fill out?

Knowing Steven, and his flair for vitriol, I understood two things to be true: First, he wasn't going to make this easy, as I had become too valuable to him. Second, he could be a downright evil bastard—behavior I had witnessed firsthand whenever he felt slighted—so I needed to prepare some collateral, especially if I ever hoped to see the $10,000 in commissions I had accrued but not received.

Late hours had become a standard part of my job, so my remaining in the office after everyone else had left didn't raise any red flags. One night I waited until the entire staff had cleared out and got to work.

My first course of business was to send emails from my personal account to my best clients—the ones I had brought in and nurtured. I informed them that I would be taking my leave from Varsoft and that I would make sure they were left in good hands. But, I added, I was not completely sure how smoothly my transition might go, so if there were any hiccups, they should feel free to be in touch. What I was really saying was: If Steven makes this difficult, I'll find a company better suited to take care of you. This was an admittedly clever way of getting around the nonsolicitation clause of my contract. I wasn't violating anything if I simply referred my dissatisfied clients to other companies.

The second step was to back up all my corporate emails, which were stored on a local Outlook server, on a DVD, and accidentally delete the local copy. There would be pandemonium if Varsoft didn't have a record of my conversations with prospects and clients, which is exactly what I wanted.

I know what all you lawyers reading this are thinking. I didn't know this was illegal then, okay?

I then sent off an email to Steven: "Hey, can we talk at 8 tomorrow morning?"

19 | TRANSFORMATION

S teven didn't respond to my email, but I knew he saw it, and I knew he knew what it meant.

I arrived at 6:00 a.m. the following day, well aware that he considered early arrival a power play, and so would try that tactic on me. I was sitting in a chair outside his office with my legs crossed when he arrived at 6:50 a.m.

He gave me a terse smile. A grudging acknowledgment that I had learned well from the master.

So as not to be outdone in this corporate cockfight, he asked for a moment to get settled, and shut the door to his office. He left me out in the hall until 8:30 a.m.

When I finally took a seat at his oversized wood desk I got right to the point: "Steven, I am going to move on from Varsoft, effective immediately. I will give you a week or two if you need."

There was no surprise in the air, he knew what I was there for. And he was prepared, as I expected. After staring at me for a few seconds, he tore a sheet of paper off a pad (monogrammed with "SL" at the top), wrote something quickly, and handed it to me. He explained that this was what he was prepared to do to keep me.

It said "100." To this day I cannot be absolutely sure what this meant.

I thanked him and quickly assured him that I had made my decision. There I sat, twenty-three years old, in my tailored suit, tightly trimmed beard, and confidence bordering on cockiness, taking on the sensei.

He remained silent—a too-obvious negotiating tactic for which I wasn't going to fall—so I got up to walk out the door and relay my departure to HR. To my surprise, he quickly stood up as I began to leave. Was I going to get a good luck hug?

He took two huge steps, grabbed me by the shoulder, and, spinning me around, knocked me back against the door, pinning me against it. "What you just did was very disrespectful," he said.

I did my best to return his gaze, but I was scared to death. Aside from a one-sided fight in high school where I knocked out a bully, I hadn't ever resorted to violence. I could now feel my resolve giving way, and the cheeky grin I tried to pull in response probably registered as more of a frightened half smile. I could feel sweat beading on my forehead.

"Let go of me, Steven," was all I could muster. It took him a few more moments of applying even more pressure against my chest until he let go. Remarkably, he wasn't done selling.

"Go home. Take the day to think about this. And tell me tonight what you need to stay here."

I did my best to not react to that statement and stormed out of the office. I started down Wabash Avenue, the metal-on-metal screeching of the L above me, and walked and walked. I was on the verge of tears, but I refused to give him that power. I sucked in fresh air, steeled my gaze, and walked until I settled down and my feet blistered, making it the almost three miles north to my apartment.

Predictably, a few hours later, I received an email from Henri: "John, the emails on your computer seem to be gone. We really need these."

"That's odd," I replied. "I make routine backups on DVDs. I must have accidentally moved them instead of copying. It's no problem, I happen to have a backup on me. Attached is the report of what commissions I am owed—about $11k. We can settle at $8k, as there's always a chance some of these pay late. If you can put the check together, I will meet you and swap for the DVD. Thanks."

I closed my laptop and went to a bar.

Not surprisingly, Steven fought back hard, until he realized that I had outmaneuvered him. He was smart enough to appreciate the leverage I had over his best clients, and how screwed Varsoft would be without my emails. Even if what I was doing was technically illegal, he'd never risk bringing in lawyers, given everything I knew about the inner workings of the company. It took weeks of back and forth, but eventually a DVD was traded for a check, and I never heard from anyone at Varsoft again.

I promptly paid off some debt and freshened up my résumé.

Yeah, right.

Nope, what I actually did was call cousin Joel. A couple of weeks later, with $8,000 ready to burn, we were flying to Europe.

The thrill, the pleasure, the freedom. I decided on this trip that no matter what happened next, I wouldn't conform ever again. No one would ever tell me which path I was supposed to be on. No one would have power over me. Damn the people who told me I couldn't do it. Damn the people who insisted I be quiet and take my seat. Damn the people who looked down on me while I rode the roller coaster to this point.

I had been told all my life, "You can't have it all." Fuck that. I was determined to defy it. Wealth, freedom, adventures, happiness. And I was right. There was a way to have my cake and eat it, too. To have a life with all the trimmings. I just didn't know at what price.

This was my mindset as I returned to America. I was going for glory.

20 | PREPARATION

"Johnny," my mother said warily, "are you sure about this? *Another* company? Maybe you should get a job instead?"

I tried to think of a response that would comfort her, show her I knew what I was doing, even if I didn't. She was the only person I felt I needed to convince—not because she would try to stop me, but because I knew how much she worried, and I didn't want to make that any worse. I loved her so much and knew she was probably right, but I had to follow my gut.

Entrepreneurship is invariably a selfish game, and it's easy to forget how many other people your decisions affect. This is an inevitable part of the journey, one you must accept. It is so consuming that you become very introspective, which isolates you from others in your life. This quickly manifests as one of the most common and negative characteristics of entrepreneurship—loneliness. You hear it admitted repeatedly when you get entrepreneurs to speak truthfully. That same loneliness links directly to the mental health issues we so often experience. When you live in mental isolation, your stressors and anxieties show up and stay put, like unwanted houseguests.

As with many such conversations with my mom, her concerns were completely justified. I was still six figures in debt. I was using credit cards to service other credit cards, and only paying minimums. My credit rating was so obliterated that I'd be lucky to qualify for a prepaid cell phone. Despite my unrelenting passion for it, I hadn't achieved any real success in entrepreneurship, but had just managed to learn a lot of painful lessons.

No matter, I would assure her. I know what I'm doing. This time is going to be different. I'm ready. This is my new life.

At least I fucking hope so. I was now probably facing my last chance, one last go at this crazy game, and I knew it. If I failed again, or let someone rip a business away from me because I wasn't careful enough or lucky enough, I would *have* to get an entry-level job somewhere and deal with financial hardship for years. No more traveling. No freedom. For a long, long time. Maybe forever. Could I handle that?

My mom wasn't the only one worried. I had started dating a girl named Lisa, who had a few opinions of her own on my "career path." She went to work every day to a very respectable job, and to her friends, being an "aspiring entrepreneur" is a thinly veiled euphemism. Like an aspiring actor in Hollywood.

I needed an idea, and a damned good one. And a cheap one,

because I only had a sliver of one credit card left to work with, and there wasn't a soul or institution who would give me money.

It was 2009, and the recession had hit Chicago hard, causing a very unexpected and fortuitous side effect: many young, smart, ambitious people were now out of work, and rather than try to rush back into the gutted workforce, they took inspiration from what was happening on the West Coast and tried their hand at tech entrepreneurship, which looked like a cash grab. Facebook had recently passed a two-billion-dollar valuation. Apple was in its second full year of the iPhone and was effectively printing money. Even Groupon, Chicago's only shiny tech star, was disrupting the entire nation.

The city's first technology coworking space had recently opened in the then-decrepit West Loop district. It represented a mecca for displaced, ambitious millennials who weren't going to be kept down by the recession, and it was the first place I felt at home in Chicago. Given that I didn't have anywhere else to be, I would spend my days and nights there, speaking with other like-minded techies and dreamers, watching pitches being presented to the embarrassingly small number of investors in the city at the time. Because I had been through the startup (to fail) phase more than almost anyone else around, I was able to answer a lot of questions and provide the best advice I could on what the journey would be like. We didn't cherish this experience at the time, but we should have. It was a beautiful utopia of entrepreneurship, with a cast of innocent, wide-eyed characters who would go on to become Chicago's tech elite.

Despite my pessimistic perspective on my entrepreneurial history, two things were true: First, I had learned a *lot*—more than I would ever have given myself credit for. Even though my efforts to date could only be categorized as failures, I had developed a genuine high-level business acumen and rigor, which left me over a decade further along than all my peers.

Second, and surprisingly, the most valuable advice and mentorship I could offer those peers wasn't about entrepreneurship or technology. It was about *design*, thanks to what I had learned at WiredLabs from Isaac. It became clear that no one in Chicago knew a damn thing about user-experience design, or UX, so virtually overnight I became the "design guy." I was the only person talking about UX, ethnography, customer needs, and information architecture. Before I knew it, I was speaking onstage at events and even being asked to join some companies as a formal adviser. It all felt a little fraudulent, because I wasn't a designer myself. But I had observed its value firsthand and recognized how much competitive differentiation some of these startups would be able to create if they, too, understood it.

This was all fine and well, but I still had to get my own act together and figure out what company I was going to start. At the time three different concepts were playing through my head.

Idea #1: I had learned quite a lot about advertising at Varsoft through my work with our agency clients. In the past few years web-based analytics tools had changed the entire industry. For the first time, advertisers had a complete, data-centric perspective on the performance of their advertising: what ads were shown when; exactly who viewed or clicked on them, at what times, and where in the world; what copy performed best; and what strategies led to conversations and sales. This left off-line advertising completely in the dust, and ads played on the radio or propped up on the side of the highway were now essentially black holes. This led to a huge backlash in the industry. Advertisers were now drunk on data, and were pulling dollars away from off-line advertising and moving all their budgets to online. Might there be a way to create an analytics plat-form that gave similar performance data for off-line? This could be huge.

Idea #2: The topic of psychographics had long fascinated me. What makes us, us? Identifying the data we have buried inside our-selves, that we might not even be aware of, would be pure gold to marketers. A Chicago-based online dating site, OkCupid, had kick-started some of my inspiration. OkCupid had published a statisti-cally significant study of its users that showed people with iPhones had significantly more sex than Android users, as did diet soda drinkers over soda drinkers. This sent a shock wave through the in-ternet (not necessarily in a positive way) and revealed the world's, not to mention marketers', insatiable desire for data and insights. Perhaps there was a way to gather other such insightful correlations at scale and sell them to marketers? Huge idea, but one that would be expensive to get off the ground.

Idea #3: Off the back of my newly acquired persona as the design guru of Chicago, I wondered if there could possibly be a business in selling my design services to startups. This seemed like the longest shot. I didn't know the first thing about consulting, and my target customer group had little to no money to pay me. But I knew my knowledge was valuable to a lot of people, so I just had to figure out how to monetize it. One inroad I felt could work would be starting with other consultancies who farmed out their work. I could surely do it faster and cheaper. Perhaps.

Three very different ideas, with very different paths to success, risk profiles, and potential outcomes. So, I did what any entrepre-neur worth their salt would do: I decided to start all three, all on the same day.

21 | FOUNTAINHEAD

Three businesses. Step one, what do I call them?

The names for the first two came to me quickly. The advertising play would be TrakLabs, because we were tracking advertising, and I loved the "Labs" moniker, which sounded scientific and smart. The data business would be SocialCrunch, because we were crunching social data. Easy.

As for the agency . . . I had no idea. The name needed to be the epitome of cool and innovative. European. Sleek. Highbrow. And because we would be constantly compared with other agencies, it not only had to stand out in a list, but it also had to appear first, and therefore should start with an A.

Naturally, I went and Googled "cool words that start with A." I came across all kinds of lists: baby names, fictional characters, exotic-sounding words. This last category is when I saw the company's name jump off the page: Äkta. What a fucking great word! *AH-ktuh.* I had no idea what it meant, precisely how to pronounce it, or even why I liked it. But this was it. (In retrospect I should have cared about what it meant. I could have unknowingly named my company "asshole" in German or something. It wasn't until a year later when someone inquired that I figured out it meant "authentic" in Swedish. Lucky.)

I rang my good friend and attorney, Brian Hartwell, and asked him if he would help me register these new businesses. The last thing I was going to do was skip around the legal process again and get screwed because of some step I missed. He figured I could run all three under one LLC until I figured out which company I would focus on. By focus on, what he was trying to say was, when I figured out which two were crap. And what he was really, really trying to say was, don't blow all of your money on LLC registrations because chances are all three are going to fail.

Here's how I weighed those odds then: TrakLabs was an industry disruptor. If someone figured out how to make this business model work, it'd be worth hundreds of millions of dollars. But it'd also be a shot in the dark, and I didn't know much about advertising. But, I still thought it had the best chance of the three. (Spoiler: I tried it, and it failed a month later.)

SocialCrunch was a wild card. What I was proposing had never been done on a commercial level. But people seemed to *love* the concept. Maybe this was the dark horse. This I put somewhere in the middle.

Äkta . . . who could know? Surely not me. I was only starting this business because it seemed like the fastest path to cash flow and I knew I could sell the shit out of it. But I felt very unsure about starting an agency. Maybe there was a book I could read.

Brian recommended I use Äkta as the parent company name, because it was so ~~odd~~ unique that it had the lowest chance of having any trademark conflicts, which I wasn't prepared to pay to investigate. I made one small tweak at this stage. I wanted the name to look big and bold, so I capitalized it as "ÄKTA" and appended "Web Studio" as a descriptor.

On February 15, 2010, ÄKTA Web Studio LLC was born.

It was easy to start. All I needed was a pretty business card, a website, and an alluring sales pitch—three things I could put to-gether in my sleep. I called up some guys I had met over the years who did good work and I figured might help me add some credibility to this new venture: Isaac from WiredLabs; this programmer Dan I had met in school; and another coder, Max, from Varsoft.

I whipped up a respectable-looking logo and stuck it on a respectable-looking website—stark white and red against a black background. To make the company look legitimate, I toed the line between exaggeration and outright invention. I never had a desire to run a company the way Steven did, but I had learned some things from him that worked.

I cited all the projects we'd done—a.k.a. the projects that Isaac, Dan, and Max had done. They were cool with my doing this, as they knew if anyone actually bought the services I was selling, I'd hire them to help me get the job done.

I explained our process—a.k.a. the process I had watched my guys at WiredLabs use to make great stuff.

I touted our unique ability to increase the probability of success for startups. To be fair, I never said we'd *done it*, just that we had the *ability to do it*.

I knew I was going to encounter serious barriers to attracting busi-ness, even apart from the fact that I didn't actually have a team or portfolio, wasn't a designer by trade, and had no network in Chicago. Not to mention I was targeting startups and digital agencies as clients, who were both notoriously challenging to reach and do business with.

I knew large digital agencies were complicated and constantly looking for vendors to help them fulfill client work, which meant there was an incredible amount of competition to get their attention.

Startups were a whole different game. They were great on paper: innovative, in heavy need of design services, and easy to target. But Chicago's investor scene was still trying to mature and startups were being funded with peanuts. They could barely afford ramen for lunch, much less premium design services.

I knew that what I was ultimately facing was a numbers game. If I could tell hundreds of companies about what I had to offer, I was bound to get at least one client out of it. And one was all I needed to kick this thing off.

I began by going through my pitiful Rolodex and emailing every contact I could think of to announce my new service. Ironically most of my "connections" were recruiters who had denied me a job over the past years. As I'd figured, the response rate wasn't great. Aside from a few courteous "Best of luck!" messages or "We already have vendors for that" cop-outs, this tactic wasn't producing a great yield.

My next move was to begin networking with anyone who would listen. Chicago at the time was so high on tech (and unemployment) that there was seemingly an unlimited number of breakfasts, luncheons, happy hours, trade shows, meet-ups, parties, panel talks, conferences, and other business gatherings. I intended to go to all of them, or at least all of them that I could afford. If an event was described by a fancy-sounding word like "gala" or "soirée," I knew the admission fee would be higher than my entire year's networking budget, so I would cross it off my list. But many of these get-togethers were free and had the unexpected benefit of offering soggy sandwiches and watered-down beer, which was a huge financial win.

This became my life. I would bounce from networking event to networking event, delivering marginally improved versions of my pitch to whatever audience would hear it, from the American Advertising Association to the American Medical Association to the latest tech programmer conference.

My pitch always started with the same bold statement: "I'm creating the best design agency in Chicago." I would then tailor my message to the particular audience, either with an anecdote about how design was changing the [insert event's topic here] industry or how ÄKTA could provide a distinct competitive advantage against [insert competitor here] with its services.

I felt like a cuckoo clock set to the minute. The same handshake. The familiar business card transfer. The adapted pitch. The empty compliments about what I was trying to sell, with some polite explanation as to why they weren't a fit at the moment. Hummingbird over to the next person. Repeat.

Despite the absolute lack of traction in this approach, I remained perpetually confident, which provided one of my great pleasures during that period of time: sitting in a cafe or park between networking sessions and daydreaming about this all working. Being surrounded by a rock star team of people in a funky, colorful, creative office with a Ping-Pong table and kegs of beer. Speaking to large audiences about our craft and selling the pants off them. Being in one of those intense pitches that Hollywood had convinced me actually existed, and getting the green light on that million-dollar contract.

Practicality is practicality, of course, so this fantasizing also brought on a very acute anxiety. What on earth was I going to do if someone actually did say yes to me?

22 | KEVIN LERASH

Assuming there was some company out there crazy enough to hire me, I had to nail the execution. And if there was one thing I knew about myself, it was that I'm absolutely awful at managing people day-to-day and seeing a project through to completion—two things that would be perfectly critical if we did win any business. So, I set out to mitigate that risk early.

Remember Kevin from a handful of chapters ago? He was still rotting away on that dank, unmarked office floor at Varsoft Audit Solutions.

I wouldn't have called Kevin a friend then—more like an oddly placed acquaintance. We had hung out a few times at happy hours during my tenure at Varsoft, and he had invited me to a "party" once that turned out to be a drug-infused rave at an abandoned warehouse on the western outskirts of Chicago. I stumbled out of that particular party at seven a.m. shirtless, stoned, and covered in neon paint to the shouts of "Cops!"

Kevin was the world's greatest anomaly. In a work setting, he was gruff, younger than he looked, and perpetually dressed in a wrinkled shirt and neutral colors. He had the presence of a beloved grandfather. Handsome, in a classic way. Trustworthy, lovable, interesting. Friendly and important to everyone. Perpetually calm. His conservative midwestern roots made him naturally incongruous to the urban sprawl in which he now lived. You could see yourself huddled up next to him by a campfire, being read stories about the war over two fingers of whiskey. In an earlier era he would have been a bank teller in a dusty cowboy town during the Gold Rush.

And that is how I knew Kevin, right up until that aforementioned party. What I learned then is that there was a bit of a looser side to him. And by "looser" I mean that his personal lifestyle would have made Jerry Garcia blush.

As it turns out, Kevin was a closet latter-day hippie who would happily plunge into any drug offered, who hung out with absolute degenerates, and who was most at home in a wrinkled tie-dye T-shirt. He played guitar and sang in an experimental jam band. The warehouse rave party was very much his scene.

Despite his employment as a tax auditor, he held a master's degree in nonprofit management—another piece in the perpetual mystery that was Kevin Lerash. This had led us to a number of conversations about starting a nonprofit organization called Digital Hope, which would use technology to connect donors with meaningful projects around the world, if I could have ever figured out how to afford to do so. We had made only slight progress getting it off the ground, but it still gave me ammunition for what came next.

Kevin was potentially the most insane person I had ever met. I loved and respected it. The question became, was he crazy enough to be on board with what I was about to ask him?

I rang him to ask if we could talk, the unspoken assumption being that the subject would be a continuation of our nonprofit talks. It was midday on a Saturday, which made me uncertain how lucid he would be from the night before, but he agreed, and said he would come pick me up in a few hours.

As I waited outside my apartment, I rehearsed what I would say to him. I had convinced people of any number of unlikely things over the years, but Kevin was a wild card. He had a natural resistance to my charm—frankly, he was too smart to fall for it. And it was clear he felt he could trust me about as far as he could throw me.

He arrived in the only car I could have expected he would drive: a dusty old Chevy Impala, off-green in color. He made a respectable salary for a twenty-four-year-old and could have driven something much more impressive. But he didn't care.

I hopped in, and he started to drive around downtown, waiting to hear where the small talk was going to lead. I finally got to the point.

"I really want to do this nonprofit," I began. "But, I have to get something going first with business before that would be possible. I think I have an idea on how to do that."

"Sure," he replied, with a facial expression that was somewhere between amused, curious, and suspicious. This look would become a staple of our relationship.

"There are tons of agencies out there. The big guys with huge budgets who are cranking out basic websites by the dozens," I said excitedly. "They charge tens of thousands a pop, and the quality is awful. I'm thinking that there's a business to be created here, doing it better and cheaper, using the guys I used to work with, and off-loading some of the more mundane work to contractors in Eastern Europe."

For those following at home, I had taken a whole different direction than what I had previously pitched as ÄKTA, but I figured this had a much better chance of resonating with him than trying to explain what UX was. He was listening, and driving, which allowed him to give very little in terms of feedback, but his silence encouraged me to continue.

"Anyway. I think this could be huge. And even though we've never worked together directly, I know that you are great at managing people and clients. If I can put this together, would you consider coming to work for me? This would also allow us to get Digital Hope up and running at the same time." I smiled at him as I finished my pitch.

He thought about this for a few blocks and then abruptly pulled over at the corner of Rush and Kinzie. There weren't many people who could make me feel uncomfortable and shake my confidence, but he was one of them. I tried to hold on to my resolve and enthusiasm. The challenge here was what hadn't been spoken. First, he knew that I knew he made a respectable $65,000 salary, and what I was going to offer was going to be only a fraction of that. Second, I knew that he instinctively didn't trust me. I represented the good-looking, smooth-talking, big-city kid that rubbed his bohemian senses the wrong way. But as ridiculous as my offer might have appeared, it did have one major selling point. Without his ever admitting it, I knew that Kevin must be absolutely miserable in his job. After all, he was still working for megalomaniac Steven Levin.

Kevin sat for a while considering what I had said. He wasn't a tech guy like me, so I knew that part of his reservation was not following at all what I was proposing this company would do.

"Well," he finally said, stoically. "It sounds intriguing. Would this be a normal salary thing?"

"Of course," I assured him. "I just have to secure the first client, and then we are off to the races. I should be able to start you at $28,000," I said, trying not to allow my voice to drop when delivering that fatal blow. "Look, I know it's a lot less than you make now. But this could be huge. And I will give you raises as soon as possible. And you'll be the first guy in. My right-hand man."

I sensed he wanted to say yes, but instead he told me he would think about it, and shook my hand as I got out of the car. Smart man.

23 | VOSGES

I felt positive about the probability of getting a client for ÄKTA, but there was no telling how long it was going to take, and I was getting shockingly close to being dead broke.

Don't get me wrong—I was already broke. Very broke. Still six figures in debt. Still using credit cards to pay off credit cards. But this was the first time I could see the end of the rope. When I maxed out this last credit card, there wasn't another one to use. I only had a few weeks of burn before I was dead in the water. There was no rainy-day fund. I was on the doorstep of what I call "fuck-off broke"—the point at which the entire world is going to tell you to fuck off, and the floor falls out from under your feet.

Thankfully, I was on the right side of good fortune, for once. My break came in April 2010 as the result of a meeting with a woman named Jennifer.

Jennifer was in a management role at a company called Endeca. Despite its having quickly rejected my job application, we had kept in touch, and she was one of the first people I invited to coffee to talk about my new venture. Though she couldn't see any potential business between ÄKTA and Endeca, she did have an off-the-cuff suggestion: I should speak with her boyfriend, Robert, who had recently begun a new role as COO of Vosges, a high-end chocolate brand in Chicago. He was in charge of a significant turnaround for the fledgling company, and e-commerce strategy and design were top priorities. Perhaps he needed help?

This was my only promising lead, and though I didn't know much about e-commerce and hated chocolate, I had to make something happen. I was empowered by the most potent force in the world: desperation.

Vosges was on the outskirts of Chicago, so rather than getting dropped off in a taxi, I borrowed my friend's Range Rover to add even a hint of credibility. The night before I had run every free search engine optimization test I could find and printed all the results. It was all total bullshit, but pretty-looking charts and graphs make everyone look as if they know what they're doing.

Vosges HQ was what I'd expected: half strewn-about open-plan offices and desks, with computers and printers and papers and rushed-looking people; half giant, loud factory space with machines and assembly lines and rushed-looking people with hairnets.

Apparently, the company was a big deal, according to the more sugar-inclined friends I had consulted with before the visit. They used fancy French words like "haut" and "couture" to describe their product, which must have justified the eight-to-twenty-dollar price per bar. I didn't know then that "couture" means "made-to-measure," which I would have found hilariously ironic while being given a tour of the robotic assembly line printing out this brown gold. Maybe it should have been an indication of things to come. The owner of Vosges was Katrina Markoff, whom I only knew from her shameless self-promotion in every luxury magazine and on every billboard in the city. She was the queen of chocolate fit for a queen, and the archetype for every feminist-powered entrepreneur statement the media cooked up. She was stunningly beautiful, wealthy, and fierce.

Robert, Vosges's COO, could have been the cover model for

Upper-Middle Management Weekly. He attempted to dress down to match his new hip environment, but he only looked as if he had forgotten his tie in his BMW due to balancing his pumpkin spiced latte in one hand and his tennis bag in the other. Apart from his outfit, there were two things I gathered about him within moments of sitting down: he was much, much more experienced than me when it came to business management, and he didn't know a damned thing about technology. Both of these would play in my favor.

"Look," he said as soon as we sat down. "I was brought in here to take over and turn this place around. We make the most high-quality, haut chocolate in the world"—he recited from the brand bible—"with the most unique flavors and ingredients. But, we've fallen behind on digital. Our website needs a lot of work. We also pay a lot of money to an agency based in London for online advertising, and I have no idea if they are doing a good job or not. We need help sorting all of this out. Is this what your company specializes in?"

This was much more of a test than a question. I knew Jennifer had given him the scoop that I was just getting started. He knew for a fact there was no "company" behind me. He was seeing if I would try to bullshit him.

"Robert"—I smiled—"my company is brand new, so you're looking at the entire team right here. But truthfully, this is what I specialize in. I've been building websites since I was thirteen, studied computer science, and I founded an online advertising company called TrakLabs. I'd be a perfect fit, and I also have an army of guys at my disposal whom I've worked with for years who I can bring in as needed."

I then produced my impressive-looking stack of papers and carefully paged through them, showing Robert how poorly the Vosges website was functioning from a search perspective, and how much room for improvement there was. Now, I had absolutely no idea if any of these graphs actually told that story, but neither did he. I had other pages in my bag that detailed the return on investment, or ROI, of certain types of internet marketing, which I left snugly packed away, as he was informed enough to have kicked my ass on the subject and killed the meeting. This is why you have to know who you're talking to.

He was clearly impressed with my presentation. There was no doubt he was stretched thin and alone on an island in this new role, and a potential partner in a hotshot tech kid could clearly bolster his cause.

"John, you know your stuff," he said. "This is great. As you can imagine, though, we are on a tight budget." I recalled the photos of Katrina on a private jet on her way to visit her truffle suppliers in France, but only nodded. "So, I would like a proposal from you, but please keep that in mind when you put the financial model together."

This was also a bit of a test. Even if his "budget" was tight, there is a truism about money that everyone in business should take advantage of. A billion is more impressive than a million. A $10,000 watch is better than a $1,000 watch. Platinum is better than silver. However valid Robert's claims, Business Psych 101 demanded that I deliver an egregiously expensive proposal just to impress him, and then allow him to negotiate down and "win" the battle.

This proposal would have to be my magnum opus. We ended the meeting and I went home to construct it, equipped with the single most important lesson about design I had learned from my time in Los Angeles.

24 | THE PROPOSAL

An interesting phenomenon had occurred in recent years around design. Apple's ferocious entrance into the smartphone business had shaken the world. The big question was why a device that functionally didn't do anything its predecessors didn't had upended the entire market, knocking out behemoths like Palm and Black-Berry, and changed how we live our lives.

The answer was simple: Apple brought design to the masses. Not design in terms of pretty interfaces and a sleek appliance, but rather, design that got into deep levels of our collective psyche to determine how we wanted to be connected to the world, talk to friends, browse the web, and consume content. They mercilessly dissected the competition's weaknesses and addressed those seemingly small details in devices that would take us from frustration to *love*. They didn't advertise the processing power or the number of pixels in the screen, but rather, all the ways that life would be better with their snazzy apps and beautiful hardware.

Apple designed the device and software specifically for the human beings they intended to sell it to, by understanding us a little better than we understood ourselves.

This approach was a reflection of one of Steve Jobs's most beloved quotes: "Design is not just what it looks and feels like. Design is how it works."

I was fascinated by and had exhaustively studied the psychological effects of good design, and I began to notice it (or the lack thereof) obsessively in my daily life. Was it clear whether you were supposed to push or pull a door without a sign's telling you? Where did an airline position power plugs in relation to the seat? How long did it take to settle an ATM transaction?

This was not only the premise on which ÄKTA was built but also became my personal differentiator. Everything I did was led with design, which sometimes made all the difference in the world. Whether you received a business card or Christmas card from me, it was design-led. I now had to translate that to a convincing proposal.

I stared at a blank screen for what felt like hours, trying to find the inspiration to get started. I tried to imagine what the readers of this document would need to *feel* to get excited about it.

I began with a personal letter "From the CEO" with a big, impressive-looking signature at the bottom. In the letter I explained how perfect a fit I was to help Vosges catch up to its competitors on the tech side, and how I had no doubt that I could meet Robert's operational goals. And most important, I suggested how much of a risk they would be taking by *not* hiring me. This final piece became one of my favorite and most effective sales tactics. More on that later.

From there the rest of the document started to flow. I knew it was going to end up in Katrina's hands, so as important as the content was, it needed to be a work of art as well. Creative executives tend to make decisions based on instinct and feeling, while more traditional, business-oriented executives will dig deeper into content and numbers. However, every human being subconsciously makes some degree of judgment about credibility and quality based on presentation alone. It's why high-end fashion companies spend such an unthinkable amount of money on packaging, retail frontage, and even the scent in their stores. A thick business card signifies a better company than a thin one. Beautifully crafted packaging implies that it holds a more valuable product than flimsy packaging.

So, a work of art is what I made—a twenty-page-long, pixel-perfect document with attractive type and convincing-looking charts. *Millions* could be added to their bottom line through a concerted digital effort, and I promised I was the guy to do it, all for the comparatively measly sum of $10,000 per month.

That figure represented the most outlandish number I could bring myself to say without laughing out loud during the negotiation. It felt completely ridiculous as I typed it into the document, but when I considered the potential return on investment I could generate, it was reasonable. At least I hoped so.

The last step was to print my masterpiece on some impressively weighty paper stock and bind it into folders for the big pitch meeting.

Here goes everything.

25 | THE PITCH

I wore the wardrobe equivalent of a mullet: a short-sleeve T-shirt with a blazer. I was doing business but also ready to party.

My confidence was high going in. It had to be. Given this was a crucial fork in the road, it didn't make sense but to go in bold and strong-spoken, ready to take on the world, and lay down my most convincing performance.

As Mike Tyson said, "Everybody has a plan until they get punched in the mouth," and this was one of those moments.

I stepped foot inside the factory and felt something was off. There was absolutely no sound but the whirring of belts and clanking of metal, even though at least one hundred people were working there. I said a loud, deep "Hello, Robert!" as he approached, only to see him wave his hands frantically and mouth *Shhh!* He took me by the arm and rushed me to a refrigerated storage area in the back.

"So, I know how weird this sounds," he said sheepishly, "but no one is allowed to talk in the office today."

You've got to be fucking kidding me.

"Katrina is here," he said in response to my baffled expression. "She apparently read some business book that talked about one valuable thing the author's company does is to have a day of silence per week—'No Talk Thursdays'—to enable everyone to focus and work with no verbal distractions. Katrina has now implemented that here at Vosges, starting today."

The book he was referencing was *Rework*, by Jason Fried and David Heinemeier Hansson. Fried was a Chicago entrepreneur who ran a software company called 37 Signals (now Basecamp). His plan to create a distraction-free environment to boost productivity worked for him because he ran a tiny software company—not a high-end chocolate factory where phones were typically ringing off the hook, people were running around hollering at one another, and dozens of staffers had to communicate verbally to keep the machinery running. Clearly, Katrina had taken the book a bit too literally without considering whether its methods were viable for Vosges. This wasn't good news for anyone involved.

I was about to ask Robert how I was supposed to make a pitch without being able to talk—perhaps I should have grabbed a couple of couture bars and used them as semaphore flags—but he was already rushing me back to the main office. On the way, I watched as customer service representatives were whispering into their phones with their heads down, inches from their desks. In every dark corner of every room, hushed conversations were taking place with eyes darting about. A half dozen people were standing outside in the bitter cold, trying to have a meeting.

Two things were evident: Katrina was feared by her employees. And, from what I could see, she might be an idiot.

There are no harder people to negotiate with and pitch business to than those who exist in their own bizarre universe. Like poker, business is a sport. And sports have rules. When everyone is playing by those rules, it works. But just like having an amateur at a professional poker table, the dynamics get thrown off when someone in a business setting does not follow the rules. This is also why amateurs so often win major poker tournaments. Similarly, I am sure her cockamamie antics are what empowered her to create a "leather-wrapped chocolate mask made with aphrodisiac ingredients" *and* get someone to actually buy it, but it wasn't going to bode well for me in this meeting.

Robert was peering at his watch, breathing a small sigh of relief that we were perfectly on time, and pushed me into the conference room.

At the small table sat Katrina Markoff. Her model-perfect public image was clearly a bit out of date. Across from me sat a disheveled woman with unkempt hair and a bag of potato chips in front of her. Potato chips would be out of place in any business meeting, but sitting in a factory that makes overpriced chocolate, it was even stranger. When I stepped toward her to introduce myself, I was stopped in my tracks by a raised hand and another overly dramatic *shhhhhhhh*, so offered a silent handshake, which she accepted with two fingers and a thumb, like the queen. I panicked as she pulled me in for a European double-cheek kiss, which I executed horribly, and then awkwardly waited for any indication of how to proceed. Great start.

Robert took a seat next to Katrina, uncomfortably close, and waved me toward the other side of her. We were now almost straddling her on each knee, like kids meeting Santa Claus. She seemed oblivious to any of it, focusing only on her potato chips. Robert leaned to within a few inches of her ear and softly muttered, "Katrina, please meet John Roa. He is the CEO of ÄKTA. He is here to tell us how he can help turn around our digital strategy."

I took the cue and produced my meticulously designed proposals and handed one to each of them. At this moment, the door opened, and a young, scared-looking girl entered. She paused, unclear on what to do, before coming over to my left side and leaning within a centimeter of my ear. "Can I get you a water or coffee?"

This was beginning to feel more and more like an *SNL* skit. I turned toward her, and she moved her hair behind her ear, as if that would make it easier to hear me. "A coffee would be lovely," I said, almost inaudibly. My lips grazed her ear.

I then turned back to Katrina as she began paging through her copy at a frenetic pace, and didn't seem to pause to read a single word or even stop to consider the visuals. When she reached the last page she registered the "$10,000 per month" figure and loudly said, "Ten thousand fucking dollars? Is this a joke, Robert?"

Half the office heard this, due to the complete silence.

"Katrina," Robert quietly pleaded. "Please hear him out." Our heads were still within inches of each other.

Instead of being able to productively walk her through my plan, I would now have to speak directly to the price, which is the worst place to start a negotiation. She was also clearly aggravated with Robert, which undermined his ability to advocate for me.

My options were to talk myself into a deeper hole, or flip the script. So, flip the script I did. Backing up to an appropriate business-discussion distance, I began calmly, in a normal tone of voice to speak. "Katrina, I can only assume that the reason your office is dead silent today is because of the book *Rework*." Assumptions are always most effective when you know you're right. "I can therefore assume you respect tech companies and technology, or else why would you take the author's advice to this level? You have another tech guy sitting in front of you right now, telling you that, respectfully, Vosges's digital strategy is an embarrassment, and you're missing out on millions of dollars in revenue. You're also holding the door open for a competitor who isn't ignoring digital to eat your lunch. Frankly, I could care less if that happens. I don't even like chocolate. But Robert asked me to come in here and explain how I can fix that problem. If you aren't interested, I'll gladly take my leave. It's no sweat off my back." That last gambit was ironic given that my back was now sweating profusely.

She stared at me irately for a few seconds, clearly not accustomed to being spoken to in such a way. I was readying my defenses in case she attacked. I was pretty sure I could spin out of my chair before she could do any real damage. But after a few more beats, she relented and asked if she could take a moment to read my proposal. She was still whispering, which now felt even more awkward after my little speech. I happily agreed and tried to act nonchalant as she paged at a more appropriate pace through my document. Normally I would have struck up some small talk with Robert, but all we could do was make awkward facial expressions at each other.

After what felt like a quiet lifetime, she whispered something to Robert that I couldn't hear, got up, gave me another queenly shake, and walked out the door. After we were confident she was outside of whispershot, he relayed her message:

"She loved it."

26 | BANKROLLED

We spent some time negotiating the terms and landed at a month-to-month contract for $4,000 per month. This was a huge number for me, and allowed Robert to boast that he had talked me down by 60 percent, which made him look like a rock star. Make your buyer look good. Start high, work down. Worked like a charm.

I was now fully funded and knew I could create serious value for Vosges with minimal effort. TrakLabs was long gone, and while SocialCrunch was still buzzing around in my head, I had a wild new optimism for ÄKTA. Perhaps because it was producing real capital, and aside from the physically awkward confrontation with my new client, it was straightforward to start. I now had both the time and capital I needed to hustle my tail off to get ÄKTA running.

My relentless networking intensified, especially now that I could afford to buy tickets to events. Serial networking is about as glamorous as researching all the ways you can kick yourself in the balls. A never-ending slog of bad food, worse presentations, and bloodthirsty corporate sponsors. Forget which shitty hotel you're in, take a name tag, pretend you know some guy, shake one sweaty palm, hand over a business card. And on and on and on.

By my best guess, I attended three hundred events in 180 days and met some four thousand people. Every drawer of my crappy apartment was littered with random business cards. My email inbox was stuffed with meaningless follow-ups and condescending responses to my business pitch. There were phone calls and meetings, but still not a single solid lead.

I had no choice but to keep going. I refined my strategy to give every prospect the absolute least amount of time possible. I'd ask a few qualifying questions, such as their role and company, to determine if they even had the ability to buy my services or had any influence over the decision. As soon as I heard someone was in accounting or the partner of one of the speakers, I'd pretend I had a phone call, or that I was being waved over by someone else, and move on.

I was almost burned-out. I just didn't have anything left in me.

On a fateful Friday, exhausted from the week, I was drunk at an Irish pub with one of my friends, a Brit named Ruairi. He lived in the same building as me and we'd met in the elevator. He played the welcome role of jester in my life, a never-ending source of comic relief and silliness, at a time when I really needed the balance of both. I sat, drinking a pint of beer that was well out of my budget, complaining to Ruairi on my lack of progress.

I noticed a girl across the bar. Pretty and lively. One benefit of having to look presentable every day and not having money to overeat was that I was in great shape and so got plenty of attention from women. She was Scottish Susan, across the pond for work. A bit older than me with a hilarious personality and, as the beers went down, an accent that sounded as if she were speaking multiple words at the same time, making her virtually incomprehensible. When my girlfriend, Lisa, arrived, I tapped my friend in. "Hey, Ruairi. Come over here and talk to Susan. She is a Brit like you. Enjoy."

They began a dialogue that not a single other person in the pub could have understood. As the whiskey shots came and the clarity of the night started to fade, Ruairi suddenly turned to me with a wry smile. "Mate!" he said. "Turns out, Susan is some big shot at a golf company. I think she needs a business like ÄKTA to help her."

27 | TOPGOLF

Susan was, in fact, the director of marketing for Topgolf, which had expanded to the United States from the United Kingdom, flush with cash from a big private equity deal. Its premise was kind of genius: imagine golf meets bowling. It featured a full-fledged driving range with large spaceship-looking circular targets placed throughout it. You swung at golf balls that had RFID chips embedded inside them, so that if you hit one of these targets, the system could detect it. You could rack up points and compete against friends, and even play games like hitting sequential targets in order. Topgolf hosted birthday parties and corporate events, complete with greasy food and alcohol, luring in non-golfers.

Its problem was that the systems and screens used to play the game—large flat-screen television monitors at each bay—had been ported over from the United Kingdom, and looked like something made in the 1980s. As it turned out, Susan was responsible for finding a vendor who could redesign these systems. Her search had turned up little thus far.

"Is this something ÄKTA could help with?" she asked me over a coffee later that week. She had gone on a date with my friend. An inside track always helps.

"Absolutely, Susan," I assured her. "We're design specialists. This could be an *amazing* project."

The timing couldn't have been better. The Vosges job was going to be done in a couple of months, thank the Lord. While that meant my sole income source was ending, it also meant I no longer had to deal with the band of ninnyhammers that was that chocolate company, even though the project had been a success.

A few days later I was invited to the Topgolf site in suburban Chicago to see its current operation firsthand and to meet their executive team, who happened to be having an all-hands meeting that day. I spent the bulk of the week preparing my pitch and designing a presentation deck that would give Steve Jobs a hard-on. This was the culmination of over half a year of relentless networking and disappointment. There wasn't a chance in hell I was going to leave this meeting empty-handed.

Chief Technology Officer Brian showed me around the facility, explaining to me in proprietary, technical terms how everything worked. I held a finger to my lips and nodded my head, as if I had any clue what he was talking about.

I took diligent notes, mostly with big question marks about things I didn't understand that I had to follow up on.

After the grand tour, I was led to a large conference room populated with a number of young people in business-casual attire, talking in huddled groups and drinking coffee. Brian announced our arrival and asked everyone to take a seat for my presentation.

I smiled and set up my laptop, trying to ignore my jackhammering heart. Even though I had delivered a hundred sales pitches, I had never presented at this level, with this much at stake, with this little to back up what I was trying to sell. A few well-placed questions that dug into who my team really consisted of or the history of my company would destroy any chances and credibility I had. My pitch would have to be so impassioned and convincing that they wouldn't feel the need to hit me in diligence.

As a businessman, I recognized that I was facing a personal conflict as well. I refused to believe I was doing anything wrong or proposing anything I couldn't figure out how to do at a high level of excellence. Despite walking a fine ethical line in my younger years, I was now hyperfocused on running ÄKTA by the book and doing right by our clients. With that said, a company like Topgolf should not have been hiring us. It would be inching very close to corporate negligence to hire an upstart agency with no full-time team, no portfolio, and no history. But that was precisely what I intended to have them do. My mind briefly trailed off, wondering how on earth any service business got its first real client. I filed that away to investigate later and dug in.

My pitch was a master class in euphemisms.

"ÄKTA is a user-experience design consultancy in Chicago. We are made up of a collective of designers and technologists that I have put together over the last seven years through my different startup companies." *No employees, yet.*

"We are new, but that makes us solely focused on progressive methods and not stuck to any legacy technology or platforms." *No portfolio, yet.*

"We have led design projects for Microsoft, Nintendo, Boeing, Motorola, and Google." *At least, my people have.*

"The design challenge Topgolf has ahead is extensive and difficult. But if executed at a high level, could provide a competitive differentiation and defensibility for years to come." *This is going to be expensive and complicated—for all of us!*

The next section I ad-libbed.

"Outside of our world-class design and technical skill, our real value is as a mitigator of risk. These types of projects have an embarrassingly high rate of failure. It is not difficult to burn hundreds of thousands of dollars and end up with nothing to show for it, which is the worst-case scenario for all of you. With ÄKTA, you can be assured of lock-tight project management processes, transparency, simple accounting, and executive accountability." *Your ass is on the line here, people. Hiring me will make you look good.*

"We have a lot more work to do in the discovery phase of the project. But from our current vantage point, this is a two-hundred-to-four-hundred-thousand-dollar job, probably stretching six to twelve months." *I have absolutely no idea what this is going to cost, but I think I could build a fucking spaceship for a few hundred grand, so that sounds like a perfectly fine number.*

"At the end, you'll have a work of art that will grow with your company and make your customers love their experience at Topgolf. We would be honored to work with you."

I let the projector hang at the "Thank You" screen while I nonchalantly refilled my coffee. I was high from my own energy. But there was absolutely nothing more critical than appearing as if this were just another day at the office.

Whispered conversations broke out across the table, which was a good thing. I retook my position, and once an appropriate amount of time had passed, asked if there were any questions. The moment of truth. Positive, project-oriented questions meant a life of riches and glory. Negative, diligence-oriented questions meant a life of bankruptcy and shame.

The questions that were raised were softballs, at best. Wanting to hear more about my entrepreneurial story. More about our design philosophy. Agreement about how perfect it was that we had experience with Nintendo given that our job with Topgolf would effectively be to produce a video game interface. Compliments about how our work was done onshore and the convenience of us both being based in Chicago. With every question, my confidence and excitement grew. We were going to get this fucking deal.

The CEO, a charming British man, had finally heard enough and stood up. He shook my hand, told me I had him convinced, and told me to work with Susan and Brian on a formal proposal that the board could review. The rest of the room followed his lead out the door until only Susan remained. Even she was impressed, not having expected so polished a presentation from the drunk guy at the pub.

Outside she gave me a hug as I hopped into my rental car, even though I felt as if I could just flap my arms and fly home.

I immediately rang Isaac, who was expecting my call, in Los Angeles. "I think we got the deal!" I screamed. I don't think he had ever heard me so excited. "However, I just committed to a load of shit that admittedly I don't know anything about. Please for the love of God tell me you know what scalable vector graphics are!"

Isaac assured me he could deliver on the scope I had sold. We were in business.

28 | IN BUSINESS

I arrived home in a trance. All my motor functions were on autopilot while my mind raced at peak speed working out everything I had to do.

Find an attorney. Get Topgolf signed. Get Topgolf's down payment. Hire Kevin. Find an office. Buy laptops. Write up an agreement for Isaac. Figure out who else has to be on the team. Work out exactly what the heck we had to deliver for Topgolf.

Nothing on earth could have broken my focus at this point. The energy that was still coursing through my body was pure electricity. I wasn't hungry; I wasn't thirsty; I wasn't thinking about friends or family; I wasn't paying attention to text messages; I didn't consider how long it had been since I'd seen my girlfriend. I didn't know what time of the day it was. There may or may not have been music playing or sirens going by. Being an entrepreneur consumed and empowered me. The lure of this feeling and mindset is what I can now identify as my greatest personal challenge. It's why I ended up trading away things I shouldn't have while chasing this dragon. This feeling is why so many parts of my life died over the next five years.

I was doing a hundred things simultaneously. Calling contacts to ask for introductions to lawyers, accountants, banks, and real estate brokers. Making overly detailed lists of every step I would need to do in the coming days to perfectly execute this start. Mentally writing the final proposal to Topgolf. Sorting out my offer to Kevin.

Folks generally stop me at this part of the story and ask, respectfully, how did my twenty-six-year-old self, with only failed startups and mistakes behind me, know how to do this? How did I learn such a massive amount of information necessary to launch so ambitious a project?

The answer is a combination of instinct, vision, drive, a bit of insanity, and honing all of the above through thousands of hours of experience. What I realize in hindsight is that I had done precisely the same thing that anyone who sought outsized success at a young age would have done: locate the magic intersection between biologically based talent, ferocious passion, and relentless perseverance to succeed. It's the same path for all of us—young athletes, musicians, scientists.

Your favorite baseball player didn't just start slamming home runs in the major leagues. Someone who observed him noticed that at five years old he had a talent for swinging a bat, and seemed to love swinging that bat, so they encouraged him to swing it a million more times. We all know the formula. Entrepreneurship is simply taking a brain attuned for it, a psyche built for it, and adding a wealth of experience.

As soon as I had taken care of the preliminary steps in setting up the business, I rang Kevin and told him we had to talk. I hadn't slept in two nights and the urgency in my voice was clear. He picked me up in his shitty car once again, taking almost the same route to almost the same street corner downtown.

While I clearly brought a newly heightened energy to my proposal, I now also had the confidence to match. I did not feel as if I were asking him to do me a favor. I was giving him the opportunity of a lifetime.

With only nonverbal cues, I knew he was in. And so did he. Which made his final statement a bit jarring.

"If we do this, we can't be friends," he said solemnly. "Or this won't work."

If anyone knew this to be true, it was me. But it was still hard to hear. Entrepreneurship is a lonely journey at the best of times, but for some reason I felt this one was going to be lonelier than my previous ones.

He told me he needed a few weeks to roll out of Varsoft. We shook hands and ÄKTA was in business.

The real estate guys I had contacted weren't interested in helping us with an office search, because their commission would probably be less than the price of the coffee they bought on the way. But, they made some suggestions on possible spaces. I called Kevin the next day and asked if he could meet me at a spot just a handful of blocks from Varsoft.

When we arrived at the mid-rise on Michigan Avenue near Grant Park, I felt an electric head-to-toe rush that would come to accompany every major moment or milestone at ÄKTA. As we headed up to see the available units, Kevin had a very peculiar smile on his face. Something was up.

"What?" I asked him. "What's going on?"

"I just fucking quit Varsoft. Grabbed my stuff and walked out at lunch. Fuck that place."

I was laughing as we approached the space. First, at just how outrageous my man Kevin was as a human being and how glad I was to have him on my team. Second, at imagining the moment Steven Levin put two and two together and realized that Kevin had left to work for *me*.

The fourth-floor office space was the business equivalent of a dorm room. Two hundred square feet of checkered carpet, drop ceilings, and beautiful floor-to-ceiling windows looking out on Michigan Avenue. I didn't need to see anything else. This was our new home.

Because the space would be occupied for another few weeks until the old tenant could move out, we were offered a small temporary office down the hall, for free. At 9:00 a.m. the following morning, Kevin and I both arrived at 155 North Michigan Avenue and walked up to our new office. As ridiculous and claustrophobic as that little space was, that first day was one of the happiest days of my life. We schemed and planned and drew on the whiteboard and brainstormed and laughed.

Nothing had felt so right in a long, long time.

PART TWO

The Turn

29 | THE GENIUS MISFITS

The earliest days of launching a new enterprise are such a critical point in time for any entrepreneur. They require a balance
of honesty and introspection to appreciate the challenges ahead,
without getting overwhelmed and letting them consume you. It is
incredibly easy to lose balance and either overplan or underplan,
which becomes a poison pill at this stage. With Kevin coming on full
time, this was the last moment it was going to be a truly solo adventure. The roller coaster ride was about to begin.

There were a lot of highs during that period—organizing the
final Topgolf contract, figuring out how to write them an invoice
for $100,000, explaining design and user experience to Kevin, re-
creating the logo and website for ÄKTA—which were matched by a
wealth of lows, including our extreme anxiety that we'd gotten ourselves in too deep, the reality of the size of the project we'd taken on,
trying to figure out how we were going to hire a local team who
could execute this work, and my own sheer panic that I had to explain to Kevin what design and user experience were, because they
were, well, our entire business.

For Kevin, though, being unbeholden to Steven finally gave him the opportunity to use his wide-ranging skills in a more fulfilling way. It was those skills that gave me the most hope in our earliest days. For some reason, Kevin seemed to have solutions to the most unexpected problems. As I was explaining one of the positions we would need to fill, he nodded his head and mentioned that he knew a guy who did that exact thing in Chicago. The guy's name was Dave, and I told Kevin to get him in to talk to us as soon as he possibly could.

But how did a municipal tax auditor know an information architect in Chicago when I didn't? When Dave showed up, the answer became clear. He had big curly hair, an amazing beard, and one completely tattooed arm. He looked like Weird Al and David Beckham's love child. I ran him through the paces of the job and explained that we weren't able to pay salaries quite yet, but could offer a (slightly under-) competitive hourly rate. He was keen and happy to be working with his friend Kevin.

For the other positions we needed to recruit, Kevin stole job descriptions from other design agencies, ran advertisements online, and reached out to his bizarrely robust network. After a few days, résumés started rolling in.

One critical position was a user researcher, who would lead the studies of various user groups and determine their requirements, which in turn would drive the entire project. Barely a day into his search, Kevin told me he had the perfect person. When Scott arrived, I was seriously bemused, as he looked exactly like the guy you would hire to play the user researcher in a made-for-TV movie: He was tall and pale as a vampire, with short blond hair and a completely lovable demeanor. He was either the nicest guy on the planet or a serial killer.

He answered each question I asked at a staccato clip, as if he had mentally written out the replies in his head and was now reading them back. He used exactly the minimum number of words possible and then sat perfectly silent, staring at me until I posed the next question. He was wildly intelligent and more knowledgeable than me about every topic I brought up. He was perfect.

We had found two needles in haystacks in a matter of weeks, and they weren't typical—not by a long shot. But I loved that, as they appealed to my own natural subversiveness. They were awkward, odd, quirky, and probably overlooked by other recruiters, which made them exactly what I wanted. We weren't going to hire only the fancy résumés coming out of top design schools. Fuck the optics. Our entire foundation was to be built on doing things exactly as we saw fit.

The last key position I needed was someone to help me drum up more business. I knew intuitively from day one that ÄKTA would have to maintain a large pipeline of business, as cash flow is the Achilles' heel of any consultancy. As these companies grow, they end up with expensive butts in expensive seats, and these people either cost tremendous amounts of money when they aren't working on billable projects or make a great profit margin when they are working. And with no investors and no piggy bank, which was our situation, it was going to be a constant struggle to always be bringing in new clients.

I hadn't been shy about notifying friends, family, and social media about my new venture. I had been creating buzz by promoting ÄKTA as the "best design firm in Chicago" and promising a reveal of our soon-to-be-named initial megaclient. I used these same platforms to announce a special career opportunity for someone to lead our business development charge. To work alongside me, *master* entrepreneur and salesman, to drive new clients and relationships. I left out the part where the salary would be effectively zero until we closed new business, and how shitty of a mentor I would probably be given how I was making things up as I went.

Lisa had a great group of friends whom I had gotten to know in my limited social time. During a night out one of them suggested that I speak to her sister, Pascale, as she was looking for work. I assumed that such a recommendation wouldn't have been made unless she had some relevant background, so I agreed to meet her. As it turned out, not only did Pascale not have experience doing long-cycle technical sales, but she had absolutely no business experience whatsoever. Her last job had been serving burgers at a restaurant on her college campus. She even spelled "employment" wrong in the subject of her email to me.

While that would have ended the conversation for most people, I did what I always try to do and evaluated her from other angles. She was healthily confrontational, intelligent, and someone I could see molding to the ways of the startup. And she certainly wasn't in a position to ask for even a competitive salary. Here was this fiery young woman who needed a start and clearly had a very natural potential.

When I told Kevin of my plans to hire her, he thought I was insane, but backed my decision.

Our core team now felt complete and we were ready to get to work. But then a curveball came.

There was always a curveball.

I received a message randomly from a high school friend who told me some extended friend of a friend was looking for work in Chicago. He was young but extremely talented and I should see him. I agreed and encountered one of the most interesting humans I have ever met—a young kid named Ryan, who I *think* had studied animation and design, but I couldn't be sure, because he stuttered and sweated throughout his interview due to social anxiety. Despite his being unable to have a productive conversation, it was clear there was a lot to this guy, and best of all, he was looking for an internship, paid or not. Well, for us it was "not," and we would look so much more professional with our very own intern. (To date I have never had anyone make me coffee.) He went on to become one of our most talented and influential designers.

This was the beginning of our band of genius misfits.

30 | THE FIRST DAY

If there was one thing I wasn't going to get tripped up on again, it was not having my legal ducks in a row. Kevin called up a colleague who was a practicing attorney and got him to work at an extremely low hourly rate (in exchange for the promise of future normal-wage work) to make sure that everyone on the team had proper paperwork when they started.

I had never really considered what the first days of our first project would be like. Kevin had brought in a couple of high-level architecture and design consultants who would help us kick off the project and add credibility. Gray beards, he called them. Apart from them, the team had little formal business experience, and most had never been part of a scrappy startup. I could see how they might have a romanticized view of a startup, thanks to Hollywood's version of them and any number of *Forbes*'s features, only to then arrive at a plain, boring office with a small group of awkward people, and have their dreams dashed before they had even had a chance to begin.

I wanted to prevent this disillusionment in any way possible.

To avoid this culture shock, my gut told me that one of the first things I had to do was to quickly (but frugally) invest in the quality of the work environment, now that the other tenant had moved out and we were ready to renovate our long-term space.

Remarkably, Kevin had gotten Topgolf to pay our down payment, so we now had $100,000 in our bank account. This was a freeing and horrifying moment all at once. Money makes everything very real. Before money was in play, either party to the deal could back out or wise up to the challenges we were facing. But once that line was crossed, the stakes went up by a factor of one hundred. Now we were bound by scary contracts that would end in lawsuits if things didn't go well. But it also meant that ÄKTA was now a funded business, and I had to be very careful about managing that.

Had I paid attention in Business 101, one of the early chapters would probably have covered the importance of first creating a budget—a plan to make sure that that $100,000 was properly earmarked. While the thought did cross my mind, I was also realistic enough to know that there was no viable way to be precise about a budget, given our current situation. There were too many unknowns, too much winging it, too little experience to fall back on. A budget would have inevitably been inexact, which could cause more harm than good. We were going to have to follow our gut.

First, I gave instructions to our landlord for the basic office renovations we needed: stark white walls and black-and-red carpet squares. "But you don't *ever* paint walls white, John! Use something off-white!" It was comedic how many times I heard this, as if my whole group of friends had suddenly become interior designers.

Second, I rounded up Kevin and Pascale for our first out-of-office mission: a trip to outfit our space. We rented a large van and set off for the suburbs of Chicago and IKEA, the perfect place for this task: cheap as dirt and with a deep selection of solid primary-colored furniture. I was determined to carry the red, black, and white color scheme through as dramatically as possible into our office setting.

For my corner, because I was the CEO and all, I chose a sheer black glass desk. For the team, thick black wood desks with black metal frames. Each would be separated by bright red bookcases and topped with red lamps. Finally, a large white conference table with black chairs that I hoped would fit in our tiny space.

The objective was clear: to look bigger and better than we were, ready to punch above our weight class. We were the "best new design agency in town," after all.

The tab for outfitting our entire office was about $8,000, a sum that was so astronomical at the time that I thought I was going to vomit. But I kept a smile on my face, which apparently convinced Kevin and Pascale that I knew what I was doing. My hand shook as I handed the business debit card to the cashier, but I made sure they didn't notice.

Our van was packed to the gills as we left the superstore, and Kevin began calling our team to arrange for everyone to meet at the new space upon our return. Assembling the office was going to be our first team-building exercise. I wanted everyone to feel a part of the office and be accountable.

We pulled into the loading bay of our building to find the crew eagerly waiting. I had one of those awkward internal dialogues about my role as CEO: *Do I join the team and help them haul boxes? Or do I leave them to do it so as to assert my position of authority?* In this case, I helped, but I knew there would be a turning point down the road when this strategy would need to change.

It gave me tremendous confidence that every member of the staff naturally gravitated to his or her role during furniture building. Kevin was managing them all and making sure everything was going smoothly. The information architects were diligently building with precise movements and all the right tools. The designers were drawing the best layout so the colors would create the right pattern. Everyone was showing medium to hilariously high levels of obsessive compulsiveness and perfectionism, which is what you want in a design group.

Me? I let them find their rhythm together and answered the important questions when asked. Mostly I sat back and observed, trying to look self-assured, while the hamster wheel in my head whirred.

This is crazy, right?

We can pull this off, right?

A non-designer can start a design agency, right?

31 | THE SHOW

The scope of our work for Topgolf was mostly clear: as the design group, we were responsible for understanding the technical and customer needs of the new software, architecting the best way to present that information, designing video-game-esque inter-faces for the new screens, and helping to deploy our work into the physical Topgolf site. My engineering background certainly helped in translating some of that. I fundamentally understood that Topgolf had some engine behind the scenes that would handle all the logic and calculations for the games, and output some kind of code in or-der to present game information on the screens. The only issue was we had to propose a solution before actually digging into this tech-nical infrastructure.

Susan, who had gotten us Topgolf as a client, was now in a steady and serious relationship with Ruairi, which meant that not only had Lisa and I become quite good friends with her but that she consis-tently gave me the inside track on what Topgolf expected of us. The sentiment within the company was that ÄKTA was a legendary de-sign group, and everyone was excited to be working with us. We were cool, noncorporate, young, and edgy—everything Topgolf wanted to be.

This information played into how I prepared for our crucial kick-off meeting, which would be held in their corporate office. I spent days preparing the sexiest damn keynote presentation that ever did exist. It was like *Starry Night* knocked up a supermodel. It was magic.

My team had been well coached.

"Have your fucking introductions memorized and buttoned up."

"Show the fuck off."

"No one fucking talk when John is talking."

"If John gives you that look, you better have something fucking interesting to say."

"Take notes and fucking smile."

I knew I was at my best when I had to put on a show and prove myself. But between you and me, I was terrified. I felt a panic attack simmering barely below the surface. I was trying so hard to ignore it.

Deep breath. Inhale through the nose. One, two, three. Exhale through the mouth. Feel your heartbeat slowing. This inner dialogue helped. Imagining my epic performance. My dominance. Winning the battle.

I stood in the hall outside the Topgolf conference room. Black shoes, black skinny jeans, black V-neck T-shirt—the same outfit I'd been wearing for weeks. I held my phone to my ear, pretending to take a call, to buy myself a little more time. Out of the corner of my eye, I saw more than twenty people milling around the room, pouring coffee, exchanging business cards with my team. Loose-fitting checkered shirts tucked into wrinkled khaki pants.

Kevin, who was already inside the room, gave me a nod. Even now I don't know if he actually believed I was on a call or was just aware that I was trying to keep the situation from spinning out from under me, but the nod helped. It was game time. Jordan from the free throw line. Phelps at the last turn. It didn't matter that my nerves were working against me. I had to go in and crush this.

One last deep breath.

I entered the room, gave a wide smile to the CEO, and apologized for my tardiness, giving him the "We CEOs know how it is!" wink. I took my place at the head of the table.

As I scanned the room, I was satisfied with the team's execution of my seating arrangement, which would ensure that the all-critical relationships needed to make this work would form: Kevin was next to Topgolf's project lead, with whom he had to become best friends. Dave was between the technical architects, in order to make small, positively reinforcing comments about my plan. Pascale sat with their business development lead. Scott had a seat alone, nearest to me. I needed him ready to deliver his speech about our proprietary ethnographic approach to user research and heuristics using longitudinal studies in order to reveal the unmet needs of the Topgolf user. Or, something.

"First off, thank you so much for having us," I began. "We could not be more excited at the opportunity to work together. Topgolf is one of the most impressive companies we have had the chance to talk to, to say the least, and we look forward to delivering what we are sure will be an industry-leading product."

A bead of sweat dripped down my spine as I flipped through the first slides of my presentation, which were just there to pump ÄKTA up: Our cumulative years in the industry. All the great clients we had worked for. A creatively cropped photo of our new office that made it look exponentially bigger than it was.

I then started to flow.

The project plan looked brilliant, even though it was a shell at best. Aside from Topgolf's project lead, no one actually cared about the details—they just needed to be convinced we had a plan. My team stepped up. As instructed, they answered questions like professionals and impressed their audience. When Scott delivered his segment, not one person in the room had a damned clue what he was talking about, but it sounded so impressive that it didn't matter.

And then, *boom*. The thank-you page. It was over before I realized. Had I blacked out?

Susan started the applause. Bless you, Susan. Smiles all around. Even a few shoulder slaps. The CEO was the first to stand and excuse himself, after thanking me. He had heard all he needed to, which was the answer to the question: "Did anyone fuck up by hiring these guys? Nope. Okay, I'm good."

Game on.

32 | EXECUTION

I still have the fondest memories of those early days of our first project: arriving before everyone else in the office, having my morning coffee, checking emails, and watching the ants march below on Michigan Avenue. My team would gradually appear, some more slowly than others . . . designers weren't known as morning people. Headphones were popped in ears; diagrams, spreadsheets, and mock-ups would start appearing on screens; and dollar signs would stream from keyboards into our bank account.

With a small handful of people and a single, high-budget client, this was as straightforward as an agency gets. As long as you didn't royally screw up on delivery, you were guaranteed to make money. But you had to think ahead, and this is where the cracks in the agency armor typically appear. Because design projects tend to go in phases (discovery, architecture, design, engineering, implementation), only certain staff would be utilized at any point in time. So, as one person or group finished their phase, you had to be ready to put them on another paying project or they would instantly start losing you money by being inactive. The alternative was the subcontractor shuffle, which I wanted to avoid.

I knew I had to get to work on finding the next Topgolf before this project was over. That was hardly a given. There was a chance this would be our only project and ÄKTA could end as quickly as it began.

I know what you're thinking: Was that *so bad*? I could probably make a hundred grand in profit off this one project. In what, six months? No one could complain about that. It would at least give me some ammunition to work on my next gig, and maybe even chip away at my mountain of debt.

At least, that is what I expect a normal person might think. I went a different direction. If this was going to be our only shot, I was going to have a *great time* failing. At least then, I could look back on an epic story. In order to potentially achieve both objectives, I would sit back and think of methods to raise public awareness for ÄKTA, in the most ridiculous ways possible. I think they call these PR stunts.

It was December 2010 and Chicago was arctic-level cold. At the time there was one device everyone was after and no one could get: the first-generation iPad. I, however, had an inside track on one, which gave me an idea: freeze it in a ten-ton block of ice along with our logo and URL, and drop the whole thing off at the busiest intersection of Michigan Avenue in the middle of the night during the peak of Christmas shopping season. People would go nuts. Great efforts would be made to free the iPad from the ice and the entire city would soon know who we were.

Typing this almost a decade later, it sounds batshit insane. But at the time, it seemed like a great idea, and Kevin was tasked with executing the plan. This wasn't the only time I'm sure he questioned just whom he had pledged his allegiance to. To my utter dismay, his response to me wasn't a plan and a budget, but a letter from the City of Chicago assuring me I would promptly be thrown in jail for disturbing the peace and inciting public recklessness if we went through with the idea. Of *course* Kevin had to spoil the fun by asking them first.

Fine. Scratch that. What else could we do?

I had recently taken up a new pastime: online poker. The sport was currently trending and I had a natural knack for it. New idea: I would host an illegal poker game in our office, the Offline Poker Club. The most prominent entrepreneurs and CEOs in Chicago would be invited. We would set up a table, provide beer, and position ÄKTA as the subversive hub for the movers and shakers of our community. Kevin was not any happier with this idea, but played along. We created a list of all the hotshots we could think of, built a cool-looking microsite with a password, and got the word out. To our amazement the game instantly filled up, with a far higher class of people than we could have expected. Chicago's top tech journalist. A prominent venture capitalist. Two badass entrepreneurs I had only read about (one of whom would go on to, temporarily, become a billionaire).

At our first game everyone had a great time. Everyone bonded. Everyone wanted to know what ÄKTA was.

I doubled down. I told Kevin to speak to the building manager about renting out the empty office next door to our current one. To expand our team? No. Rather, I intended to set up a bar, couch, and Ping-Pong table to provide even more entertainment for our players.

This was executed at an astounding pace, and we now had the ultimate tech bachelor pad. The poker game quickly became a biweekly event. I had by far the least business credentials of any player in the game, but as the host, I was the king. Plus, because I was damned good at poker, I would take home the bag of cash at the end of the evening far more often than any other player.

Except one. Enter Diane: tech goddess at the top of the Chicago startup world and a fine poker player. Want to guess where our next major client came from?

33 | EXCELERATE

Chicago is called the Second City, named as such during our battle with New York City for the Columbian Exposition in 1893, and from then on to acknowledge our Remus complex to our big brother to the east. We seemingly took this moniker seriously, as we have a tendency to adopt what happens on either coast far after it becomes trendy.

One such trend had appeared in San Francisco and New York in the mid-2000s: tech incubators. These companies would bring in super-early-stage tech companies and provide them with accelerants for success: funding, mentorship, connections, and prestige. Airbnb, PayPal, Dropbox, Stripe, and Reddit had all come from just one of these incubators, Y Combinator.

While late to the game, as always, Chicago wasn't about to miss out on the fun. In 2010 Excelerate Labs was born. One of the stand-out companies of its first class was ScholarPro, a marketplace for higher-education scholarships, led by a fiery young CEO, Diane Melville. A few games of poker in, it was clear that she was very enticed by ÄKTA, and the buying conversations began.

Excelerate Labs had recently asked me to mentor its companies on the joys and wonders of UX design. This equipped me with intimate details about Excelerate's latest funding rounds, so I knew how much room I had to sell her on the all-critical redesign of her new scholarship application. We were first on her list when she sent an RFP, or request for proposal, around to a few firms.

My strategy was simple: shock and awe with our approach and price. I intended to propose such an egregiously inflated budget that she would have no doubt that we were her highest-quality option. Or at least that was what I *hoped* she would think.

After a huddle with my team, I delivered a proposal for $180,000. Her call to me went something like this:

"We got your proposal. I knew you would be expensive, but the next highest bid is $50,000. That makes you almost four times the price. Are you fucking insane?"

She made a good point. But I was ready.

"Look, Diane," I told her. "I'm not here to compete on price. You need the best, we are the best. You can't afford to fuck this up, and we can't afford to take on any small projects. I completely understand if you decide to go with one of our cheap competitors. I might do the same thing. But I don't think you'll be satisfied. And when you come back to us, you'll be out a bunch of money, and more important, a bunch of time. I can't go down one dollar in budget. So, you'll need to decide what to do."

In poker we call this a "semi-bluff." I was going all in with tens. I had no idea what she would get for $50,000, and at that point we sort of needed to take on any project we could get, but I stood my ground.

Sometime later, I got a call that went like this:

"If your price had been closer to the other bids, I'm not sure we would go with you. But it is so stupidly high, that either you are really that good and we need you, or you are fucking with us. That takes balls. But my gut says it's the former. So, we are going with you. Let's begin."

34 | GROWING UP

We took the ScholarPro project, and those of a dozen other startups. Contrary to popular belief, startups aren't the most demanding clients, probably because they're so busy getting themselves off the ground. At least not these smaller clients. No one was hounding me at 10:00 p.m. for updates, no one expected us to be working on the weekend. Some were brilliant young companies with big potential. Some were ideas so stupid they made you lose some faith in humanity. But they could all pony up at least tens of thousands of dollars for us to knock out some great designs. Some of our work was hugely successful. Some I never want to think about again. More on this later.

Our core team was proving to be solid, which is the exception to the rule for early-stage agencies. Normally you have a revolving door spinning like a top as you try to ascertain who you want to keep around to shape your culture, or at least I've been told. But we happened upon a small handful of quirky, talented kids who instantly bled ÄKTA red. To augment this team, we had found a guy who lived in a castle in Transylvania who seemed happy to smash out front-end code for us at pennies on the dollar.

Life became a pretty happy little routine. Don black T-shirt. Be first into office. Drink a pot of coffee. Hustle emails, write pitches, assist the team, beat Kevin in Ping-Pong. Lock the door and leave work in the office until the next day.

I pushed the team hard. I guarantee the worst part of their week was having to run client deliverables by me before they went out the door. Maybe because our work was a direct reflection of me, maybe because I knew our competitors weren't going to go to this level, I'm not sure. But there was no faster way to raise my blood pressure than seeing inconsistent user-interface elements or incompatible typefaces. I could spot a misaligned pixel from a mile away and wasn't shy about communicating my sentiment on it when I did. Put another way, I could be an asshole. It was much more important to me for us to spin off perfect products for our clients than it was to swaddle my team.

Kevin was always there to step in and wipe any tears away, and I received constant coaching from him on how to deliver my feedback to lessen the emotional impact. ("Can you please say something nice before you tell them it's complete shit?") Frankly, this felt inefficient. I wanted everyone to realize that only perfection would ever leave our walls. I wanted them to be scared to present their work to me. Coddling them with false confidence and trying to mince words to make criticism easier to accept would be a step backward. If they wanted nice comments, they had to show me excellence.

But, I acquiesced to Kevin's advice . . . up to a point. My signature response to a less-than-ideal presentation was now a drawn-out "*Ooooooookayyyyy*. . . . " while giving him an evil side-eye. With this, he knew his team screwed up and he was about to get an earful from me—in the hallway, away from the group.

I later came to recognize this sort of conduct as the entry point to a mindset that would eventually bring me a lot of grief. Dressing people down is quite contrary to my normal behavior. In "real life" I am about as sensitive as they come (thanks, Mom!) and rely heavily on my emotional intelligence. Friends would generally describe me as warm, accommodating, kind, and calming. I would *hate* for someone to treat me as I found myself treating my staff at times. So why did I do it? Why does anyone do it?

Before having experienced it firsthand, I would have criticized people like Steve Jobs as emotionless pricks who lacked respect for their employees. The stories of him throwing work back in the face of a poor engineer who had dedicated weeks to a project or publicly shaming an underling are unsettling. But to my surprise, *I now kind of got it.*

He was a perfectionist creating a company that he intended to be a reflection of his perfectionism. We all know that *nothing* is perfect, but as long as it is was as perfect as nature would allow to the only constituents who mattered—customers and shareholders—he was going to succeed. He was competing in an industry of *imperfection.* His competitors, like Microsoft, were known for bugs, hacks, and failed products. They were focused on speed to market and were content with fixing problems later. People came to expect that one out of every one hundred PCs would be a lemon and that Windows would crash at the worst possible time. Things like computer viruses were acceptable problems.

Jobs disagreed with this approach. He tried only to release products that were so well thought out that it felt as if Apple had pulled apart our brains and got down into our deepest needs, desires, and wants. He wanted his products to "just work" when they were released, with as small a learning curve as possible. An extension of the human being itself. And if you've ever seen a toddler effortlessly use an iPad, then you know he just might have succeeded.

His admittedly assholeish and aggressive behavior caused a culture of perfectionism at Apple. It goes without saying that he took it too far, according to many stories, but it inspired some members of the Apple staff to work exponentially harder and be far more laser-focused than employees at other companies. "Impossible" was not a valid excuse. This wasn't a charity boxing match. There were no participation awards. This was hopping into the ring contending for a belt. If you weren't on your game, you were going to get knocked the fuck out.

This tactic is not only hotly debated but also very specific to a certain type of company. Some companies are well suited for a culture of aggressive perfectionism. Others are absolutely not, which is why both strategies can play out successfully. I have a buddy who runs a huge advertising technology firm. He is the epitome of the smiling, empathic, hugging, approachable CEO that some in the business community try to coach everyone to be. *It's okay, we missed this time, but we will get them next time!*

But the reality is, this leadership style works for him because his business is a marathon, not a sprint. As the leader of a long-tail growth company, he needs high spirits and sustainability, and doing okay is okay. His people are cold-calling, working on multiyear software releases, and attending conferences. That type of work accommodates less than perfection.

For ÄKTA, I didn't see room for imperfection. We couldn't

deliver "okay" to our clients. They were paying us for brilliance. The only way to achieve that was to set the same bar internally. I wanted my people panicking about delivering a milestone. I wanted them problem-solving in their sleep. I wanted them to know that nothing else but pure sex was going to be allowed to cross my desk. This meant holding to the same standards on my end. The moment I let my guard down, so would they.

I'm the first to admit I crossed the line a number of times. I said some things to employees that I still regret to this day. I've often wondered how things would have gone had I been softer on my staff and traded some of that perfection for quality of life. Would people have worked as hard, been as dedicated, and strived for the same level of excellence if I hadn't put as much pressure on them?

35 | NEWTON'S CRADLE

ÄKTA grew because I was living out Newton's Cradle in real time.

I began by manufacturing perception. Living my distorted reality. We are the best. We are the next big thing. We've earned it. But every time I said it, I was in doubt.

Then we would succeed. We would deliver the project. We would crush our goals. We would live up to the hype I had created. Perception became reality; doubt became belief. The metal balls smashed together. And then I would up the stakes, and the cycle would begin all over again.

Is it still hype if promises are fulfilled? Are you lying if your lies become truth?

It almost seemed as if the more ridiculous our approach became—the gimmicks, the insane bets, the ballsy strategy, the bravado and unorthodox nature of it all—the better it worked. The market almost seemed to be craving someone to come in and shake the shit out of the snow globe. Our absurdist attitude of expecting the whole enterprise to crash and burn tomorrow empowered us, pushed us harder and in more abstract ways than anyone else in our field. Ironically, the ways in which we would almost dare the company to fail ended up being the foundation for our biggest growth spurts.

After months of telling everyone I was creating the best design agency in Chicago, I started hearing others say that on our behalf. The only person who couldn't figure out whether to believe the hype was . . . me.

As much as I wanted to convince myself that this could work, I couldn't bring myself to do it. At some point we had to miss. Surely, we would not be able to live up to our claims. Surely, we would fail a client. Surely, someone would catch me in the act.

That constant doubt was mentally draining. I had no way of knowing if this was how everyone in my position was feeling and we all just hid it well, or if it was just me. Whether I was just playing the game skillfully, or if I was a fraud. All I did know was that with every claim, every hire, every interview, I felt the metal balls hit together harder.

My brain began to feel tight inside my skull and sleep no longer came as easily. My temper grew shorter like days transitioning into autumn. The weight of my newfound venture was starting to have

an impact on me. When I broke up with Lisa, I told her it was because I couldn't handle being a good boyfriend and growing a business at the same time. Looking back on it, I might have just been
afraid to have anyone close to me, as I started to sense how difficult
this journey was going to be.

36 | THE IMPOSTOR

If there was one question I wish I could have had answered at this
point, it would have been this: Is this how all startups are? Or is
ÄKTA unique?

Despite having had success with our earliest clients, we were still
flying by the seat of our pants, to say the least. To me, there wasn't
any other way to do it. No manual had been written for how to start
these companies. And being financially bootstrapped by profits from
our work, there wasn't a lot of room to figure it out any other way. It
felt mad. It felt out of control. It felt hysterical. But was it?

When I would hear other founders speak onstage at a conference
or read their interviews online, it seemed as if I were the only one
who didn't have my shit together. Everyone else seemed to be following a playbook that I hadn't seen yet.

From the outside, though, I was being talked up in interviews as
if I were a prodigy. I was gaining respect inside business circles. To
everyone else, *I* was the self-assured guy with the playbook. So, did
that mean that beneath the surface we might all be the same? Might

no one have any damned clue what they were doing—at least in their own head? Might this be how any company, failure or success, looked after a year?

My lack of perspective caused some of my first deep anxiety at ÄKTA. It was scary to consider that I was the only person out of the loop and that there might be an expiration date to my act. At any moment, I might get caught and exposed for the fraud that I was.

Impostor syndrome is in fact a universal and complex condition that occurs across every industry and profession.

The surgeon who enters the operating room on their own for the first time, thinking, *Holy shit, I don't know what I'm doing.*

The race car driver who buckles in and then is hit with the sheer horror of realizing they aren't ready to race against the true professionals lined up next to them.

The teacher who comes into the first day of class and realizes they aren't qualified to educate the youth of America.

It's the downside of the fake-it-till-you-make-it mentality. Now that you've become a success feeling like a fraud, you wait for the world to come crashing down on you.

Although my brain might be wired a bit differently than most, such feelings of anxiety and stress are ones that we all experience. To me there is nothing more critical in today's culture than setting a level on how normal this is, and rather than avoiding discussing it, we should be confronting it directly. There is a direct link to general mental health as well, as people experiencing impostor syndrome often show symptoms related to depression, generalized anxiety, and low self-confidence.

Toby Thomas, who founded Ensite Solutions, had a great quote about this. He said being an entrepreneur was like being a man riding a lion: "People look at him and think, 'This guy's really got it together! He's brave!' And the man riding the lion is thinking, 'How the hell did I get on a lion, and how do I keep from getting eaten?'"

What I learned later is that these feelings of doubt are not only normal, but omnipresent across even the highest levels of life. I've participated in conversations with NFL coaches, a former president of the United States, a bestselling author, and a platinum-selling DJ, all of whom echoed the same sentiment: There were pivotal moments in their careers where they felt this same fear. That they were impostors in their own professions. That they would be exposed and publicly shamed.

Don't just take it from me.

Sheryl Sandberg: "Every time I took a test, I was sure that it had gone badly. And every time I didn't embarrass myself—or even excelled—I believed that I had fooled everyone yet again. One day soon, the jig would be up."

Tina Fey: "The beauty of the impostor syndrome is you vacillate between extreme egomania, and a complete feeling of: 'I'm a fraud! Oh God, they're on to me! I'm a fraud!' So, you just try to ride the egomania when it comes and enjoy it, and then slide through the idea of fraud."

Howard Schultz: "Very few people, whether you've been in that job before or not, get into the seat and believe today that they are now qualified to be the CEO. They're not going to tell you that, but it's true."

Tom Hanks: "No matter what we've done, there comes a point where you think, 'How did I get here? When are they going to discover that I am, in fact, a fraud and take everything away from me?'"

While this was a refreshing realization to learn years after the fact—and I hope it will be a valuable lesson for my younger readers—it sure would have been helpful for me to have known it then.

37 | THE BROS

There's one professional pedigree that rules the tech scene in Silicon Valley: venture capital investors.

Almost religiously revered, VCs control the flow of money into startups, and like the hand of God, decide who gets a fair shot at success. And they get paid handsomely to do it. These dudes make the *Shark Tank* guys look like minnows. It's a modern-day boys club.

While firms like Sequoia and Accel were printing Escobar-levels of money out in the Valley, Chicago's cheap imitation back in 2011 was called Lightbank. Newly famous from the backing of supercompany Groupon, Lightbank had risen to the top level of Chicago investing. Like everything else in Chicago, the rumor mills buzzed with claims of iffy behavior and below-board competitive tactics inside their portfolio companies. Located in the Groupon building at 600 West Chicago Avenue, Lightbank resembled a frat house as much as an investment firm. Packed with the broiest of bros from the University of Chicago, where founder Brad Keywell taught a class, Lightbank housed a dozen companies that were promised to be the city's next big thing, the unicorns after Groupon—at least Lightbank hoped so—to prove Chicago wasn't a one-hit wonder.

My theory was that because Lightbank was pumping millions into these companies, and had everything to gain from their success, it would likely invest in whatever would increase the chances of that happening. Like good design. I intuitively didn't trust these guys, and I didn't even know them. I sensed what I would be getting myself into by engaging with them, but there was no way to get to startup heaven without doing multiple deals with the devil.

A few favors were called in to get me in the door, and I went in hot.

My pitch was much more refined by this point, and I could even show some *actual* work we'd done, which included eight concurrent subprojects for Topgolf. There is no demographic easier to sell than bros—just shine up their egos, show them you have one just as big, and make it sound as if they'd somehow earn more bro-points by working with you.

Within days, I had meetings scheduled with three of their portfolio companies. And won three deals.

With business like this now coming in, life became *busy*. For the first time, it became a regular occurrence for me to go multiple days without seeing Kevin. "You still work here?" I'd ask him with a wink when I would finally return to the office and watch him dart around, trying to manage all the work being done. I'd then drop a newly signed proposal on his desk, with a big smile. Even though it was my job to sell, and his to execute, there was something very personally rewarding to me about all of this. Every deal I was able to close represented validation that I wasn't delusional and we actually had something here at ÄKTA. There was also something slightly more . . . devious. I can't explain why, but it gave me some amount of deranged pleasure seeing Kevin squirm when trying to figure out how on earth he was going to pull the resources together to complete *another* project. We had to grow. We had to push. I loved it.

During this period we also closed a deal with a new startup called SpotOn, which was basically digitizing old-school paper punch cards at retail shops—simple technology in a crowded competitive landscape. SpotOn was financially backed by two guys whom I'll never forget, who also became key to our success.

The king bros, the Hyman brothers.

Matt and Zach Hyman were identical twins, serial entrepreneurs, professional poker players, zealous gamblers, and wickedly smart businessmen. These guys had made a bunch of money over the years from a slew of unrelated business ventures and now had their investment sights set on tech startups.

We were doing so well for SpotOn, one of their portfolio companies, that the Hymans invited me to Vegas so we could get to know one another and, I figured, see how much business we were really going to do together. I had sold, and potentially oversold, my poker skills to them, which spurred the twins to buy me into the $10,000-entry World Poker Tour's Main Event, one of the most competitive and prestigious poker tournaments in the world, in exchange for half my potential winnings.

To date I had been to Vegas only twice, and I still viewed it as a silly adult Disneyland that I couldn't afford and to which I certainly didn't have access. I had never played poker there, so this would be quite the initiation to their world, as well as a test. I flew to Nevada, reading a poker book I had ordered online, feverishly highlighting advanced strategies and trying my best to commit some key, high-level tournament elements to memory.

Poker is one of the only sports in the world where you can pay a chunk of money and instantly play at the highest level. Imagine being able to write a check and line up as quarterback at the Super Bowl. So when I arrived at the tournament and was seated at a table next to Daniel Negreanu—one of the most awarded professionals in the sport—I tried to keep my composure, while my bowels started growling and my hands were sweating so much I almost couldn't hold the cards.

The Hymans were late, of course, so I had some time to get my shit together before they arrived. I went to the bathroom, popped a Xanax (a drug that had only recently been introduced to me), and sat back down to the table, hoping not to make as big an ass of myself as I felt I was in my head.

The first hour went fine. I was mostly dealt trash, so I was able to skip a lot of the action. I dropped a few blinds, stole one or two, and started finding my groove. Suddenly a pair of kings turned up, with me on the button. For the uninitiated, this is *almost* the best way to start a poker hand. This is a hand you should win and get paid handsomely for. My heart started jackhammering, but I told myself that no one else could see it.

To my dismay, the table started folding all around. If no one wanted to play, my opportunity would be lost. I started staring at my fellow players as if I were one of the X-Men, trying to mentally will them into calling. My telepathy finally did work, but exactly where I didn't want it to. Negreanu, immediately to my right, considered his hand for an extra second, and threw in an outsized bet, in the big blind. This meant one of two things: either he was holding shit and was trying to simply steal a quick blind from me, or he had something fantastic and wanted me to think he had shit, so that I would commit.

This was going up for a block against Jordan. This was the greatest poker pro of all time—against me. While I'm playing up the drama of the moment, in reality, there wasn't much of a decision involved. The only bet I could make was to raise him, and see where he was really at with his hand. I steadied my hand as I palmed a small handful of chips, not exactly sure of how much I had even grabbed, placed them in the center, muttered, "Raise," and tried to dead stare straight again.

Out of the corner of my eye, I noticed the Hyman twins entering the room, pointing and smiling at other pros, glad-handing all around. When I looked back at my opponent I saw him doing the worst possible thing he could do: shoving all his chips to the center of the table.

At this point, I was in a rough spot. He could have aces, the only better starting hand than mine, but there was only a tiny chance of that happening. He might have been holding something powerful enough for the move, like ace and king, or had nothing and was bluffing me.

Once again I didn't have any choice, so I shoved all my chips to the center, next to his, when I felt a hand on my shoulder.

"What's up, bro!" Matt Hyman said, loudly. "Holy fuck! You're shoving against Daniel?"

I tried to smile and avoided looking back at him. With a bit of bad luck, I was about to lose my client's $10,000 only an hour into the tournament. Even worse, I'd lose their respect. Actually, fuck their respect. I was seeing all the potential revenue from them fly out the window if this went bad. I needed only the smallest amount of good fortune to get through this alive.

Then, it happened. "Kings?" Daniel asked, as he smiled at me. My heart sank. He knew what I had the entire time.

Well, fuck.

He turned over a pair of shiny aces and then stood up to give his bro friends a hug. I watched as the dealer flipped over the next five cards, praying a king would appear, while somehow knowing it wouldn't. And then I felt the twins' eyes on the back of my head.

"Bro! Oh my God, bro. You're already out? Daniel, did you just knock him out?"

I stood, shook my executioner's hand, and turned to face the twins, who were laughing hysterically.

"Oh my God, bro, that is gnarly! We just got here! Bro, you fucking *suck*!"

I heard stifled laughs from around the table and tried to hide my humiliation, but then something happened that I hadn't expected. The twins told me to meet them for dinner at midnight and began unzipping a backpack chock-full of stacks of cash. There had to have been half a million dollars inside, and I realized then that they didn't care in the slightest about the money I'd lost. In fact, their hearty laugh might have been worth dropping ten grand for in their eyes. I had never seen wealth like that.

That night, needless to say, included more things I had never seen before. The twins retired to bed after dinner and I went out with a bunch of professional poker players and businessmen from the tournament. Over a million dollars were lost, and then won, in a private room at the MGM Grand. A *Scarface*-esque pile of cocaine was openly laid out on the table of the back room of a strip club. Dessert was naked sushi. Nurses dressed as strippers arrived in the morning and jammed hydrating IVs into our arms, before we even left our beds.

38 | MOVING ON UP

I returned to the office in a state of shock. I wasn't sure what I had just experienced, except to know it had an effect on me.

While I could never imagine being as crazy as the twins, or as wild as their buddies, there was something deeply alluring about that level of wealth. Maybe because it represented real success. These guys worked hard and partied way, way harder. That felt like something I should aspire to. And there was *definitely* something alluring about Las Vegas. I was drawn to the excess and the debauchery, and though I didn't realize it at the time, what I was actually attracted to was the escape—from real life, from pressure, from what I felt was the unfairness of my situation. A lot of people are running away from something in a place like Vegas. I was observing failure but mistaking it for success.

I had met a girl named Cortney through mutual friends around this time, and we'd begun dating. There were days when it felt great to have someone around. But it also felt like a ticking time bomb. The good times were marred by my stress at work. While I never cheated, I certainly indulged in some sketchy behavior, like what had just happened in Vegas. I never believed anyone could *understand* what I was going through, so I kept it all bottled up inside.

Back at HQ, our team was growing quickly. Almost a year had passed since the first deposit from Topgolf, and we had converted our early employees from contractors to full-time roles and brought on some new top talent, including my white knight, Kyle McConnell.

McConnell looked like Conor McGregor if he gained fifty pounds and took up digital design. I found his portfolio online and had to import him from some farm town in North Carolina or somewhere. He was now in the big city, propped up as our lead guy, and ready to help us tackle our leading projects. The work he spun out for Topgolf, Lightbank, ScholarPro, and our newest client, TrainSignal, was the best we had ever done. We were hustling hard. With a half dozen concurrent projects, we were on pace to make almost a million dollars in 2011.

That was incomprehensible to me. "A million dollars" was one of the most unfathomable phrases I could think of at the time—especially because our net profit margin was over 30 percent, given how premium our services had become. We had the ability to throw off hundreds of thousands in profit in just our second year in business.

Our growing team had become cramped in the current space, and had even begun to take over my sacred Ping-Pong room, and it became clear that we had to move. There were many areas in Chicago that had begun the inevitable transition from industrial factory to commercial workspace. I envisioned ÄKTA in a big, beautiful, unrefined loft, with thick wooden beams and scars from all the businesses that had been there before us.

It took me less than ten seconds to decide I was taking the first property I saw. It was perfect: a huge open space with gorgeous, rutted wood floors, brick walls, and adjacent empty spaces that would allow us to knock down walls and expand, if we were so fortunate.

The building was willing to allot us some money for renovations, if we were willing to sign a three-year lease. While I wanted to have that kind of faith in my company, I was scared shitless to make so long a commitment. Despite our growth, we were still relying on a few big clients, augmented by a handful of smaller ones—all of which could dry up or fire us at any time.

The reality of the future hit me in this moment. We were doing well—*really* well—but unlike businesses whose risk profile lowers as they grow because of residual revenue and early investments paying off, our situation was the exact opposite. Every stage of growth to come would require more risk than the one before it. If we had the best quarter ever in sales, we'd have to beat it the following quarter, and the quarter after that, to not stagnate. I felt as if I had already put my maximum effort into getting to one million in revenue. So many pitches. So many meetings. So much hustling. So much luck. How would I get us to two million? Ten or twenty? I had no context for my uneasiness. Was this normal? Was this how all entrepreneurs felt at this point in the growth of their companies? Should we have slowed down and not made the office move?

While I didn't know the right steps to take, I certainly knew what I *wasn't* willing to do, and that was slow down. I either had lightning in a bottle or a disaster brewing. I intended to keep pushing until it became clear which it was.

I drew up what I wanted the new space to look like. Stark white walls against the natural brick. Whiteboard paint on almost every flat surface. Ample room for the Ping-Pong table. Our logo, cut from raw metal, hanging valiantly in the front entryway.

As the lawyers started getting back to me on the details of the lease, things got even scarier. As it turned out, someone had to be responsible for the total value of the lease. That meant monthly rent times thirty-six months—a guarantee of hundreds of thousands of dollars. By the owner. By *me*.

How was I supposed to pledge money I didn't have? Or might never have?

I sat alone in my apartment that night, sipping cheap whiskey and asking myself if I was making a huge mistake. I recalled the statistics I had heard so many times: 90 percent of startups fail within a year, and 99 percent after five years.

Despite my best efforts to visualize success, they weren't working. As my body tingled with bad energy and low-grade nausea, I stared out the window, letting the alcohol fog my brain and distance me from the reality I was facing. This all would be so much easier if I just didn't allow myself consider the risk, to push it away and deal with it later.

The following week, I signed the lease for our new office.

I scheduled a team meeting, which was probably the first time I had ever called one. I wonder how many employees thought I was going to announce we were going out of business. No one else had been included in the plan to move, apart from Kevin. I had made the decision to keep everything at ÄKTA under wraps from the team, whether my strategic plans, the financials, or company problems. They'd only be brought in on the good stuff. I figured there would be a lot of scary moments as we grew, and I felt it was my job to absorb them alone. From their perspective, everything should always be great.

We hadn't yet coined a term for team members, so I made one up on the spot.

"ÄKTers . . ." I began. *Fuck*, I thought, *that had sounded way less dumb in my head.* "I have an exciting announcement. As great of an experience as this little office has been, we are about to move up in the world. I'm happy to announce we've signed a long-term lease at a beautiful loft space in River North. In a few weeks, we will begin the move. This represents a huge, exciting milestone for us!"

I awaited the applause. None came.

"That is a lot farther from the subway," someone said. "Are you going to pay for transit?"

"Are there any restaurants near there?" soon followed, and then, "Can we have bigger desks?"

I had expected at least a *little* bit of excitement from these little shits for one of our first moments of glory. This, I quickly realized, was one of the inherent downfalls of having shielded the team from everything I was doing behind the scenes: they simply couldn't appreciate the risk, the effort, the weight of taking such a step. To them it was simply an office move, whereas to me, it represented unprecedented opportunity, risk, and uncertainty.

The distorted reality I had created between what was really going on, what I selectively shared with my team, and how I manipulated all of that for the world to see would turn out to be one of the most damaging psychological aspects of my role as CEO. I spent an incredible amount of energy manufacturing a version of a leader, of a CEO, that gave the team and marketplace the most confidence in my ability to lead. Part of that was being fearless, especially in the face of adversity and risk. At times, I could mimic that confidence and fearlessness internally and make decisions in my head without a second thought. Other times, the doubt and uncertainty would fester like an infection, but would never permeate out far enough for anyone to see. In these moments, no matter what I was feeling inside, I had to put on a show.

"Don't worry, Kevin will answer these questions in due time." I'd let him deal with it. I had bigger things to think about, like creating a beautiful space that was to be our new home.

Well, beautiful space on a budget. And that meant back to IKEA. We fully cleaned them out of black wooden desks, bright red cubbies, and sleek black office chairs. We now had space for twenty ÄKTA-puses (*ew, no*), a dedicated conference room, and, of course, ample room for competitive Ping-Pong.

You could have seen the pride emanating from my body when we got that big metal logo in and hung it at the entrance. Even though Kevin said it looked like a cult symbol (it did), I didn't care. We finally had a beautiful new space that would impress any potential client or employee.

It even reopened the door for SocialCrunch to potentially succeed. I had found a couple of guys who were willing to run it, and even a few others willing to put money in. And now I could house them inside my new office and give them the support they needed.

This high lasted exactly one day. The next, I was ready to murder someone.

39 | THE BATTLE

What do you mean you're quitting?" I asked, incredulously. McConnell stared at Kevin and me with nervous, beady eyes.

"I've been offered a great job elsewhere," he muttered. "I want to work on the client side. I'm sorry."

Sorry? I had given this motherfucker everything he had. Moved him here. Built him up to be the next big thing. And not even six months later, he's leaving? He was also leading the design of every significant project we had on the table. Losing him would be catastrophic.

"Well, where the fuck are you going?" I asked, a little too aggressively. Kevin shot me a look.

"I can't say," he replied defensively. "But I have to leave immediately, unfortunately. Thank you for the opportunity. I wish ÄKTA the best."

"You better be fucking kidding," was all I could think of saying, and this time I didn't even bother glancing at Kevin.

I knew there was no hope of negotiating with him and that this was a done deal. With that, he stood, offered his hand—which I couldn't bring myself to shake—and walked out of the room.

All my bluster was now gone. I thought about my signature—the one attached to the bottom of our client contracts, to the new long-term lease, and to our employment agreements. *Is this how it's going to end? One stupid kid is going to destroy everything I've built? Is this how Steven felt when I quit?* No, it wasn't the same. Right?

"What are we going to do now?"

We were first going to get drunk, apparently.

Kevin and I left the office and went straight to the bar across the street. We both sat staring at our glasses of whiskey, as if they were going to give us answers. We realized in unison that was probably not going to happen and finally began to replay the incident out loud.

Our top guy was leaving—the linchpin to our most important projects. He couldn't tell us where he was going. Why? No warning, no two-week notice.

What employer would demand that from a new hire? Only one explanation made sense: someone who was purposely trying to fuck us. But who would want to do that? How on earth had we made enemies already?

My first thought was to check with the guys at Lightbank. They still ran the Chicago tech scene, so if anyone would know, it was them. As it turned out, I was right. They knew exactly where McConnell was going. And they weren't even hesitant to tell me. He was going to Lightbank—or more specifically, to one of its portfolio companies called Belly. Which happened to be a direct competitor to our new megaclient, SpotOn, which McConnell had just been running point on. The same SpotOn that the Hyman twins were backing.

So, to summarize: Belly, backed by Lightbank—which was a client of ours via three of their portfolio companies—targeted and stole our best employee, to work on a direct competitor to our best client, putting us into not only an operational but also a legal shitshow, because we could be held responsible for allowing SpotOn's trade secrets to go to a competitor.

My mind's ethical and moral compasses were spinning in circles. How could they do this? This *had to* be illegal, didn't it? I began running through all the details of our legal agreements. *What had McConnell signed? What had SpotOn signed? Had we even considered a situation like this?*

We immediately called our attorney, who gave us the worst news imaginable: unless we could prove that McConnell took, and transferred, trade secrets that caused actual damage, there was basically nothing we could do. And if that was the case, it would be our client, SpotOn, that would have to take any legal action, because it was its secrets that were at stake. And because Belly had hired McConnell, not Lightbank, any nonsolicitation provisions, which prevented clients from courting ÄKTA employees, weren't applicable.

This put not only SpotOn at risk but also two other new projects we were planning for the twins. These accounted for over 50 percent of our revenue. We also had to consider the legal mess we could find ourselves in if SpotOn blamed us for effectively giving away their secrets.

If you had asked me before this moment if business had to be a dirty game, I would have told you I didn't believe that was necessarily true. There had to be a way to keep things aboveboard, to play by the rules, and still win. Apparently not. I was already being targeted. Others already wanted to see me lose, see me fail, to their benefit.

The rules changed for me then. Business wasn't just a game, it was also war. Survival mode. Reptilian brain. Winning might mean others losing. I would need to do whatever it took.

I would realize years later that everyone who succeeds at high-growth startups has reached this conclusion. No one wins clean. You kill or be killed. This thing isn't your baby. Your business is a cold, dark steel ball that you have to keep pushing up a hill as it grows bigger, running over anything in its way.

And people wonder why we all go crazy doing this.

40 | THE WAR

I spent most of the night pacing around my apartment. The booze was making me angrier. The pills, less. Finally, I ended up in a zombie state, and I fell into a hollow, frenetic sleep.

I awoke three hours later, exhausted. I ignored the haze in my vision and the acidic taste at the back of my throat, and focused on what could end up being the most critical phone call thus far in my career. I had to explain to the Hyman twins that we had inadvertently just lost our most important asset. Not only could we no longer deliver the same level of design quality to their project until we found a replacement, but now their strategic road map and product designs were sitting comfortably on the desk of their largest competitor.

These guys were maniacs, and I had no clue how they might react. It was a coin flip between their suing me into oblivion—after all, I had potentially just put their key investment at risk, which could mean millions of dollars lost—or our taking up collective arms to fight the good fight.

I rehearsed the script in my head and knew what I had to get across—*here is what happened, I'm sorry, please don't kill me*—but it was all going to depend on my delivery and resolve. It was noon on a Friday. I took a walk down the street, and peeked into a restaurant window, seeing smiling people enjoying their lunch, laughing over a glass of wine, not a care in the world. I hated them all at that moment.

I phoned Zach, as he seemed the marginally saner of the two. Or was it Matt? I always got them mixed up. I hoped he didn't answer, even though it wouldn't have helped.

"What's up, bro!" he shouted when he picked up.

"Hey, Zach," I exhaled, longing for simpler days. "Listen, I'm sorry to bother you, but I didn't want to wait to tell you what's going on. We have a bit of a situation. Remember Kyle? Our lead designer? He resigned yesterday. We did some digging, and found out he went to Belly."

I decided to stop there—nothing more needed to be said. These boys were beyond smart, and it took only a few seconds for him to work it all through in his head.

"Bro," he said tensely. "He knows everything about SpotOn. He's seen our road map and has literally designed the new product. No matter what we have on them legally, by Monday, he will have dropped all of it off to them, and there is nothing we are going to be able to do to stop it. Even with lawsuits, they'll just say he hasn't brought anything over with him, and that they've instructed him to not share anything confidential, and there is nothing we can do to prove it. We trusted you to keep this safe, bro." He paused, to let all this settle in. "This is bad."

My instincts told me to start defending myself—*it wasn't my fault, I had no idea, I thought he was solid*—but there was no point. In fact, it would only have made me sound as if I were trying to hide something. I had to just let him continue to absorb the news and make his own call on how to respond to it.

As I recount this incident years later, I feel overcome with the same sensations. My heart starts to race, the sides of my eyes tighten, a small pressure forms at the base of my skull, and my stomach starts sending up mixed signals. I think about how our fate lies in the hands of countless random people. All it takes is for emotion to take over and one guy to seek revenge. Or a hundred other things.

"Listen, John," Zach finally said. "You're a good guy. I know this isn't your fault. I've had employees fuck me, too. So, I'm not going to freak out at you. But we have to get nasty. Fuck these guys! You ready?"

I felt numb, even though my frontal cortex was desperately trying to invoke a recipe of emotions.

41 | SPIDER-MAN

The legal battle started on Monday, with the twins bombarding Belly with cease-and-desist letters from a fancy Bay Area law firm. All parties knew this was ultimately a meaningless exercise, and that its only real purpose was getting it on the record that Belly now possessed trade secrets from SpotOn, so if Belly released too similar a product later or engaged in any obvious competitive maneuvers, there would be a legal basis for a lawsuit.

The larger fallout came in the form of our relationship with Lightbank—to date, our most important client in Chicago. We internally made the decision to begin to wind down our engagements with them, while not indicating we were angry about what had happened with SpotOn. We cut projects short and gave bullshit reasons as to why our resource pool wouldn't allow us to continue.

Meanwhile, I had one major job to do: find Kyle's replacement. Without a lead designer, everything else was somewhat irrelevant. No matter how high the quality of our predesign work—research, experience strategy, wireframing, information architecture, et cetera— all that the world saw was the visual design. That had been and had to continue to be our strongest asset.

I spent days and days scouring dark corners of the internet to find another unicorn. I couldn't go through any mainstream routes, like job boards or LinkedIn, because we wouldn't be able to afford any designers who knew their true value. They could easily command hundreds of thousands in salary. No, I needed someone like Kyle, wandering around a dusty Podunk town or some third-world country, oblivious to their talent, whom I could get cheap and fast.

I sat head in hand, holding open my left eye, mindlessly scrolling through hundreds of pages of portfolios that designers post on websites that are basically massive artistic circle jerks. My screen looked like a slot machine, images flying by at an impossible speed, until part of my brain would signal that it saw something interesting, and I'd stop, find some reason it wasn't a fit, and keep scrolling.

Then it hit me like a slap: a beautiful mobile app concept by a freelancer. I snapped awake and clicked into his profile. Name: Isaac. Location: Chicago. Status: Seeking work. Profile photo: Spider-Man.

This was too good to be true. What was wrong with him? I started feverishly opening screens from his portfolio, and they only kept getting better: gushing colors, pixel-perfect detail, clever design hierarchy, orgasmic layering.

It was 3:00 a.m., but I shot off an email anyway.

"Isaac, John. I run the best design company in Chicago. You have some sick work. We need to talk. Will you come in ASAP and meet with me?"

I received a response five minutes later.

"Sure, I can come in tomorrow."

I immediately sent him meeting details and tried to sleep, although I knew it wouldn't happen.

Digital designers are on the whole just weird-ass people. They have the classic artistic temperament that you'd expect to find in an eighteenth-century painter. They have an obsessiveness for the process and their medium, a conspicuous lack of personal hygiene, and an unlimited amount of quirks. But they also have to be computer nerds, as their medium is the machine, which makes for a bizarre and comical blend. Imagine Rembrandt as a Trekkie.

Had I been forced to guess in advance, I would have pegged Isaac as any of the standard designer personas.

The Hipster: gauged ears, a few ironic tattoos, and over-ear headphones permanently attached to his collarbone.

The Burnout: powered by weed, resistant to direction, and as reliable as a two-dollar suitcase.

The Over-the-Hill: a print designer who peaked in the late '90s, so has taken to computers with a chip on his shoulder.

Nope. Wrong. I wasn't even close. Isaac was one of a kind. This became clear when Kevin came to my office and announced with a wide smirk, "A guy dressed as Spider-Man is waiting for you. I'm joining for *this* meeting."

I wondered what Kevin was alluding to, as a comic book shirt would hardly be newsworthy in our office.

It turns out, there was no allusion. I gave Kevin too much credit.

Sitting inside my conference room was a young kid dressed head to toe as Spider-Man. He looked as if he were wearing adult pajamas, complete with gloves. Instead of a mask, he donned a Spidey-themed winter hat, even though it was a warm day in spring.

The smile on Kevin's face couldn't have been wider. I'm surprised he hadn't prepared popcorn before sitting in. I stood in the doorway, dumbfounded.

Isaac wouldn't shake my hand—I didn't inquire why—and had an extremely hard time making eye contact. Over the next thirty minutes, though, I learned more about him than I would ever have cared to know about most human beings. At a rapid clip he told me that he was only sixteen years old, having recently dropped out of high school. He suffered from a host of mental ailments and rarely slept. The sunlight bothered him, he claimed.

He didn't fully explain the Spider-Man thing but did discuss his asexuality and obsession for skateboarding. Which was his sole form of transportation, everywhere, period.

Most people would have found plenty of reasons not to move forward with this particular candidate. I wasn't oblivious to any of those reasons, but I had to see things differently. Yeah, this kid was crazier than a bag of coked-out raccoons, but he was *so* fucking talented. And a really nice guy. There was no way he was going to survive in a traditional nine-to-five office setting, but we didn't need him to.

When I offered Isaac the job, Kevin's jaw dropped. Another loony added to the bin.

From an ensemble standpoint, Spider-Man actually slotted in quite well with our other visual designer, Sean. Sean was genius-level intelligent, lived on energy drinks and cigarettes, and was missing chunks of a couple of his front teeth. He demanded his corner of the office be kept completely dark and would leave the premises every fifteen minutes or so to have a smoke in the alley with a guy we called Homeless Batman. They played chess.

Had you asked me then, I would have told you that hiring Isaac was the luck of the draw: these genius misfits and oddities just happened to find their way to our door. But as I reflect on it now, I realize there was at least some degree of pragmatism in my hiring strategy.

I had built ÄKTA with so little structure, experience, or guidance that it felt cobbled together. Loose theories and spare parts glued together to form only a vague facsimile of a strategic agency; yet they somehow performed as a well-oiled machine. Some of my most bizarre choices in fact ended up being the smartest. I wanted to think of this sort of decision-making as one of my subconscious skills. But there was a fragility to this strategy: I never wanted anyone to analyze it or question it. My confidence would not stand up to scrutiny.

This was the real driver behind my trying to avoid hiring professionals with a wealth of relevant experience. Had someone come from a decade at a prestigious design firm, I feared they would instantly start poking holes straight through the sheer veil of strategic choices I had made, and then yank it right down. I feared this would be the fast track to my beautifully unpredictable decisions being exposed as merely lucky guesses. I feared someone would expose the fact that I didn't know what the hell I was doing, so I stacked the team with people who didn't know any better, and could be mesmerized by my brilliance.

I realize now that my never-ending battle with impostor syndrome actually led me to make a number of great decisions. My fear drove some of the most clever and valuable choices I made. I actually *did* know exactly what I was doing. I just never allowed myself to believe that.

42 | THE BIG FISH

It was a relief to avert a crisis as potentially lethal as what Lightbank had unleashed on us, and to hire a superhero, to boot, to make sure none of the plates feverishly spinning above my head came crashing to the ground. Despite the unorthodox nature of our newest key hire, he was absolutely crushing our most important projects and would occasionally even find his way into the office during business hours, always donning his Spider-Man kit. He even joined for a company beach volleyball game, wearing a full Spidey mask. There was a part of me that hoped he spent his nights fighting crime with Homeless Batman. I took great pleasure in watching all the bizarre personalities at ÄKTA comingle and try to find common ground.

While I watched the bro twins take aim at Belly, and saw some of our Chicago-based relationships deteriorate as a result, I knew I had to focus on the core business and move it to the next level. We were about done with the minor leagues and were going to have to advance to the pros, whether we were ready or not. I desperately needed to prop ÄKTA up with some world-class talent, even if it would hurt our balance sheet.

I set out to make my first executive hire, a vice president of design, who could take over the entire design organization. This would have to be a dynamic rock star who could hire, manage, strategize, pitch clients, and get their hands dirty when needed. A person who fit that bill was almost certainly already gainfully employed, and probably not looking for a new job, so I was going to have to go searching deep in the loins of some impressive companies.

My strategy was to reach out to everyone in my network whose ability to identify talent I respected, and ask them to name the best designers they had ever worked with. I would then target those individuals directly and try to lure them out of whatever comfy, overpaid position they were currently in.

Off the back of a simple mass email I received several leads. The filtering process was easy. I didn't want anyone who worked at one of ÄKTA's competitors, because I had heard horror stories of how the big guys operated and I didn't want bad practices brought into our walls. I needed someone fresh to the agency side of the business, someone who wanted to cut their teeth on a new way to crush UX work. I also didn't want someone too old. Yeah, it's not legal for this to be my criteria, but open your eyes if you think this isn't how real life works. There is a lot of bias in hiring. I don't like it any more than you do, but this is one item in the long list of common unethical practices in business. I needed someone who had raw talent and was early enough in their career that they hadn't gone from being a print designer to a web designer to an experience designer or something. Like the rest of our crew, whoever I took on would have to be a pure digital maven.

I created a shortlist of candidates and had my assistant compile information on them. That's right, I had my very own assistant! Kevin had grown so tired of chasing me around that he demanded I hire some help. One of my biggest struggles at that time was keeping all the minutiae bouncing around my skull in order, and most important, letting myself delegate small tasks, which would allow me to focus on the critical stuff. Now, thanks to Kevin's urging, I had Julia, my savior, to whom I could throw tasks, ask to do research, prepare me for meetings, and, ultimately, make me look good.

It's incredible how many decisions per day became critical at this point. I'd be asked multiple times per hour a question that could have long-running consequences, would be expected to quickly fire off an answer, and then move on to the next one. Adults make about thirty-five thousand remotely conscious decisions every day, on top of the dozens we are highly cognizant of. As it turns out, there is actually a limit to how many conscious decisions we are able to make per day before our brain goes to mush. The condition is called decision fatigue.

I had begun limiting the number of daily decisions I'd have to make by eliminating those that were noncritical. I wore the exact same black jeans and V-neck T-shirt, of which I had about a dozen each, so I wouldn't have to worry about picking out my clothes each morning. I kept a black blazer at the office, in case I had to "dress up" for a client. I ordered the same thing at Starbucks on my way to the office and ate the same salad (kale, walnuts, sunflower seeds, avocado, jalapeños, cranberries, strawberries, and raspberry vinaigrette) every day for almost three years, unless I had a client lunch.

While Albert Einstein, Steve Jobs, and Mark Zuckerberg have made dressing the same way every day the ultimate characteristic of the antisocial supernerd, it turns out there is actual merit to it. Eliminate one noncritical decision to leave room for one more critical decision.

Where was I? Right, candidates. The most impressive person on my list was a guy named Drew Davidson.

Drew had done time at Motorola Solutions, one of Chicago's few tech conglomerates, and was now biding his time at a hearing aid startup, of all places. He had a master's degree in Cognitive Psychology and Computer Information Technology from Purdue, and was the same age as me. Julia had cyberstalked her way to his phone number, and I gave him a call. To my surprise, he had heard of ÄKTA and agreed to have a chat after he returned from a few weeks' travel in Australia.

This was fine, as I had a trip of my own to make, out to the West Coast to visit the Hyman twins.

After the Lightbank dumpster fire, the twins' companies had

come to represent well over half my revenue, so I had to keep them happy. I arrived at a restaurant in San Francisco to hearty bro hugs and back slaps, and an introduction to a third guy at the table, Tedd Huff, from a company called TSYS.

I had never heard of TSYS, nor likely have you. But you've used their services almost every day of your life. They are the backbone behind the banks that handle the credit card transactions for your gasoline, blue jeans, quinoa salad, and everything else in America and almost one hundred other countries, to the tune of about one hundred million transactions per *day*, totaling three *trillion* dollars a year, across their network. As it turns out, the twins had recently sold one of their companies to TSYS, and Tedd was their main connection.

After we exchanged updates and pleasantries, the purpose of the meeting became clear. Apparently, the software that TSYS had acquired from the twins was uglier than sin, so they wanted us to redesign it, cheaply. In exchange, they would broker a conversation— with an inside track via my new friend Tedd—for what sounded like the monster project I'd been looking for: a *massive* strategic initiative by the multibillion-dollar TSYS to bring its currently behind-the-scenes payment processing technology to the public in order to compete against the newly launched Square in mobile payments.

My mind was racing as I tried to pay attention to the rest of the conversation. These are the projects you only dream about, where design agencies like ÄKTA get to own an entire product line, resulting in millions upon millions of dollars in billable work, with a big public launch, setting up an infinite amount of future work.

Tedd had seen what we'd done for the twins' other companies, and was willing to grease the wheels to get us in the door. Reading between the lines, a few things were clear. First, he wasn't in the driver's seat on this project, but he wanted to be. And having owner-ship over the agency-of-record would help that. Second, he was an ambitious corporate junkie, so his looking good to higher-ups was his top personal priority.

This was a dream come true. Huge project, a back channel, and support from our key client.

I saw only one issue with all of this: we needed Drew.

43 | AGENCIES

It surprises people that I had no design agency experience to speak of before starting ÄKTA. I get it. You'd expect the person at the helm of a fast-growing design consultancy to have cut his teeth over a decade or more at a renowned design school and agencies and take all that knowledge to create the next big thing.

I think part of the reason for our success was *not* having that tacit knowledge to fall back on. When I would spend time at other big design shops like IDEO, whose history starts with them designing the first mouse for Apple in 1980, I could feel the nostalgia and "good old days" energy present in every room and conversation. Their (and everyone else's) process was a hodgepodge of new tech-niques mixed with battle-hardened methods from yesteryear, topped off by thousands of successful projects and hundreds of high-level academic degrees.

When yours truly started ÄKTA, supported by a municipal tax au-ditor, it goes without saying we didn't have *any* of that to fall back on.

Rather, we were forced to make up our own version of a digital design agency and figure out anew how to hire, sell, manage, strategize, and execute. As we hired and formed relationships with other design companies, we could validate some things we were doing as "right." We had come to the same conclusions that others had, which was a pretty good sign, while discovering we had completely flipped the script on other aspects. We did some things completely differently than everyone else, and many times, these were areas of our greatest strength.

The business model for any professional services business—from a law firm to management consultancy—is the simplest business model in the world. Someone needs a service, we perform said service for a rate (with some margin above cost), and upon successfully delivering said service, we realize a profit.

These companies have some of the lowest variable cost ratios in the business world. We don't have parts, equipment, perishables, or maintenance to worry about. We have almost exclusively fixed cost in the form of full-time employees (roughly 70 percent of total expenses), leases, furniture, et cetera. Even line items like travel, which are normally client specific and could therefore be considered variable, are usually billed back to the client.

This means that running this kind of business over any given month has a set and predictable cost. Assuming you can perform enough business to usurp that number, you make money. But, this is also our biggest downfall. Unlike other businesses whose business models allow for a nearly unlimited amount of upside based on a fixed bottom line (for instance, an ebook: whether one, one hundred, or one million people download it, it costs them roughly the same amount), our biggest Achilles' heel is that we have living, breathing human beings performing the work, who all have a capacity for how much throughput they can produce in a forty-to-fifty-hour workweek (called utilization rate).

So, we are limited in the amount of top line we can generate at any given time, based on the size of our workforce. To compound this challenge, we are constantly stepping up the amount of fixed cost we have as we hire, expand office space, and invest more in employee satisfaction and business development. So, the window between breakeven and maximum revenue continues to step up as well, because they are linearly related. You must constantly bring in more business and increase sales to hit that breakeven point. If you have a bad month and top line is down, you cannot easily reduce cost, unless you're going to start rapidly firing and hiring people, which would be impossible.

The way most companies get around this is to leverage contractors, or temporary employees, that they bring on to supplement their full-time teams during busy periods. This creates an aspect of variable cost, because they are applied to specific deliverables over specific amounts of time, allowing the business to control cash flow.

But, there are three major downsides to contractors.

First, they are generally hired guns temporarily beholden to anyone who is willing to take them on, so their availability is always in flux. Plus, they enjoy a lot of freedom, making them notoriously flaky and unreliable. If they were to get a more interesting project in the middle of the work they're doing for you, there would be nothing you could do to stop them from jumping ship.

Second, because they aren't vested in you and your team, there is naturally no continuity or familiarity with the rest of the team, which invariably creates tension, apathy, and personality clashes. Not to mention, they may (will) have their own way of doing things.

Third, they are expensive. Contractors dollar-for-dollar are 50 to 100 percent more expensive than full-time employees, which is painful to your profit margin.

Despite those negatives, this is a widely used tactic among agencies and even by companies who exist only to place contractors at other companies. Most of our competitors used contractors for higher-level roles, like management or strategy. This way, they could save themselves the painful fixed cost of expensive employees and, instead, only bring them in when they needed them, keeping lower-level employees full time in order to squeeze out the best margins.

Before knowing *any* of this, we made a decision at ÄKTA to do everything in our power to rely on full-time staff and only leverage contractors in states of emergency. And even then, we would only ever allow contracted work to be low-level, commodity work. This way, we could focus on building a high-level team with a great team dynamic and culture, and not risk throwing unknown quantities into that mix. In order to mitigate the risk of such a high fixed cost, we would have to sell our asses off, constantly. We would have to be better than everyone else at business development. And this is how we would scale and thrive.

When others learned of this tactic, they were shocked. It was the opposite of the playbook written back in the 1950s for advertising agencies. We were constantly told we were doing it "wrong" and our model would never be sustainable. That we were taking too much risk by having to beat such a rapidly increasing fixed cost per month to achieve profitability.

What happened instead is that we were able to create a team with more chemistry and culture than anyone else in the industry. A team of passionate designers who were friends outside the office, respected each other's craft, and were all early enough in their careers to see things as a blank slate and find the best way to solve problems.

And no one could question the numbers: our profit margin was two to three times higher than our competitors'. So high, in fact, that when bankers started reviewing our books years later, they encouraged us to spend more money and bring the margins down, because no one was going to believe what we were achieving was possible.

This was one of many, many areas where we broke the mold without ever realizing we were doing it.

I think this is one of the things we millennials have in our tool kit that makes us so deadly in business today. A new business is no longer expected to pick up the playbook from the companies before them and simply try to execute better. We now completely reimagine what others would have said is a cemented way of doing things.

So, remember this if you're embarking on an entrepreneurial journey in any industry, defined or not. There is simply no right or wrong way to do *anything*. Everything is up for interpretation and reinvention. And screw anyone who tries to tell you differently.

44 | THE WARDEN

I prepped for Drew's return from Down Under. I had to lock him in and immediately set his sights on winning this business with TSYS. The day before he was scheduled to come in, I sat with Julia and Kevin, and started firing off orders.

"Get the cleaners in! This place must be sparkling!"

"Everyone needs to please be fucking normal for just a few minutes!"

"Make sure no one is working from home! I want as many seats full as possible! Well, except Spider-Man. Give that guy the day off!"

That was a bit of a dick move. But think about it—how would you feel if you walked in to see a skateboarding superhero fly by you?

I wore my Sunday best—black jeans, black T-shirt, black blazer— and waited in the conference room for his arrival.

On time to the minute, pulling a small carry-on piece of luggage, walked in the most ordinary person I've ever seen. Handsome, average height, pleasant. He looked as if he were friends with every human on the planet and had never offended any of them. My first thought was, *Oh, shit. He is way too normal for this place.*

We had an expectedly congenial, level, logical discussion about ÄKTA and his career history. I was in full sales mode, trying to impress upon him the level of opportunity on both sides. He would be the first executive hired into the hottest agency in Chicago. He would have full control of our core service offering, making him the most important person on the team. He would have autonomy—I wouldn't impart my views or even participate in hiring or design strategy. I made this sound as if it would be a big concession for me. In fact, it would be bliss not to have to worry about the team's day-to-day operations and instead focus on sales and growth strategy.

As I expected, he said he was comfortable in his current role, but was also ambitious, so his attention was piqued. The conversation then reached the inevitable question that I knew was coming, and wished wasn't. What could I pay him?

I owned 100 percent of ÄKTA. Even Kevin hadn't been cut in yet. Drew first asked if there was equity on the table. I said that in time, it might be possible—a perfectly acceptable answer at this stage of a startup. He was smart enough to know that if he became as critical to this company as I was positioning him to be, it would be an easy conversation later on. But that also meant he had to make enough money up front, via salary. I braced myself for the kill shot.

"I'm making one-fifty now. I'd want two hundred to come here," he said confidently.

It hit me like a left hook to the liver. Not only was that about the amount of profit we would make for the entire year, it was also about four times more than the next-highest employee was paid. I was still forgoing a real paycheck, and Kevin was working for peanuts—how would he feel about this? He was managing every project and running the entire back office.

The obvious flip side was, if Drew could win TSYS and execute it, $200,000 would look like what was left in a tip jar. My gut told me he was the guy we needed.

"One-fifty starting," I told him. "You win TSYS, you get a 25K bonus. That's the best I can do."

I could have pushed a lot harder, but there are times you don't want to overnegotiate. I did not want to diminish his value. He gave me a nervous look, but I knew I had him. As invigorating as I'm sure it was working on hearing aids, this represented a huge résumé piece for him, and, potentially, an opportunity for a big payday in time.

"Okay, John, you have a deal," he said after a few minutes of weighing my offer. "I'll need a few weeks to roll off what I'm doing now, but I'm in."

With Drew's hiring, the entire company's focus turned to winning the TSYS deal. We didn't neglect our current clients, but we weren't pressing them for new business or going above and beyond on any ongoing projects. TSYS could provide the vast majority of our income for the coming year, at least. The Golden Rule of service businesses is to never rely on that level of revenue concentration from one client, but, well, sometimes you must break the rules.

TSYS Tedd soon became our best friend. He desperately wanted ÄKTA to win the work so he could dig his nails into the project, and he frankly wanted to hang out with us and be one of the cool kids. Who could blame him? The culture and excitement of a multibillion-dollar back-end credit card–processing company has got to rival only that of a paper factory.

As Drew was still rolling off his old job, the work was squarely upon me and the business development team to get the deal as close to the finish line as possible before he joined us. We spent countless hours of research on the (ungodly boring) industry of credit card acquisition, issuing, and processing. It was important that we could speak their language, even though, if I'm honest, I still to this day can't tell you technically what they actually do. But the other folks on my team seemed to understand it, and that was good enough for me.

The merchant processing space was red hot at the time, with companies like Square and Stripe coming out of the woodwork and almost instantly commanding ten-figure valuations. Mobile phones and tablets had completely changed the game and threatened to up-end the hundred-trillion-dollar point-of-sale industry. New ways of paying that didn't require physically swiping a credit card were being introduced seemingly every day, and it was clear that there were going to be some serious winners—and serious losers—in this space.

At this exact point in time, T-Mobile, AT&T, and Verizon released a revolutionary mobile credit card wallet system that they regrettably called Isis, having seemingly not checked on where else this particular word was being used in the global landscape. I'll never forget the CEO of Isis having to go on public record to state, "However coincidental, we have no desire to share a name with this group and our hearts go out to those affected by this violence." That is how chaotic and fast-moving the industry was at the time.

So far, what we knew about the opportunity with TSYS was that, even though it was transacting trillions of payments a year and was the backbone of over half the credit card swipes in the country, virtually no one had ever heard of it. This wasn't necessarily a bad thing—there are tons of "invisible" companies that people use every day that are perfectly happy with not being a name brand. But with this recent revolution of credit card–processing companies becoming strong public brands, and owning things like the point-of-sale systems and terminals, some of the more observant types at TSYS said, "Gee, we shouldn't miss out on this."

There were two key issues facing them. One, they had never slapped the TSYS brand on anything the public had seen, so regardless of how big the company actually was, it effectively had to operate like a startup and build a new consumer brand. Which they had absolutely no idea how to do.

Two, they had the "burden of opportunity": TSYS could build and power virtually anything in its industry. It had all the knowledge and technology to create any consumer applications it desired related to credit cards, and with these, could theoretically do so faster and more cheaply than its competitors. It could create its own POS system, a mobile credit card reader, a new type of credit card, new technology to pay without having a card present, an online-based system like PayPal, et cetera, et cetera, et cetera. The challenge thus became not what TSYS could do but rather what it should do.

This was not a simple thing to determine, especially from within the walls of the company. This is where ÄKTA would theoretically come in.

TSYS wanted a consultancy to help with an entirely fresh perspective to identify the most fruitful opportunities from a "startup" perspective. Research had to be done, business cases generated, theories tested, and, ultimately, final recommendations made to the board of directors. And assuming all *that* went well, budgets would be opened to then execute on all those ideas, from prototyping to market release.

To say this was a significant project would be an understatement. It offered the opportunity to not only create and execute a strategic priority for a massive corporation, which could result in millions in billable work but also the chance to revolutionize one of the hottest industries around. This could be our key case study for years to come. This was big-boy work.

I became obsessed with winning this business. I dreamt about it. I let myself fantasize about the money, the growth, the notoriety. I got a sick pleasure thinking about the message it would send to our critics, our competitors, to employees who had quit on us, to the pricks at Belly. We don't need *any* of you.

TSYS would expect us to come fully loaded, with detailed plans, prototypes, design inspiration, robust research, and an introduction to the full team that would be executing the work. This meant many tens of thousands of dollars of investment on our side just to prepare for the pitch, travel out west to meet with Tedd, and shift our expensive resources to nonbillable work.

Our situation had Kevin, who was the most level and chilled-out person I had ever met, panicking, in a Kevin sort of way. He began to blink more than usual during our conversations; he responded to my requests with a nervous, high-pitched laugh; and would step out once or twice more per day for a cigarette. I had instructed him to dedicate about a third of our team to preparing for TSYS, which meant we were currently operating at a financial breakeven, at best. If anything went wrong on any current projects, we could be looking at our first down month ever, which would require dipping into our embarrassingly feeble bank account to cover expenses. I estimated that we had eight weeks of runway in the bank.

This all might sound insane, and I guess it kind of was. I am sure every MBA professor reading this right now is bleeding out of their ears. But this level of risk-taking is a defining characteristic of startups. I don't know a single early-stage company that hasn't had to bet the farm, sometimes repeatedly, to survive. I have a friend who cashed in his 401(k), sold his car on eBay, and slept at the office just to be able to make payroll. Countless companies have launched having spent every single dollar on their product, depending on it to create revenue. Decades ago even the founder of FedEx took his last $5,000 to Vegas and hit the blackjack table, returning with $27,000, which kept him afloat for another week and saved the company.

It seems crazy to admit looking back at this years later, but making this kind of bet didn't really shake me. I'm not sure if it was my confidence that had convinced me that I could win the pitch, or if I had come to accept that this type of gamble was simply part of the journey. I was steely eyed and prepared to succeed.

45 | THE SHOW

R ather than have Drew enter the madhouse without any prepa-
ration, I had him first meet Kevin and me across the street
from the office for coffee, so we could ease him in. Thankfully he
was more resilient than we had given him credit for. He knew exactly what he was walking into and was ready.

The ÄKTA office then looked like *Star Trek* meets *A Beautiful
Mind*. Hundreds of pages of diagrams and screenshots were taped to
every available flat surface. Hieroglyphic-looking text and workflows
detailing our planning process were scrawled on floor-to-ceiling
whiteboards. Little ÄKTAgons (*ehh, maybe*) were running around
in circles, shouting instructions, yelling at the designers to work
faster, snapping papers off the printer, and cycling on and off the fire
escape for cigarette breaks. Rap music was blasting nonworkplace-
appropriate obscenities from a sound system. Beer began flowing
by noon.

Poor Pascale, still my business development lead, was trying to
corral these maniacs and make sense of everything so it could be
added to her proposal, which was already the size of an encyclopedia.

I loved the chaos. These moments seemed just so *fitting*. The entire scene was a perfect representation of our current state of affairs.
Life *was* this crazy, this absurd. It was more unnerving to me when
things were calm and everyone was staring at screens or talking quietly on phones.

Our preparations went on for far longer than made sense. Weeks of pure, raw energy banged off the walls of the ÄKTA office, and as pitch day approached, I had a crew of strung out zombies, aimlessly walking in slow circles, softly muttering to themselves, getting stuck in a corner until someone grabbed them and turned them around. I felt like a proud father.

We killed no fewer than five thousand trees printing drafts of the proposal. My environmentalist mind felt bad, but my capitalist mind set the concerns aside. I filed a mental note to donate to a reforestation fund if we made any money off this.

Unlike previous pitch meetings, TSYS was bringing its team to ÄKTA HQ. It goes without saying this created its own pressure. It felt a bit like when parents visit their kid's dorm room. Time to hide the beer bong, pull the *Playboy* posters off the walls, and take the underwear off the television.

When the big day came, we were ready. Actually, I shouldn't speak for anyone else. *I* was ready, and I think Drew was. Kevin had bowed out of the pitch completely—he had never been a showy sales guy. I thought I might have to jam caffeine IVs into the arms of the business development team, and the designers looked like deer in headlights.

I could feel everyone looking at me for guidance. I kept my smiling face perfectly relaxed. And it wasn't an act. For whatever reason, I felt calmer in that moment than I would a few hours later when I was sitting on my couch back at home *trying* to relax. Those days, my heart rate seemed to drop during times of high stress. I was more comfortable in my professional self. It was moments of silence, reflection, and acceptance that I struggled with. Allowing my brain to slow down long enough to consider the absurd situation I found myself in during that time would bring panic rushing in. In those rare moments of mindfulness, all the issues that I suppressed on a daily basis would come blasting into my conscious mind like a bomb exploding. I was willing to do just about anything to never let my mind settle.

The moment finally came. Julia hurriedly signaled to us that the TSYS crew had arrived. I joined her at the front door so that I could properly greet them on the way in. I have no idea what I had expected—maybe a couple of powerful suits with Secret Service following them and snipers covering their six?—but what arrived was the only thing anyone should have assumed: smiling, affable Tedd; a woman in her midforties, with a calm demeanor and gracious Southern manners; and an older gentleman who had clearly been instructed to "dress down" for ÄKTA, as I could see the tie he had obviously just removed sticking out of his briefcase.

In a very flattering and endearing way, I could tell they were somewhat nervous as well. Entering the lair of the cool tech kids, with their brightly painted accent walls, Ping-Pong table, beer fridge, and more toys than a nursery, was not their normal Thursday. Plus, they were probably staying in the big city for at least the night. I could totally see the old guy getting wild and ordering that second spritzer later.

The next three hours were oddly serene, perfectly methodical, and somewhat boring. We had been working with Tedd through the entire process. He'd guided us through the proposal and made sure no points were missed. By this time he was as much a part of ÄKTA as he was of TSYS. The team took turns on their relevant sections for the pitch and played their parts well. Dozens of questions were lobbed at us, but nothing we couldn't handle. Based on all the questions they had about our corporate insurance, security protocols, and certifications (none of which we had, as only companies as large as TSYS would require them), there was going to be a stack of work for Kevin to do before the process started, but that was fine. They still had to "take this back to the board for approval," and though we had no illusions about how quickly large corporations moved, we also knew we had won this business.

ÄKTA had just entered the big leagues.

46 | MAXIMUS

This is the point in the story when, in its third year, things were just going right within the walls of ÄKTA.

After filling the office to the brim with my little army of ÄKTA-nauts (*liking this one*), we signed a lease for space next door, took a sledgehammer to the wall, and continued to expand. It felt as if every time I would come back from a daylong meeting or business trip, I encountered a new face. It was like rabbits multiplying. Kevin took great pleasure in telling me, "Hired another one! Come introduce yourself." I no longer even interviewed new candidates.

Checks were rolling in through the mail at a ridiculous pace. I'd pop open an envelope, see a dollar sign with a bunch of zeros after it, smile at Kevin, and Frisbee the envelope over to him. For me it was more about what the checks represented than the actual amount of money. This was proof we were succeeding.

TSYS was rolling at a *crazy* pace. Almost two-thirds of the office was focused on this one client. Teams were flying in and out of Chicago to perform studies, working overtime on prototyping. Months later the road map started to present itself. We had developed an unbelievably well-thought-out plan for tackling not only the consumer credit card–processing space but also the white-label market, across a huge platform of web, mobile, and tablet products, which would mean a metric fuck-ton of work for ÄKTA.

We could do no wrong. Every month was bigger than the last. Our team was rock solid, with near-zero attrition and high levels of satisfaction. While Kevin was losing his mind a bit and would need support soon, he had the operations down pat. HR, finance, and project management were all humming. I was running around closing deals like a maniac, generating an assembly line of contracts. And most important, I had gotten the taste of a big, big corporate client, with its limitless budgets, reasonable timelines, and big, sexy, public work.

Having been given a glimpse of the promised land, I craved more. The only problem was, these companies were extremely hard to break into. Without well-established relationships (of which we had none), ÄKTA had to try to pick off RFPs. Large public companies are legally forced to send these out in order to get fair, competitive bids from an assortment of companies. I didn't have the patience or knowledge to go down that route. I needed to kick the fucking door down. I needed a Trojan horse.

Mercifully, I wasn't doing as much networking as in years prior, but I was still a regular part of the Chicago business circuit. There had been such an insanely high amount of press for ÄKTA and me lately—from awards and recognitions to my being named one of Chicago's Most Eligible Singles—that when I did network, it was at a very high level.

While I enjoyed the recognition, it was also disconcerting. The spotlight compounded my anxiety. I had to go out and act like an impervious young CEO on a daily basis, and try to get millions of people to buy that story. I couldn't admit in an interview that I was starting to struggle mentally or that I felt as if, even now, I didn't know what I was doing. Any sign of vulnerability was not acceptable, as it wouldn't support the narrative people expected. They wanted an unflappable genius. So, that's what I gave them.

During one such event, at which I was easily the least affluent and youngest attendee, I met a guy named Dean DeBiase. Well, technically, I overheard Dean reciting the highlights of his résumé and leaned in to eavesdrop. "I was the CEO of this company; helped sell this other company for a billion dollars; used to be the chairman of that company." Fucking hell. Who was this guy? He had that unmistakable hard liquor drawl in his voice, so I stood by the bar and waited for him to come up for a refill, while watching him go around the room and glad-hand every damned person there, including the mayor.

I figured he was the better part of sixty years old. He had short hair that had been overdyed blond, probably to hide the gray. He had a personable smile and wore tennis shoes with khakis. He used his hands to talk so much that it looked as if he were speaking sign language. He was my dad, and your dad, and every dad you've ever met.

He finally walked up, and I had a mutual friend introduce us. I learned that Dean had apparently worked at every large Chicago company that I'd ever heard of, in some very interesting roles. Most people don't realize Chicago has more Fortune 500 headquarters than almost any other American city. And in this world, he seemed to know *everyone*. I had no time for beating around the bush. I laid out the history of ÄKTA and started hinting at where we needed the most help—landing more huge corporate accounts. He mentioned that he had helped a lot of companies scale through business development. I asked some ego-stroking questions.

Know anyone at Motorola? Yep, I used to work with the CEO.

Know anyone at United Airlines? Yep, the CTO is a friend.

Know anyone at Grainger? Yep, the owner is my neighbor.

He started name-dropping like a Hollywood agent and went on and on and on about the vastness of his network; his celebrity status, having recently appeared on *Celebrity Apprentice* with Donald Trump; and how many companies he had run, grown, and sold.

I loved it. I completely respected his hustle. Despite knowing in my heart he was 50 percent talking out of his ass. If that other 50 percent was legit, he could be a gold mine for ÄKTA. Now the question became, how did we get this guy on our team?

Dean and I had lunch the next day, over martinis. While he fancied himself a tech guy, and probably figured as one in his Chicago suburb, he didn't know much about the cutting-edge area of tech that we worked in. But it didn't matter. All I needed this guy for was to get me in the door with an executive or product owner, and I could do the rest.

He was a superb negotiator, so I let him take the lead on brainstorming how our partnership might work. He explained that to make it worth his time for working with companies like ÄKTA, his "normal arrangement" was to take a monthly fee, commission, and also a chunk of equity. The terms he casually laid out should have been illegal. I figured he was going to be expensive, and had conceded that one day I would have to cut some important people in on the equity table as an incentive, but I certainly wasn't going to make it *that* easy.

Over the next weeks we talked on the phone often, and each time

I wore him down a little more. I got him high on the idea of being in a leadership role at a fast-growing startup like ÄKTA, which I knew would be a huge ego play for him. I also made him fall in love with the idea of me: a kid half his age, with the energy of a bumblebee on meth, who was willing to run through any door he opened and win big deals. It would boost his reputational equity with these big companies if he could broker innovative projects for them.

I finally got him to an acceptable negotiating position, even though I could tell he didn't like it. He agreed to a very reasonable monthly retainer, a decent commission on new relationships he brought to the table, and a small piece of equity, earned over multiple years, based on strict terms of success. Basically, he had to walk the walk and help us drive millions upon millions to the top line, or else he wasn't getting shit.

This hedge was my signature move. Wherever possible I would find ways to incentivize only on absolute success, and have every legal mechanism available to take everything back from a person who didn't perform. Call this the result of scar tissue from my earlier unhappy experiences with partners, but the reality is, people will disappoint, cheat, and screw around. I had learned that any time I could take a position of power, I needed to do so.

For his part Dean knew how to play the game as well as anyone, and that made me trust him as much as I would a tarot card reader. But I didn't consider that a fault. The less you trust someone in these settings, the more you respect them. If they're actually trying to make an amicable deal, they aren't very good at the game.

So, we both applied pressure, negotiated hard, showed willingness to kill the deal, and ultimately, inked a contract a few weeks later.

Dean DeBiase was now the chairman of ÄKTA.

47 | GROW, BABY, GROW

The addition of Deanius Maximus (my pet name for him) became our most significant growth marker to date.

On his first day with us, I sat him down in a room with Kevin to strategize how we were going to work together. Kevin hadn't been very involved in the decision to hire Dean, so he sat in the conference room with the same look your dog gives the new cat. The aura was about as comfortable as a Middle East peace talk. Kevin probably also wasn't thrilled that Dean had snuck his way onto the equity table before he had.

While Maximus often seemed like the king of the 3Bs (bullshit, bluster, and bravado), he was also deeply connected, as promised. When I listed my dream companies to work with in Chicago, he had access to every one of them. Some of the connections were rock solid, like his neighbor who was the top guy at Grainger, a ten-billion-dollar industrial supply company that was doing all sorts of trendy things in digital. Others were a little looser, such as an upcoming speaking engagement at which he was going to be onstage with an executive of Motorola Solutions. ("I'll slip you a pass to the VIP event afterward and will introduce you as if you're also one of the speakers. No one will know, it'll be fine!")

The machine started. He would use one of his many methods to procure meetings with potentially extremely lucrative clients, we'd sit down, he would chum them up, and I would sell the pants right off their asses. I almost never lost a deal.

I've been asked hundreds of times for my secret. How I am able to sell like I do? I wish I had the answer. Maybe I can figure it out and make it the subject of my next book. It's either telepathy, overactive mirror neurons, or I may just be a little crazy. When I find myself in a sales setting, I can deeply sense somewhere in my subconscious the feelings and mindset of the person at the other end of the table: Whether they're comfortable, confident, happy, tired, distracted, or satisfied. What their motivations are. Why they're *really* in the room. The level and type of energy they're bringing to the table.

I use this information to manipulate the meeting. To put my opponents on their back feet; to make them uncomfortable, if they seem too confident. Or to make them feel like the most special person in the world, if they seem hesitant. I smile if I suspect someone doesn't trust me. I stare into the back of their skull if I need them to feel intimidated. I mirror their ego and rip it apart. Or put it together like a delicate puzzle. This made Dean and me an unstoppable force. He set them up, and I knocked them down.

We signed with Motorola Solutions on a seven-figure deal to design artificial intelligence emergency response software that 911 operators and first responders would use. This was technology straight out of *Minority Report*. Using a deluge of open-source data, like traffic data, police scanners, and public events, combined with robust proprietary data like criminal records, license plate databases, and police body cameras, we could get pretty damn close to predictive crime fighting. We could send police to a site where the software believed a crime might occur. Scary.

We signed Exelon, one of the largest utility companies in the country, to a massive contract to design a proprietary piece of software for their HR department to use, so they could better internally promote and manage key employees. We also became responsible for their Mobile Center of Excellence, which was a massive program that would enable them to quickly ideate, prototype, design, and deploy mobile applications internally to create efficiency or take advantage of new opportunities.

Nailing our triple backflip into the sea of enterprise companies thrust ÄKTA into an elite class of consultancies. We were now routinely pitching—and winning—against IDEO, whose books I had been reading just a couple of years earlier to try to understand this business that they had pioneered. We would find ourselves competing against the $200 billion consulting giant Deloitte, which was feverishly building its own version of ÄKTA with Deloitte Digital. We'd walk out with the cheddar, every damned time.

Winning so often against these big, intimidating incumbents was not only hard to believe but had started to build up in my head a new sort of pressure that threw off my equilibrium. I would have ferocious mental debates about the question, *Were we better at sales, or design?* Our primo competitors *had* to be extremely good at what they did, as they dwarfed us in size and resources, hired the highest-caliber talent, and had decades of experience to fall back on. They *had* to be amazing at experience design. It would be far too arrogant to assume our final output was that much better than theirs. Or better at all, in most cases. Yet, clients chose us, repeatedly.

All the work we were doing were firsts for us. I didn't even know what a fucking "Center of Excellence" was when I sold it. I sort of got the gist, and figured, *I don't see why we can't pull that off! That'll be a million dollars, please.*

These sorts of challenges weren't dissimilar from the many projects we had aced in the past, like Topgolf. We certainly didn't know what we were doing then, either. The difference now was that the stakes were much, much higher. We were designing emergency response systems that could either save lives, or create disastrous scenarios for first responders. That sounded like work a multibillion-dollar global consulting firm should be doing, not an army of millennial design gurus in a timber loft in Chicago.

What would happen if I got this wrong? If I overcommitted to a solution that truly was outside our capabilities? We weren't superhuman. There would always be a limit.

The combination of the standard day-to-day pressures with these new larger, riskier bets was starting to weigh on me. In previous years I would be able to leave work at the office when the day ended. Now it felt impossible. I was attached to my cell phone, out of fear of missing an important call or email, twenty-four hours a day. Sleep would come in restless spurts. A phantom phone vibration or sudden realization I had forgotten to do something would make me pop out of bed at regular intervals. It was around this time that the night terrors started. I'd had nightmares before, run-of-the-mill scenarios in which I felt as if I were falling or that a loved one was in danger, and I'd wake up scared.

What I was experiencing now was at a whole different level. I'd violently awaken, dripping in sweat, with my heart blasting out of my chest like a diesel engine. I'd wake up screaming or flailing my arms, as if I were fighting something away. I had a recurring dream of staring in the mirror, picking at a scab on my forehead, until the skin fell away, and a dark claw started digging out.

Often I'd find myself in a different room of my apartment, having fled the bedroom while still asleep. It could take minutes to orient myself to where I was, to discern what was real. On such nights, sleep would almost never come again.

The truth was, I was scared out of my mind about what I was doing every day. Despite the outward success of the business, I was all too aware of what we were really building: a locomotive with no brakes. Because projects were in a constant state of flux, there was always a single anchor client holding down the fort. Kevin was trying to be a prophet and predict what was going to come or go the following month, to appropriately staff up to make sure we didn't get caught with too few resources. If even a single major client at any given time changed their mind and fired us, or some overzealous manager decided to bring the work in-house, or a terrorist blew a plane out of the sky and the economy tanked, or the hundreds of other reasons these projects got randomly axed, we could be instantly ruined.

We could sustain one or maybe two months of loss before the walls would crumble. We would then have to cut costs by firing valuable full-time employees whom we could never get back, which would lead to a loss of morale, client obligations being missed, and then, bam—we'd be dead. I lived in constant fear of that one phone call—*Hey, John, look, bad news . . . the board had a change of heart and we aren't going to be able to move forward on the project*—that would finish ÄKTA once and for all.

That fear eats away at your psyche like rope rubbing against wood. Fiber by fiber, it burns away. Seeing Kevin walk up to my desk would send a wave of nausea through my body, in anticipation of his giving me bad news. Living in a state of constant fear is a horrible feeling. Your bones are uncomfortable in your skin. You find yourself being resentful of *everything*, even things that are so unreasonable that to resent them feels delusional. Positive thinking aggravated me. Optimism felt irresponsible.

Fuck you Tony Robbins. Everything is not *going to be okay.*

I began to become a little angry, and a little sad, constantly. Whether I was sitting in a movie theater or celebrating a friend's birthday, I no longer experienced any points of simple, pure joy. There was a fade, a fog to my vision. I would find myself rehearsing my concession speech. *It was a good run, guys. We did our best. I'm sorry I failed you.*

Giving myself even a moment to try to consider the situation objectively would make my heart rate jack up. The only temporary solution I found was to disconnect from it and not face it, pretend it wasn't happening. I'd tell anyone who asked that everything was fine. I'd try to tell myself that as well.

The reality—which was only apparent in retrospect—was that ÄKTA was a wildly capable, high-functioning machine, built of talented, hardworking people. We didn't have to be exponentially better than our competitors. Nor did they have any more functional credibility to do mission-critical work than we did. We were fantastic at our craft, we deserved the success, and we were on the right path. But that was never clear while we were battling.

48 | THE PROMISED LAND

In early 2013 I had finally begun taking a proper salary and dividends from profit at ÄKTA and pulled enough cash to pay off my personal debts and wipe my financial slate clean. This didn't feel as satisfying as I had hoped it would, as I had just made that money disappear, rather than keeping it on hand in case ÄKTA desperately needed it. Plus, I had so many personal guarantees with vendors at ÄKTA that if we failed, I'd go bankrupt anyway.

By the third quarter of 2013 we had begun to realize the revenue from all of Dean's monster clients, and we were flush with cash. It was insane. It felt as if every day a pile of five- and six-figure checks landed on my desk, which I would unceremoniously tear open and then fling over to Kevin. He would roll his eyes every time I did so.

So long as they didn't experience a company disaster, or a change in the macroeconomic climate that would affect spending, cutting a check for hundreds of thousands of dollars was nothing to these clients. Assuming we could quote a budget with a straight face, however outlandish, they'd pay it. Many projects we were now doing were even fixed bid, rather than hourly. This meant that we would come up with some crazy number to complete what might be six months of work, and then that number would hold firm unless we reached an agreement to raise or lower it, usually based on a change in scope. Such arrangements were the absolute Holy Grail for businesses like ÄKTA. All we had to do was to focus on project management and fulfillment, which Kevin and Drew had down to a science. Assuming we delivered milestones by pre-agreed intervals—which we almost always did—then it didn't matter how much work we put into it. So, if we could create efficiency internally, and not use as many hours as we projected we would, any excess was pure profit. There were times we spun off million-dollar contracts with over 50 percent gross profit margin.

In order to continue building our powerful business development engine, we had begun to invest heavily in marketing, PR, and events. It felt as if every day I was either being interviewed for some business publication, being photographed for an award, or speaking onstage at a conference. I would go out like a televangelist and preach the good word of ÄKTA as if I had the secret to eternal life.

By November of that year, it was time for another draw of cash for me. We had enough in the bank to keep Kevin happy, so I told the accountants to determine a draw amount and wire it over. November 21 was my last day of being twenty-nine years old. I sat alone on my couch, drinking a healthy pour of whiskey, trying to decompress from another hectic Thursday, and planning for what would undoubtedly be a big evening of partying the following night, celebrating a new decade of my life. I absentmindedly opened the banking app on my phone, because seeing how much I had in the bank was one of the few things that still gave me a spark. Money, at least, validated some of this craziness.

$1,051,918.45

Jesus. I blinked my eyes, making sure they weren't playing games with me.

I was a millionaire?

A confusing crosshatch of emotions shot through my brain. I felt happy and confused and, for some reason, heavy. This was cool, but what did it mean? What were the implications? What was I supposed to do with a million dollars?

No fireworks went off. No balloons streamed above.

I was hoping for someone to knock on my door and deliver a manual on how to be a millionaire. You hear the term all the time, you're constantly being told about the millionaire lifestyle, the access they have, the extravagant things they buy. Was I supposed to do this now? Would I feel different when I woke up the next day? I was now the only millionaire I knew, apart from some of my clients, so I certainly couldn't ask anyone for guidance. And I sensed that this was *not* a subject to bring up with friends.

The only thing I could think to do was text my mom.

"Mama . . . you won't believe it, but I'm apparently a millionaire now . . ."

Her response was the most mom response in the history of mom responses.

"That's nice, honey. It's a good thing, right?"

Her all-too-real question was still banging around in my head when I woke up the next morning, not feeling any different, but being oddly disappointed that even millionaires get hangovers.

I felt foggy, and lonely. I was barely holding it together with Cortney. While she was a good partner, I had begun to resent her, for no good reason. Perhaps because she was the one person who saw the real me, the person behind the curtain, she was somehow responsible for who I was. She was trying to make the relationship work, but soon her efforts would be of no use. She had arranged a big birthday party with friends and family for that night, about which I was equally excited and apprehensive.

On one hand, reaching thirty marked some kind of achievement. I felt very old and very young at the same time. On the other, I was going to have to talk to dozens of people at the party who recently only had a connection to me from interviews in magazines and newspapers. Every one of them was invariably going to ask me how things were going and tell me how proud they were of me. And of course, I was going to have to play along. It didn't matter if it was some guy I'd never met or my own brother. "Yes, life is good! Everything at ÄKTA is perfect and amazing! Never been better! You know, it's a grind, but we are crushing it!" Isn't it interesting how every entrepreneur is "crushing it"? Put one hundred in a room, and they all say that, even though ninety-nine of them are on their way out of business.

This was my standard set of responses, always. What else was I really supposed to say?

You know, I signed a contract last week that would make me personally liable for millions in damages—that I don't have—if this project doesn't work out.

Oh, yeah, an old client is threatening to sue us for breach of contract because we are working with one of their competitors, which is eating at my insides, but no one knows, because I am hiding it from my partners and employees.

I am totally faking that smile in all those photos you see of me because I truly fear I'm in over my head and am going to get exposed as a fraud.

I have isolated myself from my good friends, barely talk to my family, and am about to break up with my girlfriend. Oh, did I mention I have no healthy coping mechanisms, so I spend my time numbing my brain, forever dreading the next day? Fun, right!

My sister flew in from California to surprise me. My little brother and sister arrived from Michigan. I hugged friends and got updates on their lives. I realized I had barely thought about so many people I used to constantly care for and worry about. My entire family was together, which felt amazing. I was having fun behind a patina of guilt. I stood there, looking at them all, wondering if I was a worthy son or a good brother anymore. Or if anyone at the party had a valid reason to care about me. When Doug showed up, I realized I hadn't talked to him in years.

I got blind drunk. But I didn't care. It was my birthday party, dammit. Thankfully, my family had retired to bed earlier, so they didn't have to witness it.

It felt foolish to feel bad for myself. Clearly no one else was responsible for me reaching this point. I had to remind myself that I was the epitome of the American Dream. I was fully aware what most people would give to be a self-made millionaire at thirty. I thought about those other people, and how different, I assumed, their mindset was at turning thirty around friends and family.

It was a hell of a way to break in the new decade.

49 | GROWTH RATE

Y o, what's the formula to calculate a multi-year-over-year growth rate?" I asked aloud, out of nowhere.

Kevin looked at me as if it were a trick question. He didn't know, either, so we started to reverse engineer the equation on a whiteboard. This was a very male moment of being too stubborn to just Google it. Within twenty minutes we were certain we had worked it out, and then Googled it to make sure.

My question wasn't totally out of the blue. I was paging through an issue of *Inc.* magazine, reading puff pieces on superhero CEOs and accounts of unbelievably successful startups. All I could think while reading them was, *I wish I knew the real story.* This wasn't a dig at *Inc.* It's just what works in business journalism.

One of these profiles cited the company's rank on the prestigious

Inc. 500 list, which honored the fastest-growing private companies in the country, out of the thirty million or so in business. This particular company had a growth rate of about 900 percent, which sounded pretty damned impressive. Kevin was referencing our P&L statement from the last three years on his laptop, and totaling up numbers on the whiteboard. Finally, he wrote "1200" and circled it.

"Twelve hundred what?" I asked.

"Percent. You asked what our growth rate was."

Well, shit. That sounded pretty damned impressive, too. I searched the web for the complete *Inc.* list from the prior year, and started scrolling down to see if we would have been on it. I was blown away. ÄKTA would have been included as one of the five hundred fastest growing companies in the country?

As it turns out, ÄKTA now had a marketing department, so I called a meeting to figure out how we could guarantee a place for ourselves on the list for the current year. Like everything in business media, I was sure there was some pay-to-play component for inclusion on the list, but appearing on it would be very meaningful. You can't fake growth.

The process ended up being quite simple: We submitted audited financial statements to *Inc.* showing our year-over-year growth, paid an entrance fee, and after they compiled all the data, they notified you if you made the list.

That was the only part that was simple. The complex part was my ongoing realization that, despite my chronic uncertainty and doubt, maybe we *were* actually succeeding, not just appearing to? The constant ambivalence in my head was maddening. *No, this is real. We really are this good. We really are crushing it. No, we are just lucky. We don't belong on that list. Without so-and-so client, we wouldn't have had that growth. But isn't that true for every company? Of course it is. Of course it isn't. I don't know.*

Ping-pong, ping-pong.

50 | THE INCA TRAIL

W*e're not saving the fucking manatees here, guys.*
Every time Kevin and I would sit in a meeting where ÄK-TA's "purpose" was questioned, this was the line that was quoted. It was hard not to ask ourselves what we were spending our time on, and if there was any purpose or meaning to what we were doing. Did it matter?

No, ultimately, it didn't matter. ÄKTA's purpose wasn't to save the manatees, but that didn't mean we couldn't parlay at least some of our success into projects that would actually help the world.

If you recall, the initial link between Kevin and me was our desire to engage in humanitarian work. At best, ÄKTA was creating jobs and making our already well-off clients even better off. At worst, we were just another cog in the wheel that is American capitalism. Digital Hope was our dream—a nonprofit organization in which we would use our skills in technology to connect the disconnected world, to enable people doing amazing things to tell their stories and find ways to help one another.

There were multiple times during my time at ÄKTA when I would try to create a spark for this vision. I would have our designers create a promotional video to draw attention to a humanitarian project, or try to get out and do a volunteer project. But like clockwork the demands of everyday business would grab hold and we would have to shelve the meaningful stuff.

The thing I forced myself to do, regardless of how busy we were at ÄKTA, was to take volunteer trips under the Digital Hope moniker, document the experience, raise awareness on social media, and try to garner as many donations as possible to push toward the nonprofits we visited. The program was mildly successful. We outfitted a school in Costa Rica with enough school supplies to last them years, provided food to an island orphanage in eastern Guatemala, helped a group that raided black market animal trading in Vietnam, and spayed and neutered hundreds of street dogs in Colombia.

The sense of purpose these projects brought to my life was astounding. I sometimes felt guilty, as I might be getting more out of them than I was giving. I wanted to believe I was still a good person. I wanted to prove that to myself and others.

For what turned out to be the final volunteer trip, I recruited a couple of friends and went to Peru, where we volunteered in three different cities, before embarking on the Inca Trail to Machu Picchu. Beyond the physical challenge, the trek is a mental one, as you're battling altitude sickness, traversing wildly dangerous crevasses, and defending against hypothermia at the highest points.

I can vividly recall my mindset for the entire trip. The questions that spun and spun around in my mind were a reflection of myself, and of my purpose. *What really matters, and what doesn't? Am I spending my limited time on this earth in the right way? Am I selfish for choosing the entrepreneurial path?* Out here I felt good about myself, and about the world. We were literally making a difference. I could feel my anxiety lessening, and a sense of peace, even though what we were doing physically was significantly riskier than anything I'd ever done at home.

Maybe this was where I belonged. Or we all belonged, as humans. Maybe we were all wasting away, punching plastic keys and blabbing into devices attached to our head. Maybe I was the symptom, or the cause, of the lack of meaning that so many people experienced. I wondered if any of that mattered. If it made me a good or bad person to feel this way.

Staring out across the endless expanse of the Peruvian Andes, I thought to myself, *Maybe I will just stay out here forever.*

As good as it felt, I didn't focus on my sense of relief as much as I should have. The universe was effectively screaming at me, "Check it out! There are healthy ways to feel better!" and had I been more attuned, perhaps I would have made trips like this a regular occurrence to experience this release. Instead, I let the tidal wave wash me right back to sea.

51 | THE GRANDMASTER

Posttravel depression must be the most privileged ailment ever, but that doesn't make it any less real, especially given the cross fire I had to walk into when I got back.

I had fights on all fronts, and our public success was not helping matters.

ÄKTA and I were being written up more than Britney Spears during her head-shaving days. Interviews, blogs, awards, profiles.

Photos with the mayor. Invitations to the most exclusive events. There was publically no question that we were raking in the dough.

And now *everyone* wanted a fucking piece.

Our landlord was trying to take advantage of our success by jacking up our rent rates. I would have at least one screaming match with him per week.

One of our competitors had moved in directly across the hall. Clients would come see us about a project and then walk 8 feet for a meeting at our competitor's office. Of course, they were trying to cut us off at the knees by offering much lower pricing.

Motorola, our biggest client behind TSYS, was trying to squeeze us in any way they could, and dangled the prospect of canceling our contract anytime they demanded something. This was a delicate game of cat and mouse, because I had to present a strong business case while never letting them become aware that I couldn't stay in business without them.

Our work with Exelon, our third-largest account, was drawing to a close, and I desperately needed another client to replace them.

Various employees had started to recognize their increased value, and Kevin had to hand out raises like popsicles.

Drew and Kevin had formed a partnership to put increased pressure on me to cut them in on the equity table. This was something that did need to happen, but I dreaded these conversations. They were both new to this process and probably had wildly elevated expectations of how much equity they would receive as hired-in executives. The conversation would have been different if they were business partners sharing the financial risk and investment, but that wasn't the case. This is a black hole so many founders fall in. Equity grants of 1 percent or 5 percent or 10 percent sound like nothing—until the number of those slices starts to add up, quickly. Before you know it, you own less than 50 percent of the company, go through a number of diluting financing rounds, and then hold only 5 percent to 10 percent of a company you started. Just ask the founder of Pandora, who owned a paltry 2.3 percent of the company when it went public.

On top of all of this, I had a far greater adversary—motherfucking Grandmaster Chansung Tao from the American Korean Taekwondo Association.

Why? you may fairly ask.

Because the American Korean Taekwondo Association, or AKTA, owned akta.com. We therefore had to use weareakta.com as our URL, which everyone read as "Wear Eakta" or something equally baffling. It was a horrible domain name, so I wanted theirs.

A year earlier I had contacted the grandmaster, who was potentially interested in selling us the domain for a fair sum. But weeks would pass between his responses to each email, and by the time we were finally getting close to a deal, he started seeing our name all over the internet. I'm not trying to call Grandmaster Tao a prick, but let's just say, the price went through a healthy increase when he found out we had real money to spend. My feign as a poor little bootstrapped tech company went completely out the damned window.

He now wanted such an absurd sum of money for the domain that it made me sick to even consider it. I basically had to choose between using funds to acquire a tiny piece of digital property, or to hire more employees, renovate our office, and probably save a few endangered species.

And yeah, you better believe I bought it.

52 | THE BELLS

The entrepreneurial game does one of two things to a romantic relationship.

It either destroys any semblance of it, like throwing a lightbulb in a blender, or it binds two people together more strongly than almost anything else can. Partners in tough times.

It goes without saying, I fell firmly into the first camp. Shortly after my thirtieth birthday, I did break up with Cortney, having surrendered to the notion that I couldn't give my focus to anything but my business. After that I didn't date or even consider the option. My relationships were from then on generally measured in hours.

Kevin, meanwhile, had been off and on with a partner since the day I met him—a lovely woman named Shannon who was just as weird as he was. I always had the feeling she didn't care for me much, but I assumed it was because she blamed me for the state Kevin was in when he would return from the office. One day out of the blue he gave me one hell of a personal update: he had proposed to Shannon, and they planned to get married the following year.

Two questions shot through my head concurrently: *How in the fuck are you able to think about a wedding in the middle of all of this?* and more important, *Where are we doing the bachelor party?*

The first question really tested my psyche. Until that moment I would have said it was utterly impossible to have a relationship in this chaos, and any effort devoted to it would wind up being a lost cause. But that clearly wasn't true. Maybe it was me. Maybe it actually wasn't an unmanageable amount of stress, but rather my inability to handle it. Maybe I was broken. How did Kevin do it? These were rough thoughts. To this day I think about how different, and likely better, this journey would have been with someone at my side whom I could trust and who supported me. I would even go so far as to say this may be one of the greatest keys to success that I completely missed out on.

The second question was much simpler, and rhetorical.

53 | THE DESERT

Kevin drove, I sat in the passenger seat. This was the safe bet, as my vision was blurred, and there was a ringing in my ears. My eyelids felt sunburned and my joints ached.

We were doing a hundred miles an hour down US 93 from Las Vegas to Phoenix. This is the most dangerous road in America, which felt fitting. I sat slouched with my right leg hanging over the door of the Ferrari we had rented that morning, a position that assured grisly paralysis if the airbag had to fire out. We probably weren't supposed to take the car two hundred miles through the desert and we definitely had no idea how we were going to get it back to Vegas, but hey, we were celebrating.

We'd spent the last three days in Vegas for Kevin's bachelor party, a hedonistic blur of bottles, drugs, and women that would have made Hunter S. Thompson become a monk. But we were now on our way to the main event, heading for some sterile golf resort in

Scottsdale to be told how amazing we were in the form of the *Inc.* 500 Award. ÄKTA was officially recognized as one of the five hundred fastest-growing companies in the whole damned country; 1,147 percent annual growth, to be exact. And now we were going to join hundreds of other masochists who had also grown their companies at a ridiculous rate for a weekend of standard banquet food, tuxedos, and speeches.

At least that is how most of the conference goers would probably experience the event. But given the combination of me, Kevin, the chemical levels in our bloodstream, open bars, and a feverish appetite to milk a few days out of the office for all their worth, things were guaranteed to go bad.

The first night was a theme party, complete with Hawaiian music and everyone oh-so-cleverly getting "lei'd" at the door. We sat in the corner, trying to drink off our hangovers. I can't recall if we even had business cards on us, but if we did, I doubt we had any intention of handing any out, lest we link ÄKTA to our upcoming bad behavior.

The attendees had some common traits: young(er), ambitious, and excited to be away from work. Most looked an order of magnitude more bright-eyed and bushy-tailed than we did. We felt out of place, given the mayhem we had just caused in Vegas. Maybe we were the exception. Maybe there was a way to win at this game without being degenerates. Or maybe, you just couldn't tell by looking around that we were all masking our realities.

I was standing at the bar, ordering yet another glass of whiskey, when two pretty blondes with conference passes around their necks walked up and ordered drinks. The best part about attending business conferences is that they provide an automatic opener: "So, what company are you two with?"

Unlike most of the attendees, these two weren't entrepreneurs, but Americans living in Denmark who had been sent by the Danish government as business delegates. Both were twenty-nine years old and had five kids and two husbands between them.

A clearer-minded version of myself would have respected that fact and not pursued them. I'm not a home-wrecker. And I can't explain my behavior that night as well as I would like to, but one thing I did know was that the pressure had finally gotten to me. I was pissed off at myself and at the world for putting me in this position. The chemical aftermath of Vegas wasn't helping. I had the same mindset that compels some young celebrity to do two hundred miles an hour in his new Lamborghini, or to punch a paparazzo in the face. While I should have been happy with my success, I was instead resentful at the sacrifice it required. I blamed myself, instead of congratulating myself. *You did this!* Frankly, I wanted to go out and break things. I wanted anarchy.

Kevin and I and the two women took seats at a table in the resort bar, laying waste to a series of tequila shots. Nothing is as straightforward as tequila. There is no question of intent, no delusion of its effect. It's an evil little monster that sits on your shoulder for the rest of the night, cheerleading for chaos and pain.

At some point the "Danes" announced they were on their last drink, as they had an obligation at 8:00 a.m. Kevin and I also had our one scheduled meeting of the conference the following morning, but I figured that that gave us at least nine hours to do something stupid.

There was certainly no fun to be found in this lame resort bar, so I called an SUV. "Let's go find a bar, just one drink," I assured the girls, whom it took less than five seconds to convince.

"We need tequila. Take us to a bar!" I yelled to the driver. To which I got the most pitiful news I could imagine: Apparently, bars closed at 11:00 p.m. in the area. As did liquor stores. The whole town went dry right around the time any drinker worth his salt would want to get going. I guess that was the point.

"Where can we get liquor?" I asked the driver. There is always a way.

"Everything is closed. I promise you."

"Call your friends!" I told him. "I have two thousand dollars in my pocket. Tell them I will buy what they have."

He stared at me in the rearview mirror, clearly thinking he had misheard me. The look I gave back to him made it clear that I meant what I had said. He hesitantly fingered his cell phone, and a loud ringer soon sounded on the car's speakers. *"Hola?"* a sleepy voice answered. Rapid Spanish was exchanged. I recognized a few words, one of which was *loco.*

"Okay," the driver said when he hung up. "Uh . . . he has a bottle of rum and white wine."

Fucking perfect. Let's start there. I peeled off $200 and handed it to the driver.

Twenty minutes later we pulled into an alley behind small houses in a run-down suburb. A man emerged, in white underwear and a matching tank top, carrying a plastic bag. Words were exchanged, and the driver handed me the bag, which held the promised cheap rum and cheaper white wine.

Over the next hour we made three more stops at three more friends' houses and ended up with two bottles of tequila, a bag of loose weed, what we believed was cocaine, a stack of cups, and six packs of cigarettes. I handed the remaining $500 to the driver and told him it was his tip.

I was pouring shots in my guests' mouths and trying to work out how we were going to smoke the weed when the driver decided the party was really going to start.

"Uh, hey, do you guys want to go swimming?" he asked. "I have a Jacuzzi."

I screamed something like "Let's fucking go!" as the car made a violent U-turn and started off toward another suburb. The girls were loving it. Kevin was on the fence. I stuck my head out the back window and watched the lights fly by, without a care in the world.

When we finally pulled into a driveway, it was clear that we had been oversold. The driver's "Jacuzzi" was actually a communal hot tub in a shitty apartment complex behind a high fence, but we'd make do. I groggily looked at my watch; it was 1:30 a.m. We had all night.

The driver told us to have fun, and said he would wait in the car. In the amount of time it took me to smash the top of the wine bottle with a rock, Kevin was naked and running toward the hot tub like an Olympic long jumper. I caught sight of his bare ass out of the corner of my eye. There was nothing I could do to stop him from killing himself, so I just watched the spectacle while trying to pour wine into a Solo cup through cracked glass.

He leapt from a very impressive distance and hit the water with a perfectly formed cannonball, displacing dozens of gallons from the hot tub in a nuclear-explosion-shaped plume. His head finally popped above the surface, where he immediately demanded a line of coke and for two naked women to join him, ASAP.

I handed cups of wine to the girls, oblivious to the fact that there could be shards of glass at the bottom. I then took a huge swig of rum, stripped off my clothes, and joined everyone in the tub.

It's common knowledge that alcohol and hot tubs aren't a great combination. The heat sucks water out of your body like a vacuum, adding to the alcohol's already impressive dehydrating qualities. It also jacks up your heart rate, pumping all the toxins in your bloodstream to your brain like a fire hose.

What we were doing was stupid, on so many levels, and I knew it, somewhere deep in my mind. My brain stem was alight with activity as it pleaded with my motor functions to stop. But there was a far more powerful factor at work. Despite the egregious harm I was currently doing to my body and mind, it was in these times of substance and excess that I could pretend, if only for a moment, that nothing mattered. I was not risking my livelihood, my adulthood, my chance at happiness and success on a company that I felt I had accidentally formed. I wasn't a CEO. I wasn't being photographed for awards and interviewed on radio shows. No one cared about me. I was a leaf blowing in the wind at the edge of the earth, inanimate and invisible to everyone.

There are only a few fleeting memories I can recall from the rest of that night: Blood. Yelling. Naked bodies. Crying. And the unmistakable sound of a shotgun being cocked.

54 | THE GALA

Somewhere in my subconscious, I didn't entirely believe I was going to wake up. Somewhere deep in my psyche, layers removed from my conscious mind, there was an assessment of the situation taking place and a voice was saying, *This may be the end.* Perhaps that was the point.

I was asleep, I think, or in a semilucid hallucinatory state. I drifted between varying levels of brain activity for hours, with a simmering sensation of dread and terror. It almost felt as if I had a choice whether to ever open my eyes again. When I finally summoned the will to do so, I was frightened at what I would see.

Above me was a white ceiling with maroon accents. I felt something hard resting against my head, and for a few minutes I didn't dare move. I attempted a brief examination of my body parts by slightly moving each, and ran my tongue over my front teeth. Satisfied I still had all my critical pieces, I began to get up. As I went to raise my foot, it stuck to the bed and burned as if it were covered in acid. A large pool of blood had formed beneath it, the duvet cover acting as a bandage. I turned to confirm that I was, in fact, in my hotel room, which was surprising.

My naked body was twisted in the top cover. The hard object propping up my head was a half-empty bottle of tequila, smeared with dried blood. I moved in slow motion, dreading a further surprise. When I finally freed myself, I painfully peeled the cover from the bottom of my foot, which released a stream of deep crimson, viscous blood. At the sight of it, I violently vomited all over my chest and the bed. I stood, shaking, supporting myself on the side of my foot, and made my way to the bathroom, picking up my cell phone, which was lying on the floor next to the front door to the room, its screen shattered, on the way. The jeans I had been wearing were crumpled in the corner, slightly keeping the door ajar.

"Kev . . . what the fuck happened?" I texted him, in a message that took about five minutes to type. I climbed carefully into the bathtub and watched it slowly fill with hot water, tinted pink, feeling a flurry of emotions and questions course through my head like an electric current.

Nearly two hours later, at four o'clock in the afternoon, I finally left the room. All else being equal, I would have lain in that bloody bathtub for the next week, but I was seriously worried about Kevin. I didn't give a thought to the important meeting that had come and gone eight hours earlier.

My first stop was the pro shop near the lobby. I bought a golf hat and pulled it down over my eyes as far as it would go. I limped across the main hotel hallway, avoiding direct eye contact with other attendees, but glancing up now and then to make sure I didn't miss Kevin walking by. By the time I got to the main room, I was convinced he was dead. I had killed Kevin.

I walked out the grand front gates of the hotel to sit on the front steps and consider my options. *I for sure have to find the body. And isn't the desert where you're meant to bury bodies anyway? This is convenient.* And that's when I found him, in the exact place I had intended to sit. He was slumped against a marble column, blindly staring ahead, coffee in hand. I gingerly settled down next to him and looked over at a man whom I loved, and feared for. Had I broken him? Had I made a mistake bringing him into this world?

No words were exchanged for at least five minutes, until he finally asked, "You okay?"

This was a loaded question and made me emotional. We were alive, which was good. But the amount of unanswered questions haunted me. *Where were the girls? Did I come back naked? Why did I recall a shotgun?*

We did our best to piece together the night, with little success. One of the only details he could unequivocally confirm was that yes, there had been a shotgun, waved in our direction by a very angry Mexican man whom we had awoken, and whom I had then proceeded to shout profanities at when he told us to be quiet. And yes, Kevin believed that we had all been naked when we got back to the hotel.

There was a lot more detective work to be done, but then I caught sight of something that almost made me sick again. In the large circular driveway before us a man got out of a black car dressed in a tailored tuxedo and flashing an ear-to-ear smile.

Jesus Christ. The gala. The purpose of being here. ÄKTA's being awarded a very prestigious award in front of thousands of people. The event was tonight. Check that, in ninety minutes.

I made my way back to my room, balancing on one leg as I attempted to get dressed. The thudding in my head was so severe that my vision briefly went dark every time my heart pumped. I was seeing the tuxedo form around my broken body through a strobe light. As I struggled to tie the bow tie, I asked myself in the mirror, *What the fuck are you doing?*

The pressure of this life had made me push too hard to escape from it. If I didn't reevaluate my behavior, I knew deep down I might not wake up from one of these nights. I could hear the horn of the train coming directly at me and hoped I had the strength to get out of the way, but given the fear that was staring straight back at me in the mirror, I couldn't be sure.

I finally made my way downstairs and found Kevin. He looked like I felt.

We slowly walked into the massive banquet hall, to hundreds of tuxedo- and gown-clad guests, talking, drinking, finding their seats. I was limping and supporting myself by bracing against Kevin, trying to make it look as if I were giving him a prolonged chummy shoulder slap. *Hey man! How great is this event?*

As we approached our table I felt an aggressive tap on my shoulder. I turned to see the Danes. They were about four inches taller and much more sparkly, looking at us with an expression I couldn't place. Amusement? Apathy? Thankfully they were just as confused about how the events of the previous night had unfolded. But they did supply a handful of details about what had taken place that I would have preferred to remain a mystery.

Fancy businesspeople gathered onstage to welcome us, as Kevin and I politely declined all the food offered. We attempted to keep our gaze forward as acknowledgments and announcements were made, and then came the big moment. The names of the recipients of the prestigious award that had brought us all to the room tonight started flashing across a massive screen onstage. When ÄKTA appeared, I felt pride, mixed with a bit of shame and regret.

This was supposed to be why we worked so hard and risked so much. We had achieved a goal reserved for only the most elite companies. We had defied the odds and the statistics and the warnings that assured us that we would never get there. But having done so I wanted to stand up and scream, "Now fucking what?" The pressures that had brought us to this moment had been unbearable. And I knew they were just a taste of what was to come if we were going to charge forward and achieve ultimate success. What are you supposed to do when you find yourself higher up that mountain than you could ever imagine, already having expended your physical and mental capacity, already taken too many risks, to then realize you may not even be halfway to the top?

In these dark moments of introspection and despair, I didn't ever truly give credence to the option that there might be healthy avenues of support, like therapy or confiding in a friend. Seeking any means of support would have demanded that I be honest about the true state of the situation I was in, and I was not ready to confront that. I couldn't allow myself to think about it, much less explain it to anyone else.

Kevin retrieved our award—a heavy glass cube, emblazoned with the ÄKTA name and our achievement.

The ceremony concluded, and we made our way outside to light up a celebratory cigar. We were now smiling and laughing about the events of the previous night, thankful everyone had survived.

And that should have been it: Glass of champagne. Cheers. Congrats. Hugs. Time for bed.

But you don't put two people like Kevin and me together, off the back of a five-day bender, with one night to go, and expect us to call it an early night. Tomorrow was back to the office. Back to reality. Someone was sinning tonight.

We found our girls and reminisced over a cocktail, only to then be told that it was one of their birthdays.

I spent $20,000 at the biggest strip club in Arizona that night, having rented out an entire private room for the four of us. We had almost every dancer from the club in that space, piled on each one of us, taking a special liking to the Danes, teaching them to dance, and happily breaking any rules for big enough tips. I then regretfully realized we had left our shiny glass award in the limo and had a bouncer fetch it. It then became a prop for photos with every dancer. By the end of the night, it had enough DNA on it to be considered a biological weapon.

The party continued back at my room, where the birthday girl wanted to act out her fantasy, which included a guy like me and a girl like her friend. My last memory of the night was me, mid-act with both girls on the bed, looking over at Kevin, holding a cigar and a glass of champagne, legs crossed, bow tie undone, watching the show the same way he would a jazz trio. Finally, he gave me a half nod, stood, and took his leave.

These feeble attempts to remove myself from reality were becoming less and less effective. I awoke the next morning, between the wives, not quite as close to the grave as on the previous day, but in a tremendous amount of pain, panicking that I had missed my flight back home. I called Kevin, who informed me he was in Chicago.

He had left my hotel room and gone straight to the airport, and in the wee hours boarded the first flight home. He flew in his stained tuxedo, leaving his luggage and personal effects back at the hotel, and was just getting into his own bed with his fiancée when I called him.

I respected him for this power move, but it also depressed me further. The only person deep in the trenches with me was now lying in bed in a safe place with a person who loved him. Sadness washed over me. That must be an incredible feeling.

I let that thought remain in my head for only a millisecond before I forced it away. I had to get up. I had to go back to work. None of the problems I had left behind had changed. In fact, there were probably going to be more tomorrow. I wanted to shut my eyes again and make it all go away.

55 | FUELED

The next evening, my head was a construction site of dust and jackhammers. The pressure behind my eyes threatened to shoot them out like a cannon, followed by the remnants of my bleeding brain. Acid that could melt steel was built up in the back of my throat. I sat slumped in the conference room with Dean. He was using his dad voice. I knew I should be listening, but every word was painfully bouncing around inside my skull like a pinball machine.

". . . my son Logan . . . working at a company called Fueled. You should meet with them . . . maybe we partner with them . . . or buy them . . ."

He was telling me all of this as casually as if he were suggesting getting a gallon of milk from the market. Buy another company? How the hell do you do such a thing?

But I quickly agreed, in an effort to end the conversation, and then promptly leaned my head down for a nap and forgot everything he had said.

The following day I saw a meeting with Fueled noted on my calendar. I had to ask Dean again who I was supposed to be meeting and why.

"Fueled, John," he said a little impatiently. "I just told you yesterday. They make mobile apps. Logan says they are amazing at what they do. The two owners are coming to talk to you. I need you to sell the shit out of them and position us well in case there is an opportunity. This is how we rapidly scale our growth."

That afternoon Julia grabbed me from my desk and told me two guys were in the conference room waiting for me. That was my cue to take a stroll down the outside hallway and stretch my legs. Despite my general obsession with being on time, I had learned from my Varsoft days the power dynamics of first impressions, and showing someone you're trying to sell that he is on *your* schedule is an important tactic.

After some light yoga near the fire escape and making sure I hadn't missed anything important on Reddit, I started toward the conference room. I had done absolutely no research to prepare for this meeting, because I intuitively knew everything I needed to.

Because Fueled was a boutique mobile app development agency, a number of things were true:

First, their owners were going to be proper nerds who would be easily dazzled.

Second, they were probably great at building apps and shit at running a business.

Third, they probably hated running a business and wished they could just build apps.

I entered the room with my signature bluster, smile, and strong handshake, and waited for my assistant to bring me my coffee, which I had handed to her ten minutes earlier.

The two guys sitting there were the exact Tom and Jerry duo I expected. The first introduced himself as Matt. He was tall, hefty, and, I could see from his eyes, instantly hated or at least distrusted me. He didn't want to be here, and was not interested in being talked down to by a guy who looked like me.

The second introduced himself as Tony. He looked like the uncle you would stop inviting to Thanksgiving once you had children.

Short, overweight, with silly black glasses and a baggy shirt, he wore a perpetual smirk on his face that made him look as if he knew something you didn't. He might not be the sharpest knife in the drawer, but he clearly had some street smarts.

My objectives were quite simple: prop ÄKTA up to look like the Lord's work, determine if these guys had anything I wanted, and if so, position our dominance to aid in whatever negotiations might take place. Matt was going to be a lot of work, and Tony might pee on the floor if he got too excited. I had to be careful and quickly made the call in my mind: flip the script. Make this their idea, make them sell *me*.

"Gentlemen, I really appreciate you coming in, and sorry I was late," I started. "It's been busy around here lately, as you can see." I fanned my arm across the glass wall behind me, showing all my worker bees making me money. "I also have to apologize that Dean and I only had a moment to talk yesterday, and I don't have a lot of context about the purpose of our meeting here. Can you give me some background on yourselves and what you'd like to discuss?"

This put them both off guard. "Uh . . ." Tony started, "well, we're the founders of Fueled, a mobile app agency on Wacker Drive. We have been around for five years and make some of the best apps in town. Uh, Dean talked to us last week and told us a bit about ÄKTA and said . . . that you might be . . . interested in some form of partnership . . ."

"Interesting," I replied, through steepled fingers. "We already partner with some great app agencies now, so I'm not exactly sure about what he had in mind, but I would love to learn more about your company."

This was now an interview—exactly how I wanted it to feel.

Matt and Tony both squirmed their way to sitting fully upright and started their sales pitch. Tony opened a keynote presentation and swung his laptop around.

"Key clients include Starbucks, Verizon, and Porsche." Bullshit. Those companies never hired boutique engineering shops for any projects of importance. This was an obvious giveaway that Fueled was subcontracted by agencies and didn't have these major businesses as direct clients.

"We partner with a prestigious digital agency and share an office." That explained their posh address: they were just subleasing desks.

"Tripled in size each of the first three years." Doing the quick math on this revealed it wasn't an impressive record at all, given the current size of their company. This also meant that their growth hadn't sustained over the previous two years, given they were five years old.

"Matt used to work at the CIA and is the technical guy. Tony has been a designer for his whole life and runs that group." Game over. I had all I needed.

I didn't fault them for their embellishment dance. Hell, I'd been doing the same thing for years. I was just a lot better at it.

"Fellas," I told them solemnly, "this is damned impressive. I appreciate the overview. It sounds like our companies are similar in some respects. We are on the design side and you're development— and it's clear you're smart guys who share a similar mindset. Let me give you a little bit of info about ÄKTA."

I opened our presentation up on a 70-inch flat screen on the wall, and the difference in professionalism and quality was palpable. It's in these moments that the business card scene from *American Psycho* hits home. "Look at that subtle off-white coloring. The tasteful thickness of it. Oh, my God, it even has a watermark . . ."

I carried on at a casual pace, feigning a level of indifference. My real intent was to directly and fiercely drive home the superiority of ÄKTA in all the areas in which I knew they had weaknesses. I wanted them green with envy.

Then I went for the jugular. Our philosophy, I told them, was to have a *real* CEO in the driver's seat, and hire the best innovation, design, and technical leads, enabling them to focus on their craft, and not on running the business and selling. That strategy had worked brilliantly for us.

It took every ounce of strength I had to not smile when I watched the look they exchanged. This, beyond everything else, was the reason they were in the room right now.

Let me explain.

Logic dictates that folks with a certain high-level of expertise are the ones who create professional services companies. An accomplished lawyer is who you'd expect to start a law firm. A rock star public relations professional is probably behind the hot new PR boutique. And undoubtedly, designers and developers are the ones who start mobile app agencies. The guru gives the company credibility and expertise.

While this makes complete sense, it also creates the ultimate Achilles' heel, which has been the demise of an uncountable number of such companies.

When the guru is also the founder, they are responsible for all high-level aspects of the business. They are in the room pitching the business, creating the project plan, doing the hard work on the project, and delivering the end result to the client. And the client wants them to be doing that exact thing. If they are positioning themselves as the expert at the beginning, there's no way the client is going to allow them to pass the work off to an underling.

This creates an obvious scale problem. No matter how many folks you're able to hire under the guru, they are still going to be in feverish demand from all parties. Employees, clients, partners. That can sustain in a very small, boutique company, but certainly not at scale. The limit to this growth is around twenty to thirty employees.

For a lifestyle business, this can work just fine. We've all seen small agencies who employ eight people crank out a hundred grand in profit; they work on sustainable projects so everyone can take home a reasonable salary and the owner can drive a BMW 3 Series.

But, some of us entrepreneurs aren't that satiable. We want growth. We want millions. We want glory.

Therefore, there are only two outcomes: either the guru finds a way to distance himself from the sales, operations, and client relations side of the business so he can focus on his craft (either by aggressively hiring above and below him, or not being presented as the guru), or they get stretched too thin, the pipeline dries up, projects are flubbed, and the business crashes and burns. The latter is the far more common outcome.

While logic defying, the real potential of a professional services business is realized when there is a clear distinction between the CEO and the guru, or gurus. When one person can be meticulously focused on sales, strategy, and finance, while others can be just as focused on hiring, client delivery, and success. The reason this is so rare is that most non-designers aren't creating design firms, just as non-lawyers aren't starting law firms.

So, as you're probably gathering, this became my rallying cry. This is what set ÄKTA apart. The foresight to create a company positioned for rapid growth by having me, mister award-winning-rock-star-master-selling-CEO driving the company forward, and gurus like Drew positioned to be laser-focused on their craft. And if we got too busy, we could hire another Drew, allowing for the holy grail: a professional services business that could scale. This is also why someone like Matt, the technical guru, and his team would slot so perfectly into the ÄKTA structure.

This even became a hook in my sales efforts. One of my classic lines to say to a new client was "My job is to discuss what makes ÄKTA so unique and put together a great strategy. But the folks on my team are the real designers. I just own the shop. So, once we have a plan in place and that contract is signed, you'll be put with your team, and you won't need me anymore." As counterintuitive as it sounds, clients *ate up* that focus and confidence.

The part I obviously left out during my pitch was that ... well ... I did this totally by accident. I had no idea this was going to be the differentiator for ÄKTA. In fact, I fancied myself a designer when we started. And I was so desperate I would have founded any company I thought could have worked. It wasn't until I began to hire people much more qualified than myself, whom I could delegate huge parts of the business to, allowing me to focus on selling, that I realized we had stumbled upon the magic formula.

But that pitch sounded damned good. And it was also the *exact* thing I knew was burning Tony and Matt in the ass. They were above the size of a sustainable lifestyle business, but not equipped to properly scale. Every time they thought about growth, they would get sucked back into the monotony of day-to-day operations, never allowing themselves to get to that next level. And the whole time, constantly having to dodge the never-ending potholes of service businesses, which meant even their little business could fail if they weren't careful. They were salivating at the idea of just being able to focus on their craft while having a guy like me leading.

I leaned back in my chair, sipping my cold coffee, giving them the time to process the backhanded analysis of their business I just gave them, and waited.

Finally, Matt spoke up with the exact words I wanted to hear. "That is really impressive, John. Where do we go from here?"

I hid my smile. "I don't know, Matt. I don't have anything in mind, honestly. It seems like you guys have a great thing going on, and we can certainly keep you in mind if there might be synergy on a future project," I lazily offered.

They swapped a glance again. "When we were talking to Dean, he insinuated there might be a larger conversation here. A deeper partnership . . ."

I offered a ponderous look. "Hmm. I can huddle with him and see what is on his mind."

Tony prodded me along. "It seems like we have very complementary businesses. . . . Do you think you would ever merge with a company like ours?"

"Merge?" I repeated, surprised. "I don't know, Tony. While the idea of being able to do mobile development in-house is interesting, ÄKTA is much, much larger than Fueled, and operates at a higher level with our clients. Likely, we will end up just growing our own development team over the next year or two."

This was a multilevel feign. I needed them to feel a bit uncomfortable. Subtly telling them I might create a competitor to them would certainly do the trick. Tony pushed on. "We should really talk more about this, John," he said. "We know how much bigger ÄKTA is. I don't want to be too forward—it's just our first conversation—but if this feels right, I am sure we can work something out."

I had no doubt.

56 | THE THESIS

Y ou want to ... buy another company?" Kevin asked.

The look on his face was a combination of bemusement, skepticism, and terror. The latter because he knew I was crazy enough to actually want to do this, and that the heavy lifting would then fall on him.

"Yeah, man. I didn't know what on earth Dean was thinking when he first brought it up. But it now makes perfect sense. These guys have dozens of amazing engineers who are very hard to hire, who are all at average or below-par salaries. They also have really impressive leadership in Matt, who is incredibly gifted and working for nothing because he is running the place. Finding a guy like that to build our own engineering group would be extremely difficult and expensive. They have a few good clients we could double up on because they suck at design, so we could take them over. And best yet, their average billing rate is $125 an hour, because they are a straight dev shop. We could instantly double that just because they are under the ÄKTA umbrella, so they are now 'consultants.' We would instantly be making a profit on them. It would be huge PR for us, and we could now offer full service to our clients. It's brilliant."

I had spent the weekend obsessing about this. Kevin just kept staring at me dubiously, but I ignored him and continued.

"And I think we can get them fucking cheap. They are stuck in the mud, I'm sure of it. And this relieves them of risk, allows them to focus on what they want, and, because our plan is to sell this thing one day, they will see a path to cash."

The entire rationale for acquiring Fueled that I had just delivered to Kevin had no formulaic basis. I had spent a few days working it out in my head, as far as my intuition allowed, and then convinced myself this was the best plan. This was the same process by which I had done everything so far. I felt as if I had never actually *known* anything.

I had so few people close to me at this point that it was critical they backed me on new crazy ideas. If they didn't—if they pushed back or showed a lot of doubt or poked holes in my arguments—it would completely take the wind out of my sails. It was very difficult for me to regain my enthusiasm for an idea once this happened. I had never admitted to Kevin that I needed his support, in fear of his manufacturing it, which would leave me never knowing how compelling my ideas actually were.

Despite his natural apprehension, and a comment about how far-fetched the proposal was, Kevin was positive and encouraged my pushing forward. I had overlooked one part of the plan that turned out to entice him the most. If we pulled this off, we would have more senior managers at the company who could share his greatest burden: dealing with me.

I brought Tony and Matt back into the office a few times to continue to impress ÄKTA's superiority. I also stopped by their "office" once, under the guise of wanting to see their team dynamics, but in actuality to confirm all of my suspicions about their operation and office sublease situation.

As the smarter of the duo, Matt quickly started seeing the advantages a prospective partnership would bring.

Tony was trickier, and it was the dollar signs that hung in his purview that drove his interest. But because he was both emotional and egocentric, during our conversations he would vacillate between reluctance ("Would I be giving up my business?") to sheer excitement ("How fast can we do this?") to battling his ego ("Could I still have the CEO title?") to showing his . . . looser side.

The latter came in the form of his vice, which just so happened to be my own vice: Las Vegas. In order to consummate our prospective partnership and potential friendship, he demanded we pay a visit there. That trip solidified the deal and also gave me insight into the real "Uncle Tony": hilariously funny with a horrifying, jaded view of the world. He softened his insecurities with excessive gambling and strip club marathons, where he prided himself on staying for breakfast. Our weekend there became a case study in debauchery, at a level that would impress even the bro twins. We talked deal terms, and in between hands of blackjack, came to a high-level agreement.

After Vegas, Tony believed he had brokered a killer deal for himself and Matt, one that would lessen his workload, ramp up his clout, and give him a weapon like me to rally behind. He would be able to get on the equity cap table, and if we achieved our goal of selling the company, he'd be rich.

We also became friends. He was now the only ÄKTAtron (*nope*) whom I would see outside the office on a regular basis. He was my boy. My silly little maniac of a friend to help me blow off steam. In another life Tony would have been a stand-up comedian, as long as there was an audience with the same level of depraved humor in which he specialized. I would get texts from him at all hours of the day and night that would send me into wild fits of laughter. He forced me to wear one of his Rolexes to a client pitch meeting, appalled that I didn't wear a proper timepiece. I honestly had never had interest in one until he made me realize how much such signifiers matter in high-level business. I quickly became a watch guy.

Friends and business partners. The chemical formula of tragedy.

57 | PRINTING MONEY

The negotiations between ÄKTA and Fueled progressed, and soon contracts were drafted. Expensive lawyers yelled at one another for a few weeks, while we sat back and watched, wholly uninterested by most of the points they were arguing about. They call these the Act of God clauses—the insane what-ifs that make up 90 percent of a contract like this.

What if a day before the third round of vesting, one of the partners quits . . . what happens to the equity? What if they quit a day later?

What if John gets hit by a bus?

What if Godzilla smashes into the office and lights all our programmers on fire?

I had learned my lesson when it came to contracts—I wouldn't sign a purchase order for office pencils without a lawyer's reviewing it—so I didn't try to usurp the legal process.

The real challenge for us became figuring out what would happen when the ink was dry. We were going to import a big team of brand-new people into our space—virtuosos of a different ilk. These were programmers. Code slingers. Binary bandits. Console cowboys. Left-brained supernerds who were now going to be joined at the hip to hipsters. Monster Energy meets Pabst Blue Ribbon. If you were to walk through the startup graveyard and read the headstones, you'd find that for the majority of companies that died during an integration, it was usually the casualty of chemistry and personality clashes.

Kevin, Dean, and I tried to brainstorm ways to prevent such a disaster.

There were a lot of emotions at play, at least according to Kevin. Our guys were going to feel less important in a bigger family, while theirs were going to feel as if they'd lost their identity and had their world flipped upside down. There would be a lot of confusion, and a lot of questions. There would be power struggles and some folks getting left in the dust.

I cared more about Indonesian politics than I did the feelings of either team. I want to be honest here. Being attuned to their emotions and personal needs would have prevented me from doing my job in the way I had to do it. It may sound harsh, but your boss's boss probably feels the same way. For his part, Dean was only focused on how much more money we could make. Thankfully, we had Kevin, the patriarch, fully focused on everyone's emotional well-being.

As I mentioned earlier, our greatest immediate opportunity, outside of the positive PR we'd get for acquiring another company, was that ÄKTA had now positioned itself in a very elite group of service providers: strategic consultants. We had developed the ability to sell in at the top level of a company, sign on for mission-critical work, and charge rates that only major management consultancies like Accenture would normally be able to command. I was hustling Drew out for $600 an hour. That amounted to over $1.2 million in annual billings, or 700 percent gross ROI, for just one guy.

As a result of their acquisition by ÄKTA, every single Fueled employee instantly became more valuable. Like most development firms, Fueled's workforce was considered a commodity and beat to death on hourly rates. A developer making a $75,000 salary would be able to bill out at $100 an hour, tops. That meant a 100 percent ROI, if they were lucky. Under the ÄKTA umbrella, I could instantly get $520,000 out of that same developer, at a 600 percent ROI.

In addition, almost every project we were doing at the time had a significant development component for which ÄKTA's core design team was responsible. We could now immediately sell in our newly available services and create instant utilization, while punting some of the trash clients that were wasting Fueled's time.

This was called printing money. Assuming we didn't fuck it up.

Kevin and Drew had all sorts of clever ideas for how to mesh the companies together, including staged integrations, keeping the offices separate for a while, or hiring change management consultants to support us.

"Why don't we just have a party?" I asked.

They looked at me as if I had just proposed an orgy. The fact was, at the end of the day, this was supposed to be a celebration—or at least we wanted it to appear that way. If there were stuffy consultants running around, it would only raise the general air of apprehension. By throwing a party for both teams in the ÄKTA office before formally announcing the deal, featuring pizza, booze, and music, we would see how everyone got along.

"This might be a bit simplistic," I acknowledged, "but I'm not hearing a better plan."

So, we did just that. We announced to our ÄKTA group that another company was going to hang out with us on a random Thursday after work. Though we were careful to use words like "partnership," there was no mystery among the staff as to what was really going on. On Fueled's side the group was told that they were going to check out ÄKTA's new offices. Again, a thin façade.

Hours before the event, the new partners—Dean, Drew, Kevin, Tony, and Matt—sat in the office having beers and feeling proud of themselves. The Fueled executives were drunk on the ÄKTA Kool-Aid. They felt as if they'd made the deal of the century. Maybe they had. While acquiring another company should have felt like a big, exciting win for me, it actually didn't register as much of an accomplishment at all. I got no high fives from Kevin, no compliments from Dean. It was just another business transaction. Nothing felt very personal anymore.

The time finally came for the teams to meet. Awkward guys and girls with more awkward haircuts, donning logo-ed hoodies and huge laptop backpacks, started filing into the office. Kevin went from desk to desk to pull our team off whatever they were working on, which was an almost hopeless effort. He finally announced he was going to start cutting the power to the desks, so they had better save their work.

The first thirty minutes was junior prom. Designers on one side, developers on the other. A flirty glance would be shot across the void, to no avail. No one was taking the bait. We partners stood in the DMZ at the dead center of the office, laughing, drinking beer, and trying to show everyone that we could all be friends. This was going exactly how you're seeing it in your head. That ridiculous and hilarious.

Finally, one of our fearless hybrids (a designer *and* developer) made the journey across the great expanse, liquid confidence brimming from his first beer, and started speaking to his geeky brethren. Like in a Discovery Channel documentary, the herds started mingling. The designer Trekkie found the developer Trekkie. Two guys bonded over a game of Ping-Pong. A guy and a girl discovered an overt sexual connection. Less than an hour in, there were no longer two teams, but one. Everyone was trading stories. Work was being shown off on screens. Techniques were being shared. Obscure nerd references were being thrown around.

This was the last time I could remember that all the bullshit had fallen away, and things felt amazing. I made my way out of the mix, watched this spectacle play out in real time, and thought to myself, *Damn, this really is cool.*

PART THREE

The Prestige

58 | MACHINA

The conference room became my battleground. I began to look at every prospective client as an enemy I had to defeat. It's shocking to me to recall how aggressive and cocky I'd get in that room. "If you don't like the price, that's fine. I am not giving you a dollar off. Go hire one of our competitors and call me when they fuck it up." I'd end too many meetings by slamming my fist down on the table.

Something savage had appeared in my eyes, which I realized only by how the rest of the employees looked at me after a pitch. Kevin tried to warn me that I was scaring them. *Fuck 'em*, I'd think to myself. *They don't understand what I do when they aren't looking. They don't understand the strain I'm under to keep their paychecks flowing and interesting client work on the table.*

It didn't help the situation that on any given day, I wasn't more than a short distance ahead of or behind some kind of bender. I had made a group of friends in Vegas that ran the town, which made going there even more fun than it normally would be. Now it was a constant stream of private jets, expensive cars, models, bottles, lines, and celebrities.

Vegas has everyone's vice—it's just a matter of meeting your personal devil. I encountered so many of my own there that it's hard to believe there are any left in hell. The town became my playground, the perfect way to leave the real world's injustices behind and blow my mind into outer space for a few days.

Trips there went from being something I did for a special event, like a conference or a birthday party, to a quarterly visit, to a monthly visit, to the point where I would fly there on any random night when I felt I'd had too much of reality, as long as I wasn't missing vital client engagements. The story I told anyone who asked about my frequent absences was that I was playing professional poker, which is in fact why I had started to go so often initially, but that had long ceased to be the case. I am not exactly sure how many dozens of times I flew into that city during ÄKTA's short life span, roaming my way into the hazy utopia and losing two or four days of my life on each visit. The drinking, the drugs were a critical reprieve from my conscious mind. The gambling was a shot of adrenaline.

The women, they were a challenge to my confidence—a game, like everything else. It could have been the same swagger that I displayed in the boardroom, or some level of fervency in my eyes, but it was a rare occurrence that I'd leave the club alone. As far as they knew, I was Trevor, or Joe, or Jared. There wasn't a single occurrence of my ever wanting to see one of them again, and I'm sure the feeling was mutual. It wasn't even about the sex, which was almost always either a train wreck or a blacked-out fog of a memory anyway. It was just another drug. I refused to think about what kind of person this made me.

The downside of drowning in pleasure and pumping your body full of party drugs during the weekend is that your brain's neurotransmitters get hijacked. The highest of highs on Saturday turns into the lowest of lows a few days later, when your brain has stopped producing dopamine and serotonin because too much had been forced into it, and it thinks it must recalibrate. You exist at the bottom of a dark hole. This is what we call Suicide Tuesday.

Some people engage in this sort of behavior because they become truly addicted to the substances at hand. That wasn't true of me. I had something I needed to numb and would have turned to just about anything to do so. My self-destructiveness was a byproduct. I vacillated between having too much and too little control of my life. Faced with too many critical decisions and too many people depending on me, I craved anything that relieved me of that control, even for a little while, as I knew I would have to return to asserting an abundance of it. This is why billionaires and politicians are often found to lead such depraved lifestyles, or indulge in sexual perversities. Often, with more success, comes more power and potentially more self-destruction.

Recalling this now feels as if I were telling someone else's story, given how detached I had become from reality. I had pushed my mind and body to become a machine, to maximize my effectiveness in business and reduce my emotional capacity. This way, the realities of ÄKTA couldn't faze me. Nothing really made me happy; nothing made me sad. I neglected everything—friends, family, anyone who could have provided emotional comfort. Acknowledging any of them would mean admitting to myself just how close to the edge I was, just how close to snapping I felt. It was far easier to keep everyone at a distance. This included the team at the office, and even Kevin.

Ask a tightrope walker what they feel when they are up on the rope and they'll all tell you the same thing: nothing.

Any emotion could be the vibration that forces a mistake. One mistake, and you're done. Imagine what that does to a nervous system to be that suppressed, that disengaged, while you inch back and forth on that rope, over and over, in my case, for years.

59 | THE EMPTY CHAIR

The first days of walking into an office with a whole new integrated company were truly surreal. I didn't know people's names, didn't have a clue what they were working on, and had no idea what they thought of me. I now had a whole team of employees with whom I had literally never had a conversation.

While this might be typical for upper leadership in any midsized or larger company, for me the isolation it created was unnerving.

But we were in full-fledged growth mode, and the only way to keep our newly supersized beast growing was to pump up our already robust sales efforts. Each month we had to sell what had formerly been quarterly or annual targets. I needed more soldiers. And a lieutenant.

I had been alerted to a guy named Jimmy, who was leading sales efforts at a competitive shop. His background was in traditional management consulting, meaning he could speak the language. His headshot on LinkedIn was that of a stereotypical corporate sales guy, and when I invited him in for a meeting, I was hardly surprised that he showed up wearing a suit and tie, which stuck out more in our office than a Spider-Man costume.

Jimmy considered his words carefully, had a few gray hairs, a perfect family, and undoubtedly lived in an upper-middle-class sub-urb, with 2.3 kids, a fixed-rate thirty-year mortgage, and a French bulldog. He had come up through the corporate chain at management consulting firms big and small. He wasn't going to wow anyone in a room, but he would be able to thoroughly and coherently speak through every stage of a process, and deliver a firm value proposition.

What made Jimmy unique was his experience in managing sales *teams*. Sales at ÄKTA was currently me running around like a rabid mongoose, and the rest of my biz dev team hopelessly chasing after me. We had almost no structure, pipeline planning, or funnel prior-itization. We were able to generate millions upon millions in sales while being hilariously unorganized, but the model clearly wouldn't sustain. We needed a Jimmy to come in and add some maturity to my . . . system.

Jimmy would be the fourth key member of the ÄKTA executive team, with Kevin running ops, Matt running development, and Drew running design. Adding him would free up an incredible amount of time in my day to focus on only the highest-level activities. I needed to get to a point where I could parachute into a huge client pitch, do my magic act, disappear in a cloud of smoke, and let a highly crafted team close the deal. Jimmy would also be responsible for long-term account management, which was critically important. If we couldn't keep our best clients happy, while surgically removing more dollars from their wallets, we would find ourselves in dire straits. It's infinitely cheaper to maintain and grow existing clients than to solicit new ones.

The biggest value Jimmy brought, however, was taking me away from the negotiating table. I call this the Empty Chair Effect, and there isn't a single more powerful sales-side negotiating tactic. When the decision maker is taken out of the equation, the negotiator has the ability to partner with the buyer to get a deal done. They are effectively members on the same team.

If I am at the table, a potential client might say, "John, we want to work together, but I need 20 percent off or we have to walk away." This could either be true or a feign, but either way, it puts me in a very disadvantaged position. I either say no, which is combative and harsh and may kill the deal, or I concede and lose money. Either way, I have no excuse to not make a decision. Lose-lose.

Now replace me with Jimmy, and when the same demand is made, he can say, "Look, I want to give you the 20 percent off. If it were up to me, I would. But unfortunately it isn't. John is the ultimate decision maker, and I can tell you, he won't go for it. We are just too busy, and I already had to battle even to get to *this* budget—John wanted to charge more! If I ask him for another discount, he may fire me on the spot. Neither of us wants that. We are on the same team here. What if I go beg and fight for 5 percent off? Could we get going then?" Teamwork. Empathy. Concession. It almost never fails.

This is why actors have agents and politicians have delegates. It works on both sides of the table.

60 | NOUVEAU

With the acquisition of Fueled we instantly started realizing 100 percent more revenue from key clients who needed development work. Even the TSYS project, which the design team had been working on for well over a year, was just entering the development phase to bring our amazing design work to life, and we now had a group who could perform that work internally, so they didn't need to go shopping for another development partner. How convenient! Millions in additional revenue were generated by that project alone. The Fueled team, which was previously working on meaningless apps for advertising clients and unpaid prototypes, was now diving into commercial-grade stuff—big, challenging, sexy products that were going to end up being used by hundreds of thousands of people. They loved the structure, organization, and professionalism they now had. Plus, they had the rigorous design work from the original ÄKTA team, which made their lives significantly easier than working with the hacks at the ad agency with which they used to cohabitate.

Everyone seemed happy . . . with one notable exception.

My new pal Tony had quickly found himself in an awkward position. At Fueled he had been the CEO, which didn't mean a lot because they appeared to have zero strategic planning. But he was a designer by trade, so he served as creative director for their projects, as well as managing clients and running sales.

At ÄKTA, though, those roles had become redundant. We had a massive team of talented designers, led by true design guru Drew. Matt, Tony's former partner, became Drew's counterpart as the vice president of engineering and was running the Fueled team at ÄKTA like a champion. I handled the chief executive tasks, and now that we had Jimmy on board, we had plenty of sales muscle.

But Tony was well-liked—at least by everyone but Jimmy. To everybody else, he was the funny, affable dork who would come and go throughout the day, crack a solid joke, and bring in a box of donuts for the team. He was also the only person who could get me laughing at the office. I'll never forget the day he called a helicopter company—on speakerphone—to ask how much it would cost to drop off a hot tub on the rooftop terrace of the apartment I was thinking about renting. The entire office could hear the exchange, especially when he turned to my desk, and from about twenty feet away, yelled, "Roa! They're asking how big the hot tub is! Should I tell them the biggest one they fucking make?"

In an effort to include him, I invited him to everything—sales meetings, networking events, social events. We were friends, but I also wanted him to feel good as my business partner. He and Matt had been given a small amount of equity as part of the deal, so at this point, no matter what happened, we were in this venture together. Even while my life behind the scenes was rapidly deteriorating, I forced myself to remain overly positive for Tony, an effort I didn't make for anyone else. He needed to feel optimistic about what the company was accomplishing, and for the first few months I think he did.

After a while, though, I began to notice some changes in Tony's behavior. It was like watching a teenager go through puberty. Little things that didn't seem relevant at the time were signs that a serious change in his attitude was taking place.

In order to make him feel he was in the loop, I would give him tasks and assignments to do—that may not have been high value— but seemed important, and I felt they would give him purpose to come in every day. But Tony soon began going dark for days at a time—no emails, no texts, no invitations out for drinks. He would occasionally pass through the office, but only for quick visits, and always with large headphones covering his ears. I could sense the tension in someone who normally was a very tension-free man. He

had a persistent look on his face that registered as something between confusion and mourning. Like he was constantly being told
"Your cat hasn't come home for a few days, but I'm sure she's fine."
Even my beloved obscene text messages stopped arriving. For my
part I didn't give his obvious discontentment much thought beyond
that. I was then struggling to connect with anyone on an emotional
level, as the relevant areas of my brain had long since gone into a
prolonged hibernation.

Regardless of Tony's dissatisfaction with his current role, there
was a potential bright light ahead. Maybe in a year, maybe in ten
years, even his modest slice of equity would make him rich if we
pulled off a sale. That meant all that had to pass was time, and that
time seemed as if it would pass far more quickly than expected. As
one of the rock star companies in Chicago—wildly fast-growing,
profitable, prestigious, clean as a whistle—we had begun to attract
the attention of a few private equity companies, who asked us if we
would consider selling. I didn't know the answer to that. Maybe? It
felt too early; we still had work to do. But then one such firm in New
York City tried to make me an offer I couldn't refuse.

61 | THE CATAMARAN

Hendrix was a character. He was the better part of eighty years
old, looked fifty, and acted twenty. A billionaire as the result
of various successful ventures, he had all the resources he needed to
live his best life.

That life included running a private equity firm in New York, which was very interested in acquiring ÄKTA.

That life also included hosting parties and getaways that had become almost legendary, and made Hugh Hefner look like a frat boy. They seemed like myths until I was invited on one such trip. In an effort to woo me into seriously considering selling ÄKTA, Hendrix told me to pack a bag and be ready for sun and beaches on a "boys' trip" with "business leaders," one of whom was a guy I had done some partying with and who had brokered the connection. A private jet would be wheels up from Teterboro Airport in New Jersey at noon on Friday. Don't be late.

I was never late. I flew in the night before, got a good sleep, and headed to the terminal. When I reached the private lobby and strolled up to Hendrix to give him a handshake, still thinking this was a business trip, he turned around, called me a motherfucker, gave me a hug, and introduced me to five more gentlemen who were joining us. They were all aged somewhere in the fifty-year gap between me and Hendrix, were all good-looking, clearly had some wealth to their names, and all had a smirk that suggested they knew something I didn't.

As we walked out to Hendrix's beautiful jet, I noticed a matching one directly behind it. Each easily seated sixteen people, and we were seven. I figured the answer to this riddle would be revealed in time.

Butts hit seats, bags were stowed, champagne was poured, and we took off, the other plane following directly behind us. Only then did I ask, "Hendrix, where the fuck are we going?"

"Bahamas, my man!" he shouted back at me. "I hope you like sailing."

We touched down at Marsh Harbour Airport in the Abaco Islands, where waiting for us on the tarmac was a marching band.

They banged on various instruments and sang traditional Bahamian songs, while Hendrix laughed and danced with them. Out of the corner of my eye, I saw the big clamshell door in the jet that had followed ours open and the stairs float down. A dozen women disembarked, every one of them in colorful dresses and big sunglasses, every one of them stunning.

The girls walked over and happily joined Hendrix's dance. When the band finally finished its performance, everyone was properly introduced. Given Hendrix's reputation, I had assumed these women were professionals, paid well for their time with us. Imagine my surprise when I learned that many of them were in fact professionals, but of a very different sort.

As it turned out, Hendrix had a knack for meeting, and courting, some incredibly successful and interesting women to accompany him on these trips—from an Olympic athlete to a well-known actress to a model I immediately recognized. Everything was off the record; no cameras were allowed. It was just some fun between friends.

Hendrix had chartered a catamaran that was the size of a small city, with, myths be damned, seven guest rooms. A professional crew with pressed white shirts and big smiles greeted us.

We spent five days sailing between knockout beaches and bars. Upon arrival at each new isle, a huge table would be set up and fully stocked with fresh food and an absurd amount of alcohol. For the nights we stayed on an island, guest rooms would be ready for us at a beautiful local hotel.

Hendrix and I would sit at the front of the catamaran, strong pours of rum in hand, talking business as the boat cruised through the teal sea. We could be partners, he told me. He could make me rich, he told me. I thought about the future. About what he was offering. This was yet another moment that seemed inconceivable. Yet another experience that had absolutely nothing, and everything, to do with this crazy game I had found myself in. Is this really how deals got done? Was I the rule or the exception? I glanced behind us at the row of gorgeous bodies lounging in various states of nudity in the blistering sun. Sex. Power. I've never encountered one without the other.

I didn't have an answer for Hendrix. There was too much to consider. But he wasn't going to let me give him a nonanswer.

62 | THE DEMONS

He told me to join him in—of all places—Las Vegas, the very next weekend.

Hendrix was hosting a big conference there with all his partners and wanted me to present ÄKTA. I've gone to that hellhole for a lot worse reasons. Private jet. Rolls-Royce. That tremor that comes along with looking out the window of a suite that overlooks the glowing neon playground. The smirk as that glass of whiskey is poured from the minibar.

My presentation was the very first night. I donned my favorite suit and headed to the sprawling conference hall at the ARIA. My pitch was so well honed at this point that it felt as if all anyone had to do was pull a string on my back and it would come flowing out. I painted a glowing picture of the future. Of innovation. Design excellence. Entrepreneurial genius. And of course, lots of money to be made all around.

Afterward the old finance guys looked at me as if I were a super-model, so badly did they want my goods. I smiled and glad-handed, biding my time until they put themselves to bed, so I could acquiesce to the little horned motherfucker sitting on my shoulder begging me to go get into trouble.

Apparently if you're famous, you feel a need to do everything—which is how Paris Hilton was now a DJ, putting on her first show at a Vegas club that night after only recently being allowed to return to the hot spot after her cocaine-linked ban years prior. An invite from my boy who ran Vegas to see this firsthand could not be passed up.

The night started in a huge suite at the Wynn. My favorite DJ, Avicii, sat next to us, playing piano. Chuck Liddell was yelling a story about his time in the Ultimate Fighting Championship to a girl who was way too scared to move away from him. A few Instagram "models" were taking selfies and drooling in the corner. Paris was screaming at her poor assistant about a certain piece of DJ gear being absent from her setup, while simultaneously posing for photos with her personal photographer.

I, meanwhile, was arranging a very specific pattern of drugs on a table, attempting to coordinate my consumption of them with the cadence of the night. There wasn't a single thought in my head about the potential multimillion-dollar speech I had just finished.

The drugs kicked in just as Paris took the stage, and by a few songs in, I realized I might have overestimated just how much MDMA was appropriate.

The serotonin was blasting through my brain like a dam had

broken. I could taste the music. I was standing next to Paris onstage, pupils as wide as dinner plates, staring out at the thousands of guests. My jaw was grinding uncontrollably, trying to eat my face. Only someone who has been that high will understand my next strategy: *Perhaps a bit of cocaine will even me out*, I thought. Not surprisingly, that was my last memory for the next handful of hours.

I woke up facedown in the plush bedding of my California king. My brain was still on tilt, but something was afoot in my room. I turned my head around to a spectacle that I couldn't process. Through a haze, I saw several figures in my room, swaying. Loud music was playing. I was wearing only a bathrobe and a watch. I thought I recognized some of the silhouettes, but the chemicals in my brain were doing a good job of disguising everyone, and everything. I then figured those details were irrelevant and it was time to join the fun.

Somewhere between seconds and hours later, my phone's alarm started blasting, and I remembered I had to take an important sales conference call. I dialed the number and made the universal *shhhhh* motion to my new friends. Kevin was the first to greet me on the line. "Where the fuck are you?"

"Brother," I muttered to him, "this is one of those times it's better not to ask."

I lay back in the bed and delivered an impassioned sales pitch, periodically rubbing ketamine on my gums and taking sips of tequila. I divided my attention between answering questions about ÄKTA's ethnographic research processes and watching two beautiful girls fooling around and playfully trying to distract me from my work at the end of the bed.

By the time the last guests left, it was late afternoon. I thought, *How is this possible?* It felt like the worst kind of time travel.

I had committed to having dinner with a friend, so I attempted a nap, cobbled together an outfit and headed downstairs. I walked into the restaurant looking as if I had just come out from under a tent in a dank alley—ripped jeans, baggy shirt, baggier eyes—all dark in color. It felt as if my beard were three times longer than the night prior.

What I thought was to be a casual meal was instead a quasi-business meeting with my friend and his associates. I was the only one not in a collared shirt and blazer. Identical twin Pakistanis were sitting next to my friend—or maybe it was just one, and my mind was still doing amphetamine magic tricks. A few of the other guys rounded out the table, all glancing in my direction as if they had expected me to ask them if they could spare a few bucks. Their brightly colored clothes and clear eyes were a stark contrast to every-thing about me.

I didn't say anything that would indicate my occupation, fearing there might be some connection to the very serious business meeting I'd held the night prior. My best efforts at ending the festivities after that dinner were thwarted when my friend questioned *just* how con-nected I was in Vegas and teased me that *no one* knew the city better than he. I wound up showing them a night that few humans could ever imagine.

Fourteen hours later I was sitting in a meeting with Hendrix. From a Vegas perspective, I was sober enough to have an adult con-versation. He was still in full sales mode, but I knew we weren't go-ing to get a deal done. If anything, he bolstered my conviction that we had something special that needed a bit more time to mature. But he also brought up a lot of good points that I had to seriously con-sider. How much more runway did we have? What kind of business did I want to sell ÄKTA to? How close were we to the proverbial cliff, when risk would completely outweigh potential gain? Was any of this real life?

Before leaving Las Vegas, I officially told Hendrix the business wasn't for sale, and within moments I wondered if I had just made a monumental mistake.

I had just turned down an offer potentially worth tens of millions of dollars. The reality of Hendrix's proposal left me tense and nervous when I returned to HQ. I felt in my heart that I had made the right decision, but that is generally the last place from which you want to make these decisions.

63 | THE TAKEOVER

To accommodate the size of ÄKTA's new team, we leased a third space in our building—the basement. It was home to a large population of mice and the creepy building maintenance guy, Howard, who literally lived in a cubbyhole under the stairs. We were reasonably sure he was a fugitive from the Polish government, which was fine with us. We would bring him cold beers, and he would look after our stuff. Most of the engineering team chose to relocate there, which shouldn't surprise anyone who has ever met a programmer.

We did our best to ÄKTA-fy that huge, musty space. Our designers painted a sprawling, bizarre LSD-trip mural on the main wall, featuring a grasshopper getting electrocuted in a wall socket, next to the phrase "The More I Mess Up, the Better It Gets." Next to that was a portrait of Abraham Lincoln staring at an octopus

(ÄKTApus) that was firing a machine gun at Super Mario–style pixel hearts that were bleeding.

My personal environment was changing, too. I had signed a lease for a ridiculous twenty-sixth-floor penthouse in Chicago's River North, with two levels, a 3,000-square-foot party terrace, and the most breathtaking, sweeping views of the city anyone had ever seen. I had no need for a home this size, and knew I would hardly spend any time there, apart from the terrace, which became my hedonistic playground. The parties that regularly took place up there were a bit notorious in the city, mostly due to just how inappropriate the activities became when the moon hit that certain point in the night sky. I recall sitting on the couch, staring at the snapping flames from my fire pit, with a million city lights glaring back at me in the background and some naked girl balancing on the railing of the terrace, the fatal drop behind her not more than a subtle breeze away.

I picked up a $170,000 black Maserati GranTurismo after I saw it at a charity event, just because I could. There was no reason to have a car in Chicago, but it sure did sound impressive flying through the tunnels of lower Wacker. When I got bored with that, it was the R8, then the Ferrari, then the Bentley. I enjoyed the view through the windshields over the shine of my Rolex, or IWC, or Audemars Piguet, or one of the other high-end watches I now owned, a collection that cost hundreds of thousands of dollars. They sat in a case in my closet, mesmerizingly, endlessly spinning. If money talks and wealth whispers, I was shouting.

None of these things made me particularly happy. I couldn't even begin to explain why I bought them. Because I could? Or should? What was I thinking? Why did I want any of this? I guess it felt like a rite of passage. The answer wasn't clear, even today. Older me is the first to criticize such excessiveness and recklessness, the first to disapprove of the professional athletes who spend their first millions on cars, women, and jewelry, only to blow out an ACL and end up bankrupt. *Fools*, I'd think, and I'd be right. But younger me barely questioned any of it.

In the office, I was now operating more and more often on autopilot, my emotional range having narrowed to a fraction of what it had once been. Closing a new million-dollar client was just another event, like having pizza delivered or stopping at a red light. A client would threaten to fire us, or refuse to pay, and we would have to engage in a firefight or pull in lawyers. Ultimately it all felt irrelevant.

Master networker Dean had put together a series of public events in ÄKTA's new space, to which he would invite a few hundred people to watch him interview a CEO from a large Chicago company. These gatherings not only put ÄKTA front and center to a huge swath of influential Chicago business types but also placed executives who *always* happened to be from companies with which we intended to do business in a power seat within our walls. If they weren't impressed with us after this shine-up, they weren't human.

The sight of this big group of important people, including the ÄKTA team, corralled in our beautiful office, energized and beaming, should have been the occasion for intense levels of pride. But it was yet another marker of success that only shook my confidence. I'd find myself swallowing pills to keep calm enough to introduce Dean and the speaker. I once even had to flee from the room, claiming I had to take a phone call, because I felt a panic attack coming on. When I was onstage at a conference elsewhere, I had no problem with public speaking. But being on home territory placed ÄKTA, and therefore me, at the center of attention.

Maybe it was still the fear of being "caught." That this reality still felt like a façade I was weaving in front of everyone's eyes, hoping they didn't push it aside to reveal the truth. The Wizard of Oz of the tech game. Even the money was ephemeral. If ÄKTA went south, I'd have to give it right back. So, it felt fake, temporary.

I was convinced our success wasn't sustainable, but I was determined to hold on tight, no matter how much this was all starting to afflict me. An ending, of some kind, wasn't far away. That much I knew.

64 | THE PLUME

Against all odds, we hadn't fucked up any of our critical projects, which is almost unheard of for a client services business. TSYS had its mobile payment platform, Motorola Solutions had its crime-fighting software, SpotOn was kicking Belly's ass in the local market. And because everyone and their mother was trying to get a foothold in the tech startup game, we even took on some celebrity clients.

Jimmy Chamberlin, the drummer from the Smashing Pumpkins, came to us for his new live-video-streaming platform. He was on the fence until he challenged me to Ping-Pong, which he prided himself a pro at, and I whipped his ass. Some say I should have let the client take that one, but I am far too competitive for that. He clearly respected it. We've been great friends since.

Hunter Hillenmeyer, of the Chicago Bears, brought his weird multiplayer, mostly illegal gaming idea to us, called OverDog. It was

JOHN ROA

a completely silly idea, but hey, he wanted to fund it. This was extremely common.

"But why would you take a project like that on if you knew it was crap?" a young entrepreneur once asked me after I gave a speech about successful versus unsuccessful projects.

I told him that if a client services business, of any kind, ever tries to tell you they are selective about what projects they take on, realize they are lying through their teeth. The only selectiveness is if the client has the money to pay you or not, and if you have available resources to perform the work. The client services business *does not care* how good or bad your idea is, even if we use that as part of our core sales pitch. One of my favorite lines after a client pitch was to say, "Well, we both have a decision to make. On your side, you have to determine if ÄKTA is the right fit to execute this vision for you. On our side, we have to huddle and determine if we want to take your project on. We are *very* busy, and only take on work that we believe in and think will be massively successful in the market."

To that young entrepreneur, I said, "There is arguably no greater sales tactic than convincing the other side you might not want them. And not just in business. When you fully have a girl's attention at a bar, suddenly tell her you aren't interested, and she will want to fuck you in half." There was probably a better way to say it, but I'm sure he hasn't forgotten the lesson.

ÄKTA HQ had taken on a new level of energy. I'd walk the rows of desks in complete awe of what I saw on the screens. Beautiful designs, complex workflows, cutting-edge code. I'd see work for clients I didn't even recognize. We had such a powerful business development engine at this point that I wasn't even aware of many of the new deals being signed.

"You still work here?" I said when I got to Kevin's desk. It had lost its humor. Now, it felt like more of an omen. "By the way, who is that girl in the black shirt?"

"That's Macy."

"Interesting. What is she working on?"

Incredulous look. "Whirlpool."

"You're shitting me. Whirlpool is our client? That's rad."

His incredulous look intensified.

Whatever. Fuck off, Kevin. How on earth was I supposed to keep up with all of this? We had even hired people to hire people to hire other people. The rabbits were multiplying so fast that even Kevin couldn't keep up with it, so we now had an HR department.

No, I wasn't worried about people's names. I was giving all my focus to two things.

First, landing a couple more monster clients. I wanted to crush our prior year. This would put us in such an elite category of revenue that absolutely no one would be able to ignore us. To do that, I had to find one or two more mammoths.

Second, we were growing out of our recently expanded headquarters, again. What used to be a conference room was now stuffed to the gills with desks. My beloved Ping-Pong table's space had been so compromised that an overswing could easily put out some programmer's eye. What I had designed as cubby seating for lunch was now someone's workspace; 3D printers, servers, and other blinking, buzzing tech was stacked on every flat service. Lines would form at the bathrooms. It was impossible to find an available meeting room. Poor Kevin didn't even have a desk anymore.

This was daunting to consider. When you do an office upgrade like we were due for, you don't just go for a small step up. You have

JOHN ROA

to invest in what could be three, five, or more years of growth, which means exponentially expanding on what you currently have.

In our case, that would mean tens and tens of thousands of square feet. We'd be measuring in basketball courts. And with that level of space comes construction, morbidly expensive furniture, equipment, security, and technology. Untold millions in investment.

The thought of it ran chills down my spine. I honestly didn't know if I could handle it. I started to become aware of the increased instability in my mind. It had begun playing tricks on me. Dreams would come in wicked waves, and I would awaken with no sense of what was real or not. I would go from feeling completely numb to desperately emotional in a flash. My isolation felt completely natural. The thought of having other human beings around me outside the office felt obscene.

65 | ICARUS

It was now the summer of 2014. Almost four years after Topgolf cut us that first check. Three years since Lightbank tried to break us. Two years since Drew and TSYS shot us into outer space. And one year since Maximus and I started rolling through Chicago's Fortune 500 like a hurricane.

It felt at times as if decades, and at others, only moments had passed. Detailed memories from the past years were sparse and distant. Core early team members like Pascale had come and gone. I hadn't seen Spider-Man, Sean, Dave, or Ryan in what felt like months.

Did they still work here? Kevin was holding on tight, but I could see the pressure and stress getting to him. I know now that he was struggling with some of the same issues as I was. I know now that he was drowning himself in booze after a rough day. I know now that he spent a lot of energy hiding problems from me. I know now that his marriage was being tested. I only wish I had known then, as our mutually acknowledging the toll that running the company was taking on us could have lessened at least some of the damage.

Every two weeks he had to hit the payroll button, sending a king's ransom flying out of our bank account. While we were making a huge amount, we were spending more and more. We had to overhire to anticipate new contracts closing. We had made bad bets on some employees, and were forced to spend a fortune dealing with issues they caused. A team lunch could now cost thousands of dollars; a holiday party, tens of thousands. Our insurance bill was now more than what we used to make per year in revenue. Unlike so many of our tech brethren, we still hadn't taken a dollar in investor capital, so there was no war chest to offset tough times.

As I became more entrenched in the design agency industry, I learned that very few of the companies I looked up to were thriving as much as it seemed. Near-nil profits, heavy turnover, and stifled growth were more common than riches and glory. *This is what I have to look forward to?* I thought. It now felt as if we were just racing to a cliff.

Dean had cleverly featured BMW, and their head of engineering, at a recent ÄKTA event. The company was trying to lead the electronic luxury automotive market to the future with its i8, which looked like something out of a Will Smith dystopian film. It was effectively a giant computer with wheels. That meant that for the first time, a core component of a BMW vehicle's success would be its digital user experience.

Signing a flagship client like BMW would solidify our dominance in the market. This is the kind of deal for which you'd hire a PR company to announce to the entire world how cool you are. Not since TSYS had we deployed so aggressive a full-court press. Excited whispers echoed around the office that we might be able to partake in the design of digital apps that would control and manage a *car*. Our team had designed screens for airplanes, police stations, and luxury coffee shops. But to participate in design that the mainstream world would see . . . that was a dream.

It was also a big test for the team. I could no longer be expected to be single-handedly responsible for closing major deals. The team had to be able to bag a whale without my holding their hand, so I kept everyone at arm's length, only requesting daily updates from the sales group, but obsessively monitoring the progress in secret.

The team performed, and outperformed. BMW ate up our pitch and plan like hungry wolves. Our presentation made the other agencies pitching, including Accenture Interactive, Deloitte Digital, and IDEO, look old-fashioned.

While most companies do contingency planning for when things go remarkably bad, Kevin and I had spent all our time planning for the unbelievable phenomenon of things going too right. When the ink dried and the scope became clear with BMW, we might need to dedicate 60 percent of our design team to a single client, putting a dozen other projects potentially at risk. We would have to quickly hire scores of new people to accommodate the new workload, adding potentially millions to the top line.

In the good old days when these insane moments would occur,

Kevin and I would share a whiskey and a wink, making some premonitory comments like, "Well, let's see what happens, my friend!" Not anymore. Now we'd maybe share a terse look, but never on purpose. Our meetings were all business. We no longer cared about each other's weekends or had a beer after work to relax. The pressure had changed everything.

I wanted to crawl into a hole and hibernate, only to emerge when the project was over to see if ÄKTA had survived. I had lost my love for all of this—the hustle, the grind, the battles. There was absolutely no joy left. My brain hurt. I found myself confused about what was real and what was not. I wanted to just disappear.

Fast-forward to Vegas.

Fast-forward to four days of excess.

Fast-forward to fleeting memories of ink being drilled into my forearm, bottles of tequila, naked bodies, and a haze of drugs.

Fast-forward to the episode with the poor maid at the door.

66 | THE CRASH

Twelve hours later, I was in the back of an ambulance. I knew I was dying.

That night, the worst of my life, began on my rooftop, shortly after returning from Vegas.

I was so high I could barely see straight. The prodigious amount of weed I'd smoked was doing its best to counteract the cocktail of chemicals in my bloodstream that had trailed me back from Sin City.

A dozen people were milling around on the terrace, excited to be partying at my house, even though it was a nothing Tuesday. I couldn't even tell you now what the girl who was sitting on my lap, sharing joints, looked like. Let's call her Tina.

As the night went on, Tina began staring at me, clearly trying to get more attention than I was capable of giving. By 2:00 a.m. everyone had cleared out, but she had no intention of going home. "Can we go to bed?" she asked.

I answered by taking another hit and a long draw of whiskey.

"John? Come on," she said. I could hear some concern in her voice.

Just then I felt a sensation that started at the base of my skull, right at the top of my spine. My vision started to bend and twitch. I heard a loud, impossibly high-pitched ringing noise. The floor folded toward me; the night sky came down to crush me.

"What the fuck was that?" I asked, in a panic.

"What did you say?" she answered, the look on her face a combination of fear and confusion.

The frenzy happened again. Bright flashes strobed across my vision. I was being pressed into the couch by an unseen force. The pain cut like a blade.

"What the fuck *is* that?" I repeated shrilly. "What is going on?"

"You're just mumbling. I can't understand a word you're saying," she said, now genuinely frightened.

I tried to speak again, but only heard myself talking gibberish, mere noise billowing out of my mouth.

I panicked and tried to stand up, but I found that my legs wouldn't move. Then more pain set in, only now making me feel as if my skin were on fire, the heat being generated from inside me. Every fiber of my being was burning with nerve pain.

It was followed by an intense pressure at the back of my head in the soft spot where the pain had first started. It felt as if someone were hammering a chisel into my occipital nerve.

Tina was suddenly gone.

I fumbled around and managed to get my phone out of my pocket and tried to call Kevin. His line started ringing. I began to black out. My heart was jackhammering so hard I could feel it in my throat. I thought it was going to explode. I realized I was crying.

The next thing I recalled, EMTs were rushing across the roof toward me.

Then I was out again. When I came to, my skin felt as if tiny live wires had been routed through my muscles and then hooked up to an overpowered battery. The pain would surge whenever I tried to move my arm to wipe the tears from my eyes. The pressure in my skull was unbearable.

As I was wheeled to the front of my building I could see the worried expressions of three people I couldn't identify then; they were looking at me through the rear window of the ambulance into which I'd been placed. One of them, a man, was waving his hands, trying to be let into the ambulance.

Even as I was climbing in and out of consciousness, I was keenly aware of one mortifying aspect of the situation: I was being asked basic questions that I was incapable of answering. "What is your name? Do you know where you are right now?"

I figured that I had to be experiencing a stroke or aneurysm or some other condition that I didn't understand. My brain might be dying, and my insides were going haywire. I felt movement and then realized I was now in a hospital, where a few masked people were staring down at me.

My eyes just registered chaotic shapes, and my thoughts were racing at an impossible speed, completely incomprehensible, as if I were staring out of a train window at the memories of my life. I was stuck in a middle ground of consciousness, where I had no control. I heard my cell phone buzzing on a stand next to the bed and started to reach to grab it, only my body didn't obey me.

Why was my pillow soaked? It must have been the crying. At least I figured as much—I couldn't feel the tears. Why was I alone? There had to be someone who cared or knew I was here?

As the nerve pain increased to levels that I had never experienced, I started to feel detached. Floating. An observer of my own body and mind.

Time was passing in a vacuum.

Darkness came again. This time it felt warm and intentional. The doctors had administered something through the IV jammed in my arm to calm my racing heart. The pain began to lessen, but the relief was not comforting, as I feared it might be the last thing I would ever feel. This was it—the final calmness.

67 | THE LIGHT

When I opened my eyes, I saw white, which for a moment made me believe in God. As my conscious mind kicked in, I realized I was midconversation with a pleasant-looking doctor, who was sitting next to the bed, gently touching my arm and asking me similar questions to the ones I couldn't previously answer.

After I replied to a few of them correctly, he asked, "Do you know what day it is?"

When I gave no response, he said, "Okay, that's okay. It's Thursday night, John. Your friend Kevin is here. He's been waiting for you to be ready to talk. Do you want to see him?"

When I told him no, he rose and said, "Then please rest. We'll be back."

Thursday night. I had been in the hospital for almost forty-eight hours. I could recall only about three minutes of it. I couldn't believe Kevin was in the waiting room, which left me feeling ashamed. Angry at myself. Hurt. Sad. Scared. Who else knew I was here?

Various doctors, nurses, and psychologists came to talk to me. They feared I had tried to kill myself. They feared I had suffered a stroke.

I went through a battery of tests on my brain and heart. I was so weak that I had to be helped between stations. The staff kept me under watch and plugged in for another day. My sleep was frantic and fitful, my eyes snapping open at random intervals, and I would momentarily forget I was in a hospital.

Finally, the medical team came to speak to me. I was ready to be told I had finally pushed too far. That I was permanently damaged.

The doctors told me that they suspected I had experienced an acute psychological disorder called dissociative amnesia, triggered by a psychotic break as a result of the pressure, stress, and abuse to which I had been subjecting my mind and body for years. My brain had been working so hard to sequester the pressure and damage I was causing myself that it finally ran out of space, and the dam broke. The breakdown created a temporary new identity as a defense mechanism, a fugue state.

I couldn't process any of this. My only thoughts were that I was alive, and that no one had heard from me in almost three days. I couldn't imagine the stress that had already caused.

The doctors called Kevin that night to inform him that I was ready to go home, and he came to pick me up. I gingerly changed back into the jeans and shirt in which I'd arrived. I was still moving in slow motion, my mind a thick swamp.

"You still work here?" I offered, in a soft, broken voice when Kevin entered my room. The expression on his face made me fight back tears. As he bent down to help me get my shoes on, he looked up and gave me the most emotional look I'd ever seen from him. It said *I'm glad you're alive. I'm sorry we're in this position. But Jesus Christ, don't ever do that again.*

I lay in my bed for the next few days, alone with my thoughts. Kevin crafted a story for the office: I had to unexpectedly return to the Bahamas to meet with a business partner, which accounted for why I had suddenly gone off the radar.

I remained severely depressed, so much so that the prescriptions they gave me didn't seem to stand a chance. What had I done to myself? Was any of this worth it?

I sent a few texts to loved ones explaining that I'd had a busy week, just so they wouldn't worry. Kevin was my only visitor, as only he knew what had happened to me. He asked if he could bring a doctor over, and I agreed; though I didn't want to talk to anyone, I felt I at least owed it to Kevin. This doctor was a psychiatrist who looked at my test results, explained in more detail what had probably caused my episode, and told me what I might expect.

Apart from indulging my academic fascination with how crafty the human brain is to be able to decide, "You know what? This sucks.

Fuck it! Let's make a new version of our human," she didn't have a lot of good news to deliver. Not only did this episode mean that I was extremely susceptible to it happening again, but she believed that, in a weird way, I had (for the most part) trained my brain to handle the stress and pressure, so that any attempt to "fix" me could actually make things worse. Obviously, the drugs and excess had to stop, and I had to find ways to actually sleep at night, but there wasn't a lot more to be done. If I were to do the therapy and recovery necessary to return my brain to homeostasis, I might struggle to perform my work duties, as I would break down far more quickly and more violently.

So, until I stepped away from my intense role at ÄKTA, I couldn't even think about "getting better."

I remained in my quiet bedroom, turned my phone off to support Kevin's white lie about my whereabouts, and let my thoughts wander, absorbing every emotion that came along. I found a strange peace to this. I thought about my choices. About how normal people conducted their lives. I had taken the red pill and was well down the rabbit hole. I was a mess, with debris littered everywhere. But this was also the chance of a lifetime. I had survived, and now, maybe, I could actually get to the finish line.

68 | POT OF GOLD

Failure is an important concept—in life and especially in entrepreneurship. And please don't believe those cute quotes you read about it.

If you learned from defeat, you didn't really lose.

We learn from failure, not from success.

There is no such thing as failure. There are only results.

Fuck. Off.

I've come to despise the culture of inspirational sayings and motivational seminars. I believe it drives faux positivity and optimism that set dangerous standards and expectations.

Here is the truth: Failure sucks. It is painful, scarring, and sometimes permanent. In interviews I did during my time at ÄKTA, I talked a lot about failure, and spewed the same bullshit as everyone else—that I embraced failure and credited it for my success. That I *enjoyed* failing, because it led me to bigger and better opportunities.

The truth is that I said those things for only two reasons. First, it made me sound smart and powerful, which is probably the basis for most motivational quotes. Second, because they made me feel better. Marginalizing failure like this allowed me to build another layer of self-defense: If ÄKTA failed to succeed, it would just be another life lesson!

But I recognized now that genuine failure would not only have destroyed my ability to ever be an entrepreneur again, but would have put me in a devastating position both mentally and financially. Even bankruptcy wouldn't rectify it. Failure would follow me around for the rest of my life, like a disease, and there would be almost no coming back from it.

The level of risk I needed to take had not been completely clear to me when I was starting ÄKTA. Of course, I knew the effort was going to be hard; my own experience up to that point had told me as much, as did any number of movies and news articles. But no one is ever *really* completely cognizant of the level of risk they may take on.

Lawyers will tell you what a contract says, but as anyone who has ever worked with a corporate attorney can attest, there is a big gap between legalese and real-life consequences.

Sadly, this is the basis for so many of the horrific accounts of failed businesses, which are too often overshadowed by the more enticing success stories. Kids take millions from investors, secure prestigious partnerships, accumulate massive amount of overhead, attach their reputation to their bold claims, and then it all comes crashing down around them, because they were never qualified in the first place, or failed for one of a million other reasons, and never considered the consequences of the risk they were assuming. Rather than finding a way out or seeking the support that would help them, they melt down like I did, or jump in front of a train, or swallow a handful of pills. This epidemic can also be found in the arts, academia, sports, or any aspirational, competitive field to which young people aspire, especially in America.

That inflection point of success, failure, and risk is one that entrepreneurs end up holding in the back of their minds, twenty-four hours a day. High risk is justifiable for the high reward it can bring. The potential for failure is worth accepting for the right risk profile. Every decision we make, every deal we close, every conversation we have involves an adjustment of these psychological meters, and consciously or subconsciously affects how we decide to make our next moves.

For me the end of 2014 was when the scales finally tipped.

ÄKTA was a massive success, by any measurable index. We were one of the fastest-growing companies in the United States. We were at the top of our field in almost every meaningful statistic: top- and bottom-line growth, profit margin, attrition, churn, repeat revenue, client concentration, average billable rates. We employed a big team of happy, intelligent, impactful practitioners. Our clients were an agency's dream—blue-chip companies in every meaningful industry. Our brand reputation was spotless. As far as the world was concerned, ÄKTA was a masterpiece.

What no onlookers could have seen was what I knew to be true: our growth was not sustainable, every higher tier we reached only made us more unstable. A lot of luck and good fortune had contributed to our success—some of our biggest wins could have easily gone the other way. Cracks were beginning to appear among some of our most important personnel. Drew was being courted by every one of our competitors, Dean had become frustrated that I had outgrown his influence, Kevin was succumbing to the pressure of his role, and Tony was preparing to burn the house down.

We had become victims of the law of exponential growth. If every future deal had to be twice as large as the previous one, at some point, we'd simply run out of potential clients. BMW was about as big of a contract as we could ever expect to get from a single client; deals in our industry simply didn't get any larger. Which meant we now needed *multiple* BMWs to continue growing. Where could we go from there?

We could keep stacking new directors under Drew, but at some point, he wouldn't be able to handle his role as their leader anymore. That meant we would need more Drews. It was hard to imagine how much time and money that would entail.

I had heard a lot of entrepreneurs use the house of cards analogy (behind closed doors), which is precisely what it felt as if I had built. At any given moment a house of cards can be carefully planned, stable, and seemingly expandable. Even beautiful. But it is vulnerable to an innumerable amount of forces that can cause it to collapse.

I realized we were approaching our limit—of growth, of sustainability, of good fortune. I had beat the house, cleaned out the casino. And now it was time to walk away from the table.

69 | CONCRETE BOXES

I spent quite a bit of time trying to imagine what it would be like to go back to work on the following Monday. I had no tan to show for my private island getaway and had lost about ten pounds, which I hoped a well-tailored suit could hide.

When I arrived, my new trusty assistant, Valerie, was smart enough not to ask where I had actually been, although her gentle, over-accommodating attitude revealed that she was aware it hadn't been a good week for me. I had finally opened my email inbox the night before, to hundreds and hundreds of unread messages, staring at me, judging. My desk was littered with notes—questions and reminders employees had left for me due to not being able to reach me by phone.

When Kevin walked in I understood I was the only person who could have noticed that the look on his face wasn't normal. He had the burden of knowing what had really happened, had seen me reduced to a mere vulnerable human. He brought me a coffee and asked when I would be open to catching up on everything I had "missed." I dreaded what this might mean.

Though not as much as the gut punch I felt on being told that I was going to be picked up in thirty minutes by our commercial real estate broker to do another citywide tour of office space. We were so overcrowded in our current location that we were probably violating some labor laws. I had already looked at dozens of options across Chicago, but had yet to find a suitable new home. Returning to the hospital actually sounded better than another real estate tour.

The problem was that we were now looking for a minimum of 20,000 square feet of office space, expandable to up to 60,000 square feet, to accommodate our growth. You don't sign on for a parcel like that for less than a seven- or eight-year term, and a commitment of millions of dollars sunk into the build-out. This was, literally, the biggest decision I would have to make, and even just thinking about the perils involved brought the now-familiar buzzing pressure to the back of my skull.

We went shopping, concrete box to concrete box, discussing footage rates, egress, signage, materials, and the tenant improvement allowance. All I could see was potential risk. We'd be committing to spending what could be a hundred grand a month on rent, for almost a decade. That was twice as long as the company had been in existence. And I would be responsible for that payment if the company folded.

In commercial real estate, brokers and architects have a tendency to discuss everything in terms of dollars per square foot, in order to normalize costs. For instance, wood flooring might be five dollars a square foot, or custom paint might be two dollars a square foot. So, as you're touring a space, you might ask how much it would cost to polish all the raw concrete. Their response is likely to be, "Oh, I don't know, maybe nine bucks?" It sounds cheap, right? I can afford that! Nine dollars is about two lattes, isn't it?

What they're *really* saying is $9 x 30,000 square feet . . . or $270,000. For fucking polished concrete.

"Finishing the raw ceiling is simple—maybe a dollar fifty"—a.k.a. $45,000.

"Demolition on a space like this is about ten, eleven dollars"—a.k.a. almost half a million.

I guess it makes the sting easier to say it this way. Until you realize just how many of these line items occur on a budget for custom built-out space. It quickly becomes unfathomable just how expensive these kinds of projects are.

While many businesses in recent years have moved away from expensive physical space to virtual teams or coworking, we didn't have that luxury. ÄKTA relied on constant in-person collaboration, and when our clients visited they expected to see a big, beautiful space, with a lot of smart-looking people hard at work. Our office was directly representative of our creativity, power, and success.

The only person more miserable than I during this process was our broker, Ryan Foran. His job was difficult enough without having me as a client during this period. I was constantly irritated, impatient, demanding, and ready to snap at just about anyone who told me something I didn't want to hear. I would walk into a space, decide within a matter of seconds that it wasn't for me, and demand that we leave, to the chagrin of the other brokers who had prepared a big show.

I'm also sure that Ryan understood that this was the easy part in the grand scheme of the commercial real estate process. He could well imagine the kicking he was going to endure once I actually found a property I liked.

Sometime that afternoon, after ruining the day for a handful of brokers, I walked onto the twenty-second floor of 205 West Wacker, right on the Chicago River, and had that familiar sensation course through me. This felt *right*. Despite standing in a massive, U-shaped abandoned office that looked like a stock-trading boiler room, something told me this was special. I asked to see a raw floor, and I knew we had it: high ceilings, a view of the river and downtown, vintage charm, direct elevator access, and thick, soundproof floors.

I kept my poker face on, not wanting to give any indication to either side of the brokerage deal that I was interested. But Ryan must have assumed something, solely based on the fact that I didn't scoff and walk out.

After completing the tour and subsequent dog and pony show, we walked downstairs for a coffee before he intended to carry on the tour. No need, I told him. This was it. Go beat the shit out of their offering, and give me a term sheet, as soon as possible.

70 | THE MESSIAH

We all looked haggard.

The ÄKTA executive team—Dean, Kevin, Drew, Matt, Jimmy, and I—sat in our conference room, drinking beers and silently reflecting on what had just taken place. Our faces could all have used some sun and a shave. The only color in the room came from our Christmas sweaters, which we had been mandated to wear for the party taking place throughout the rest of the office.

It was the middle of December 2014 and we had just finished a day of meetings with investment banks. We had assembled to determine whether, in the current marketplace, and based on ÄKTA's growth and success, it would be possible to sell the business to a qualified acquirer for a good chunk of money.

We had provided each bank with a healthy amount of diligence and financials weeks prior. The first group was a bunch of well-heeled Harvard Business School guys from a global megabank who told us that we were still too young and too small to be meaningfully acquired. To me, an email would have been more convenient than wasting two hours of my time only to have them end with a shitty punch line. But if there is one thing MBAs love, it's hearing themselves sound smart.

The second group was a significant industry player that had taken a number of companies like ÄKTA to market, with varying levels of success. Their specialty seemed to be sales to industry holding companies—essentially, huge conglomerates that own dozens or hundreds of independent agencies. These were notoriously bad deals for companies like mine. You were bought for the promise of future money, based on goals and metrics that were intentionally just short of impossible to achieve. Effectively, for the next five or seven years, you'd be working for someone else on your own business—just pushing the finish line farther out. The stories I had heard of companies doing this could have been Hollywood horror scripts.

Then our messiah arrived.

Enter Chuck DelGrande. Chuck represented a boutique bank in Boston, but was essentially a one-man band. He and Dean had some business history, and he came in all smiles. I liked Chuck from that first meeting, and two things about him were immediately clear. This man was irritatingly smart, so naturally intelligent that you felt like a Neanderthal just talking to him. He had a photographic memory and was a human calculator. But he had also channeled that intelligence into becoming a natural killer in business. He had already processed and discarded any new thought or idea you might propose. He was one step ahead of everything.

Second, he was utterly free of bullshit. The first half of his presentation featured issues he'd identified that might be hurdles in ÄKTA's sale. His concerns were fully justified. I had built this company from scratch, on a blank canvas, and it went without saying that a lot of things could have been done better. He succinctly and unemotionally walked us through what would have to be cleaned up in order to give us the best chance in the open market. With that acknowledged, he also thought we were perfectly positioned—a perfect size, growth rate, and level of clout—to attract some very interested acquirers. And then he dropped the magic number—the price he thought we could get in the marketplace. It took my breath away. For a split second I allowed myself to imagine that actually happening. Life would change, forever.

I snapped out of that reverie to hear the weight of his final message. Selling a company like ÄKTA was a terminal process, one way or another. The amount of investment, focus, and strategic changes that we'd have to make would create a situation that would be just about impossible to reverse. If we chose to head down this path, it would lead to a sale, or to the company rapidly failing.

We contemplated the gravity of the choice we faced during our beer-drinking session, while the rest of the office played Secret Santa and prepared for their holidays off. Was this the right time to try to sell? Were we trying to do so too early, as the MBAssholes had warned? We were only four and a half years old, for Chrissake. Could we survive another year if we didn't sell?

71 | DOUBLE BARREL

Chicago is a small town, both in size, when measured against our coastal brethren, and societal fabric. Everyone knows everyone. Business doesn't stay private for very long. Rumors spread like a disease.

So, it wasn't completely surprising when I started hearing rumors of what had happened with me and Tony.

"Is it true you stole his company and fired him?"

"I heard you screwed Tony over."

Weeks earlier, we had met to try to address his concerns.

"I want what's best for you, Tony," I said, as we sat in a scuzzy Italian beef deli near the office, where he had laid into a giant beef sandwich, not enjoying any of it.

I had never seen him so depressed. Months had passed since he had even stepped foot in the office. I rarely talked to him. I had hoped that spending so much time away from the business would have enabled him to clear his head and see he had a very fortuitous position. He held a valuable equity stake in ÄKTA, worth exponentially more than anything he would have created at Fueled, and I had offered to keep him on at his six-figure salary, without needing to work.

"I want what's best for you," I told him. "Give me some time to sell this bitch, and we will all be rich. I know you feel as if you've lost something, but as you can see, everything's in very good hands, and we have the ability to make something out of it."

I meant every word I said, but for whatever reason Tony wasn't having any of it. He stared at me with such undisguised malice that I realized that no amount of logic was going to break through. He had come to believe that he had been suckered into a bad deal. Pushed out of his company. Left with nothing. Outplayed, outsold.

Some switch deep down inside this man had been flipped. The look in his eyes actually scared me. This was a guy who was willing to handcuff himself to a ship he was sinking, so long as I was also onboard. He would rather end up with nothing than come to a sensible agreement. This was the worst-case scenario. There was no one harder to deal with than someone who felt he had nothing left to lose. There was no reversing our deal, even if I had wanted to. That meant that I would now have to prepare to go to war internally. Our meeting ended, and I knew that that was the last time I'd ever see Tony as a friend.

The weird thing was, this was the only situation I was currently dealing with at ÄKTA to which I had any emotional attachment. The day-to-day issues involved in running the company that had once kept me up at night now all just felt like cogs in a machine. The executive functions in my brain were so jacked, and the emotional centers so suppressed, that I had become horrifyingly optimized to do my job.

The Tony situation was one of the only problems that would light up my struggling limbic system. He was an actual friend whom I genuinely wanted to do right by. I didn't care that the rumor mill now had me pegged as an asshole, but I certainly cared he believed that. It was so unfair, and upsetting. I wanted to grab him by his little head and shake this out of him.

I was in a low place over the Christmas holiday and did very little on New Year's. My mental episode months earlier had frightened me sufficiently to avoid overindulging or partying much since then. This was overall a good thing, but just meant I had more time to spend in my own head, which remained a complicated and messy place. My depression had worsened, stranding me in a constant fog. The world had the volume turned down and lacked color. My characteristic urge to break things and party had been replaced with no urges at all. I was either at the office or lying in bed at home. The loneliness was suffocating. Did the outside world notice? I didn't really know. I could still put on a gracious smile at dinner and deliver my trademark impassioned sales pitch, but the moment the cameras were off, I didn't have a lot left in me.

One particular morning was especially bad. I woke up on the verge of tears, for no obvious reason. I felt a slight tremor in my body, and it hurt my eyes to look out the window. Mental illness is so much more complicated a condition than we give it credit for. Everything becomes up for grabs. Your very existence, your sanity, your self-worth. The control your brain has is haunting. Reason, logic, and choice vanish. You can't identify new thoughts from old. *Have I always felt this way? What is normal? Will I ever feel it again?* Intrusive thoughts take root in the darkest parts of your brain. It's the nastiest trick your mind can play. Coupled with the social stigma, it's inexorable torture.

I didn't know then how typical my experiences were in people suffering from depression. I felt as if I were the first and only person to deal with it. In fact, about half of all entrepreneurs have a diagnosable mental health condition. Students with severe ADHD are twice as likely to start a business. An entrepreneur is more likely to have a mental issue than the other members of their family. Founders are ten times more likely to suffer from bipolar disorder than the general population, three times more likely to suffer from substance abuse, and are twice as suicidal.

Entrepreneurs get hit by two powerful forces: biology and society. Our brains are predisposed to be affected by certain mental illnesses, with depression, anxiety, and ADHD being the most common conditions. Society's contribution comes in the form of the particular culture of entrepreneurship, especially as it has evolved in the millennial generation. Those individuals who go for glory take on remarkable challenges for which no human is really built. As mammals, we are supposed to do nothing but eat, sleep, reproduce, and fight. Making hundreds of decisions a day, managing thousands of people, and being responsible for billions of dollars is not normal, or part of nature's blueprint. We are pressured to take an extraordinary amount of risk, and push our minds and bodies further than we are really prepared or equipped to. The result is systemic isolation and mental anguish on a brain that is already a bit shaky. The chronic stress prevents the endocrine system, which is responsible for fight or flight responses, from returning to a healthy, relaxed state. Normal, critical bodily functions like sleep and regeneration are deprioritized, because the body believes it's fighting to survive. For many of us, this becomes an infinite loop of mental chaos, until we can find a way—healthy or unhealthy—to disrupt the cycle, or the dam breaks.

The saddest part is that there are a number of beneficial ways to deal with these issues, including therapy, wellness treatment, and the responsible use of medication. But at that moment, I didn't feel that any of these were acceptable solutions for myself. Therapy would have meant admitting to someone all of the fucked-up things I had done to reach the point at which I had arrived. That frightened me more than I could articulate. Other forms of treatment would have meant taking my foot off the gas pedal. That wouldn't fly. I certainly couldn't verbalize this to my team or partners, fearful as I was that everyone would turn their backs on me, because they would have discovered that rather than working for an impervious genius, their boss was a mere mortal.

That morning, though, Kevin needed to speak to me, which I imagined wouldn't involve good news, as there wasn't a lot of it to go around those days. I used this as my motivation to get out of bed, or else I would have lain there until it grew dark and I could pretend nothing outside was real.

When I arrived at the office Kevin was waiting in the conference room, with a pile of papers in front of him and a despondent look on his face. This was worse than I thought. He started speaking before I even had a chance to sit down.

"Do you want the bad news? Or the worse news? Eh, fuck it. We are getting sued. Well, to be more accurate, we are getting sued by two different people, at the same time."

Tony. Who was the other?

"Remember those asshole clients from Florida that Fueled brought with them?" he asked. "We fired them shortly after the acquisition and never heard anything else. It looks as if they're now coming after us for breach of contract."

It didn't take much effort to connect the dots. Tony had called and explained the situation, and spurred them into taking legal action.

The American legal system has limitless problems, but one of the most critical for entrepreneurs is the nature of our litigation practices. Anyone can sue anyone else for any claim they want to make, from breach of contract to tagging someone in an unflattering photo—and the receiving party must defend itself. In most situations, frivolous lawsuits are quickly dismissed, but in business, they can be destructive. Even the process of getting something thrown out can cost tens of thousands of dollars in legal fees. And if there is any kind of merit or discovery, going into arbitration, subrogation, or, heaven forbid, an actual trial could easily involve seven figures in fees and years of time. While it's clearly an abuse of the system, deep-pocketed plaintiffs commonly use this tactic to severely handicap or ruin competitors.

Not only was Tony prepared to drop a nuke inside a company he was an *owner* of, but he was willing to spend his own hard-earned money to watch it happen. And he had seemingly persuaded another party to join him in this insane game.

Kevin was short on details regarding Tony's case, as he had just been alerted to it by our counsel. But it didn't really matter what he was suing for, or what he hoped to achieve. Whatever his case's merit, it meant we would have to engage in an expensive, time-consuming, and public legal dispute. The gathering of contracts, emails, text messages, testimonies, and interviews, and attending any number of hearings, were about to take over our lives. Tony knew that we had officially started the process to sell the company. Which meant that he also knew that we would be legally obliged to reveal that we had active lawsuits pending against us in that discovery process. Having an equity holder and client suing you, regardless of the reason, is not exactly a good look to a prospective buyer, especially in a client services business.

Even if we were able to get through the sale process with active lawsuits pending, any purchaser would require us to resolve the disputes before the deal closed, making us pay off our accusers in the form of settlements. Tony knew this, too.

72 | FOUR-THIRDS

After squeezing the life out of the brokers on both sides of the deal, I finally executed a seven-year commercial lease on our new office space. We hired a design and architecture firm just two floors below us in our current space to assist in the build-out. They seemed like unpretentious professionals, and were close enough that I could run down and scream at them at any time if there were problems.

My intensity was now locked in at a solid ten. I thoroughly intimidated anyone meeting with me. One prospective assistant fled an interview in tears. Another simply went mute. Kevin had to constantly remind me to "be nice," but even when I tried, I couldn't mask my ferocious fervor.

The kickoff meeting with the architectural firm was no different, and I made it clear I was going to accept absolutely no bullshit on this project.

"I don't have time for introductions or small talk. You know who

I am, and we are already contracted, so no need to shine anything up or sell me further. This is a huge, expensive, critical project for us. I expect fucking brilliance every step of the way. If you tell me something, make sure you mean it. If you give me a date I can expect something, you better not miss it. I will make decisions quickly and decisively. There will be no backtracking. I know what I want, and I need you to deliver it in that exact way. I intend to design every square inch of this space and have a very distinct vision in my mind, and it's your job to bring it to reality. I am open to your opinions, but you are not to make a single decision without my oversight on it. If any of this is not taken seriously, I will fire you faster than you can blink your eye and hold back every fucking penny you were supposed to be paid. But if you do as I say and we pull this off, I will be your biggest advocate and spokesperson. That's it."

I must have been a *joy* to work with at this point in time.

I could take some measure of solace in assuring myself that such behavior did not reflect who I *really* was. I was still fundamentally a nice person, just under a lot of stress. I was still capable of caring for people, just not at that moment. I could still love and want to be loved. Right?

It is intimidating to ask these questions, to wonder whether you've killed the parts of yourself that make you most human. But there simply wasn't enough time to worry about such concerns. I was too high up the mountain. But there was no doubt I would have to confront them once all of this was over.

My time during this period was strictly divided into thirds.

One third was taken up with designing and planning the new office. This had to be done on time and on budget.

A second third involved working with Chuck on the sale of the company. He and his associates were giving ÄKTA a colonoscopy, rooting deep into every contract and decision we had made over the past five years in order to get an accurate picture of the business.

Another third was spent hunting down our next megaclient. Chuck told me that we would need some major wins during the sale process so that we could enter meetings armed with good news, as an assurance that we were still rapidly growing.

A final third was preparing to take on two active lawsuits, sitting with overpaid attorneys, and developing a strategy to mitigate the risk these posed, both short and long term.

For those keeping score, yes, that adds up to four-thirds. There was no outside world. I couldn't tell you who was going to the Super Bowl, if our government was still operating, or what films were currently playing. I didn't know which of my friends still lived in Chicago or if there were any significant developments in my family. I was in full cyborg work mode, again.

Everyone around me sensed my mood. I did not respond well to any missteps, omissions, or mistakes. Kevin kept his distance, as did the rest of the executive team. They knew not to ask for any updates, knowing I would tell them what I thought they needed to hear, when they needed to hear it, and to speak to me only if there was something truly mission-critical for me to be aware of. I didn't care about employees coming or going, issues with deliverables, or new contracts.

Days were managed to the minute. Every meeting lasted for the exact length of time necessary, and then I was off to the next. It was pure wrath for anyone who was unprepared. Inefficiency was a terminable offense.

I would bounce between ÄKTA HQ, the construction site, lawyers' offices, and the architects downstairs. Pop in and pitch a client. Shine up some prospective partner over dinner. Fly to a meeting in the morning, back at night. Live and die by the calendar. To keep me in the best headspace possible, we even began planning my days by the emotional toll each meeting would take. High-energy, exciting client pitches were scheduled for the mornings. Construction was early afternoon. Lawyers were as late as possible. I could then go straight home and be alone.

Chuck was my only reprieve. I felt a little less lifeless when I would confer with him. Good meetings gave me hope that there might be an end to all of this. Bad meetings scared the hell out of me, as he had begun exposing cracks in our armor that I had done a good job of hiding for years. Kevin and I had developed all sorts of cheeky tricks for attributing revenue and profit to various projects and quarters to maintain our growth story. We had a whole arsenal of ways to make our stats look superhuman. They involved nothing illegal or unethical, but there were a lot of ways to quantify ÄKTA, and we had learned to work them in our favor. Chuck saw through all of it.

73 | THE FLORIDA MAN

Most lawsuits don't go to trial, as the American court system would crumble under its own weight if they did. Instead, it encourages conflicting parties to behave like adults and try to resolve legal problems on their own, outside the system. This would normally start with informal discussions between the plaintiff and defendant, then move on to an exchange of nasty letters between each side's attorneys, hoping the other side will fold. Next would come arbitration, which is basically the legal equivalent of couples therapy—an independent third party attempts to bring the two parties "closer together" to form an amicable resolution. There are versions that are binding, whatever the arbitrator decides must be legally enforced, or nonbinding, where both sides pretend to play nice in the room, and then go back to quarreling as soon as the session is over. If a resolution is mutually agreed upon, which generally is a matter of one side paying off the other, realizing it's cheaper than the legal process itself, then the suit is dropped. Otherwise, you go to jury trial.

My lawyers were starting this process for both of our battles, and while such efforts are typically slower than erosion, we didn't have the luxury of time. The longer these suits stayed on the books, the more exposure I had. They negatively affected everything—morale, focus, acquisition discussions. So, I had to figure out how to get these plaintiffs to back off.

It turned out that the Florida accusers were a husband and wife duo. I had never met or even spoken to them and obviously couldn't ask Tony for any relevant background. I told my attorneys to get in touch with them to arrange a meeting. I would turn the charm up to one hundred and see if I could put this matter to rest.

The meeting was arranged to take place at a steak house in the Orlando airport at noon. This felt like the setup for a prank show.

There I sat in the first-class cabin of yet another American Airlines flight, eating miserable oatmeal, in a suit that was now surely wrinkled to hell. I had become accustomed to flying in the closest thing to pajamas that I could get away with, so having to be fully suited and booted going to Orlando of all fucking places put me in a bad mood. I could only imagine this fake-tanned jackass smiling when he thought about what he was making me do.

My mental picture of this guy wasn't far off. He was the personification of Florida. Middle-aged, orange skin, baseball cap, tight-fitting Polo shirt, ring on pinky finger. He sat waiting for me at a tiny table outside an airport restaurant, smiling as I walked up, clearly loving the fact that I had had to come down and do this.

The meeting itself went about as well as expected. He felt wronged that we had fired him as a client after the acquisition, even though we hadn't charged him a dime past what we had already delivered, and he even had a standing balance that we hadn't made him pay. "Prejudiced," as he put it. This was clearly a word his lawyers had given him to use.

After ninety minutes it became clear that absolutely no forward progress was going to be made. Trying to be nice wasn't getting me anywhere. New tactic.

"Look, man. I came down here to have an adult discussion about clearing this lawsuit up. You obviously have no interest in doing so. You also seemingly know this is all crap, and you're just wasting my time and money—two things I care a lot about. So, here's what's going to happen now. I am getting back on a plane away from this shithole immediately. And my first call when I land is going to be to my attorneys, instructing them to file a lawsuit against you, for monies owed, and for any other charges they can think up. I'm going to file the lawsuit in Delaware, which is the jurisdiction of the contract. Have you ever been to Delaware, motherfucker? I haven't, either. But you'll soon become very familiar with it, because that's where you'll need to travel to in order to fight me on this. Will I be there? No. I will send my overpriced lawyers, because I can afford to. But you can't. So, I am going to use every means I have possible to bleed you of your money and make you regret coming after me like this. We can go through all of this together and see what happens at the end. Have a great day."

Subtle, but I think he got the message. I stood up and walked out, stiffing him with the bill for my iced tea.

The hypocrisy of the situation was not lost on me. I had just threatened to do to the guy the exact thing that he and Tony were doing to me. But I didn't feel as if I had any other options, and, well, it was effective. As my great-great-grandfather used to say, "Don't hate the player, hate the broken litigious American legal system."

My meeting with Tony was one of the most awkward of my life. An arbitration had been set up, at which we both had to be present.

My lawyer and I sat directly across the table from Tony and his. I stared at Tony the entire time, never taking my gaze off him, daring him to look back at me, which he managed to never do.

Despite the impassioned efforts of my attorney, Tony obviously had no intention of settling the suit. After an hour of thinly veiled threats between the lawyers, everyone stood at once to leave, knowing that if anything, this effort had only made the situation worse.

74 | THE ROAD SHOW

Chuck had finally finished his investigation of ÄKTA. The result was a seventy-five-page document called a PPM, or private placement memorandum. This was basically a reverse-engineered business plan that covered ÄKTA's history, growth, financials, management structure, key clients, projects, sales process, et cetera, with no stone left unturned. It was so thorough that *I* even learned things about the company when I read it. The PPM was supplemented by a one-page summary of its findings, which would serve as an anonymous teaser citing the company's highlights.

The goal was now to get this summarized version into the hands of as many corporate development teams as possible and, depending on their level of interest, they would then sign nondisclosure agreements, or NDAs, and be granted access to the PPM.

Chuck, Dean, and I gathered in the conference room to discuss potential acquirers. We started with the blue-chip tech companies like Apple, Microsoft, and Google, then major consultancies like Accenture and Deloitte. We extrapolated from there, and a few hours later had filled the whiteboard with about a hundred names. The anonymous memo was sent to all of them over the coming week, plus a few dozen more potential buyers we had either missed or Chuck's office had identified.

To my amazement Chuck was bombarded with responses. Within a few weeks dozens of companies had signed NDAs and had requested the full PPM.

I tried to wrap my brain around what this meant. On one hand, it was the best news possible—a lot of corporations were seriously interested in acquiring ÄKTA.

On the other hand, I had come to terms with how much work this would require to execute. Chuck had informed me that the first conversation for companies outside of Chicago would be held over the phone, but any additional meetings would have to take place in person. These would include initial presentations, management presentations, "get-to-know-you" dinners, and any follow-ups. He got very serious when he was explaining the process, which made me want to ask him if he thought I was truly ready for what lay ahead.

For the next few weeks I sat in my office, taking conference call after conference call with interested parties. These still had to be conducted in almost humorously anonymous terms, so I could not actually say my name or anything about ÄKTA. I would answer questions nonspecifically but provide enough information to interest them in proceeding to a more formal, in-person conversation. I quickly became a broken record of canned responses, speed dating for cash.

For a long time I had considered myself a very passionate traveler. I would get excited when going to the airport and loved arriving in any new city. But I now quickly reached the tipping point when travel was no longer enjoyable, but just work. As soon as companies began to respond and sign NDAs, I was heading for New York, San Francisco, London, Austin, and Los Angeles. I started to live and breathe recycled air and midrange hotels. Fly out at the crack of dawn, breakfast meeting with a suitor. Back on a plane. Dinner meeting with another. Four hours of sleep. Early presentation. Plane. Late presentation. Sleep.

After a while I wasn't sure which city I was in or with whom I was meeting. For all intents and purposes, it didn't really matter. I would get off the plane, find my driver, and head for the conference room of whatever company was on the schedule for that day. I would give the same overly rehearsed presentation, answer some basic questions, and perform like a Broadway actor, day in and day out.

The upside to this assembly-line approach to an acquisition is that it consumed 100 percent of my focus. I didn't have one iota of energy left when I would crawl into whatever bed I was assigned to that night. My brain was too tired to run wild or even have any fleeting thoughts. It was probably the easiest time I'd had falling asleep in years.

The downsides were stark. While I was out doing my road show, there was still a company called ÄKTA back in Chicago that was still running a mile a minute. The executive team had been coached to handle the stress of my being away from the office, but no one else knew what I was out doing. Despite our best efforts, the trickle-down effects of my absence were going to be disruptive.

I now deeply understood why Chuck had warned me that this process would be a point of no return. Major decisions at ÄKTA had to be made with its potential sale in mind, whether they involved hiring, firing, or acquiring clients or prioritizing clients differently. Everything now had to "meet the narrative" of what we were saying on the road show, regardless of whether they were the right decisions for the company over the long term. We'd massively discount a deal just to add another client to our list, even knowing we had taken on a dumpster fire of a project. I pressured Kevin into a key executive hire we would otherwise have never considered, because it made a great piece in the story I was selling. Internal departments, ranging from accounting to marketing, were being reengineered to paint us in the absolute best light, irrespective of if they were intelligent business decisions. I didn't even know this was *possible* to do, before we were forced to do it.

I was having to learn the art of high-level business in real time, and execute it flawlessly. Chuck later made the comment that this was like me getting a fast-track MBA, while treading water, and juggling.

75 | THE HAWKS

Those months were so insane I would sometimes forget there was still a perfectly normal world out there, doing things like celebrating birthdays, taking vacations, and watching sports.

As it turned out, the Chicago Blackhawks were having another breakout season. It came as news to me, having been delivered by a close friend in Chicago during one of my rare visits back home. The Blackhawks were doing so well, in fact, that they were heading to Game 6 of the Stanley Cup—a potential championship game, which was scheduled to take place on the evening I returned to town.

Fuck it, I decided. *One night out. A few drinks with friends and doing something normal might be just what I need.*

We bought some overpriced tickets and headed to the stadium, where it was pure chaos outside. Probably because we exist in a frozen wasteland for half the year, Chicagoans *love* their hockey. Sirens were blaring, fans were shouting, fights were already breaking out. For some strange reason, the pandemonium comforted me.

I tried to focus on the game and calm my mind down, something I hadn't attempted in months, and the roar of the crowd helped. The action of the game helped. And the result especially helped: victory over Tampa Bay, 2-0.

We yelled and cheered and hugged. The postgame celebrations were in full swing. I got a text from a friend: "We're at the Mid. The team is coming. Let's fucking party."

The Mid was a long-standing nightclub in the recently gentrified

West Loop district of Chicago. It was a grumpy old man screaming at the kids nearby to get off his lawn. It was gritty and dark, like the city itself. The chances of meeting a beautiful woman or getting stabbed there were about the same.

A bunch of the Blackhawks players had settled in on the private upper deck behind the DJ, along with all the usual Chicago cool kids. Showers of champagne rained down, piles of women careened to attract the attention of the players, and an endless train of tequila shots found their way into every mouth in the place.

It had been months since I had done this kind of partying. Part of me was scared it might trigger something bad. Even the smell of tequila gave me *Fear and Loathing* flashbacks. But it also felt good. For just a few hours. Screw everything else. I wanted to scream this at the top of my lungs.

A wave of anxiety hit me. It wasn't a panic attack, but something else entirely. My mind was warning me that something was very wrong in my immediate surroundings. I was tangled around a girl who was sitting on my lap, a shot halfway to my mouth, when I saw him.

Standing in front of me, partly in the shadow, was Tony, staring at me with a nasty look on his face. He was clearly annihilated, but was still focused directly on me. The look in his eyes was crazy. My fight-or-flight instincts immediately kicked in. I realized I was bracing for him to attack.

As he walked toward me, I slid the girl off my lap and tried to stand up, as the room gently spun. Tony's belly made him a bit heavier than me, but I still had about four inches of height and a lot more aggression. By the time I had my feet set, he was within arm's reach. I reflexively grabbed the front of his shirt and slammed him against the wall to my right. "Stop!" I growled. The viciousness in my eyes matched his.

The look on his face didn't change until I took the pressure off his chest and stepped back. He calmed, gave me his signature smirk, and walked away.

My heart was thrashing. The adrenaline was counteracting the alcohol. I was now completely lucid and could hear every beat of the music and every word being spoken around me. Unnerved to my core, I went to the bathroom to splash water across my face, and when I saw myself in the mirror I knew it was time to leave before anything else happened. I didn't want to know what Tony was capable of.

I walked outside to find a taxi, and the scene outside was just as frenzied as in the bar. Lights from police cruisers strobed at my eyeballs. I just wanted to get away.

I heard Tony before I saw him. He was screaming in the face of a police officer. The cop had his right hand on his belt. I couldn't tell if he was reaching for a gun or a Taser. Something was about to snap. I started moving before my mind could acknowledge it.

I jumped in between Tony and the officer with my hands raised, trying to show I only wanted peace. I shouted at the cop that he was my brother, he was drunk, and to let me take Tony home. I gestured that I was not a threat, as this was not worth getting shot or stunned over, but I was already in.

The officer reacted by slamming his left hand into my chest, to move me back. I tripped over Tony's leg, then the curb, and went down hard. My right hand landed in broken glass as my elbow and knee collided violently with the cement. I closed my eyes and tried to lift my hands up to my face, and braced for pain.

The next thing I felt was Tony's hand grabbing my bloodied wrist and yanking me to my feet, and then down the block. Seeing that I was disoriented and limping, he sat me down at the next street corner and dropped down next to me. We didn't speak for a few minutes, then he began.

"You didn't need to do that," he said quietly. "But thank you. You fucking asshole."

Not knowing how to respond, I continued to stare at the ground, picking tiny shards of glass from my palm and trying to figure out why I had been compelled to save the guy who was trying to ruin me. I suppose it's because I saw my friend, my business partner. I still saw a person who believed I had wronged him. And somehow, even though I didn't think I had, I wanted to make it right.

"You took everything from me!" he finally shouted. And then, his voice quieting, "You stole my business, and my life. I have nothing." He was speaking more from the heart than I had ever heard before.

Legally we weren't supposed to speak without lawyers present. I assumed that doing so while drunk and bleeding on a street corner after an altercation with the police would be severely out of bounds. But I had no choice but to say what needed to be said.

"Tony," I told him, "I am truly sorry you feel that way. But man . . . I have to say that I don't think you're seeing the world clearly. You hate me. You think I am some devil who robbed you. But that just isn't the case. We all know the business you had created was plateauing, and your reckoning was going to come sooner than later. Every one of your employees was looking for other jobs and saw the writing on the wall. Even your business partner wasn't happy. While I realize your role wasn't as important at ÄKTA, the reality is, you own part of the damned company. And we are worth something. I've been living on airplanes for months talking to dozens of companies who want to give us fuck-off money for this business. We'll all be fucking *rich*, Tony! You'll be a millionaire! It's already happening. It's real. If I can do that for all of us, how on earth isn't that worth it? It's what you've always wanted. And now one of the biggest threats we have to that success is you suing your own business. It's a smear on an otherwise beautiful painting. A struggle every time I must explain it to a buyer. You're cutting off your nose to slight your face."

I paused and thought, *I hope I got that phrase right.*

The look in his eye told me that his ego and frontal lobe were fighting it out. However much he *felt* robbed and slighted, he *knew* rationally that that wasn't the case. I couldn't control the outcome of that battle, so I just waited for him to speak.

"So what now?" he finally uttered.

I was getting woozy. Blood was dripping from my pinky finger at a staccato pace into a little design on the cement. I was out of long-winded speeches and clever idioms.

"Drop the lawsuit, man," I told him. "Let me finish this. Please. I am begging you."

76 | THE DREAM

My memory of the next few months is like watching a VHS tape on fast-forward, with fleeting memories of airports, dinners, and conference rooms broken up by flashes of black-and-white static.

Every day, the giant Jenga game that was my psyche got taller and taller. Good news. Bad news. This prospective buyer gave us a no. This client said yes. This employee quit. This meeting went well. We are over budget here. We made money there.

Battles were taking place on every front, both internal and external. Not a day went by without a fight. I had fully accepted we were on wartime footing. I had stopped judging anyone for taking shots at me, but I also made it clear that I would burn anyone to the ground who missed.

I would wake up to the heinous sound of my phone's alarm, tears welling in my eyes and a layer of sweat beneath my body, even though the room was freezing. "No, no, no," I would repeat, pleading with time to slow down so I could have just one more minute in bed. As if that would change anything.

The combination of drugs I would consume each day depended on how lucid I had to be and how likely the environment I'd be in was to send me into a panic. Conference call from my hotel room? Mild antidepressant and a green tea. Big in-person presentation? A handful of beta-blockers and anti-anxiety pills, an hour before. More if I had too many drinks the night prior trying to wind down and was shaky. Even these didn't do the trick at times. I'd be in the bathroom before an important meeting, an inch from the mirror, staring into my own eyes, trembling. Begging my mind to cooperate so I didn't melt down.

But that never actually happened, as I always managed to deliver my presentation with my patented zeal and confidence. If midsentence I would feel a shock wave of panic begin to course down my spine, like a steel rod across a xylophone, I would grit my teeth, take a sip of water, and scream silently to myself, *Stop, relax*. I somehow found a way to stay consistently at exactly 1 percent above a break-down. This was my superpower.

Back in Chicago, construction was underway on our new office—an unbelievable operation with hundreds of people hard at work. I would storm in like a bat out of hell and demand updates. The poor project manager would scramble to keep up with me as I marched around the site, mentally checking up on hundreds of different items. When the hard-as-nails, six-foot-four construction manager yelled back at me on one such visit on a particularly bad day, I grabbed him by the collar of his shirt and threatened to throw him out of the huge hole in the wall next to us, two hundred feet down to Wacker Drive. He didn't make eye contact with me again.

In fact, under his management, the office was coming along like a dream. My goal was to create a half-acre advertisement for how progressive, creative, and innovative we were at ÄKTA. Living plant walls, reclaimed wood headings with vintage lanterns, a huge recreation room with an Olympic-sized Ping-Pong area, and a luxury executive suite.

On a daily basis, I would make decisions that would make any seasoned architect's eyes bulge. Yes, I did intend that conference room to float one foot off the ground. Yes, I did want each meeting room to be completely different, with unique furniture, seating heights, lighting, colors, layout, electronics. A feature I demanded was a fire hazard? I don't care. Figure it out.

Even though in my heart I knew that ÄKTA was either going to be acquired or burn to the ground (figuratively) in a few short months, I still wanted this office to be my legacy, an enduring memorial to me and all the blood, sweat, and tears that had gone into this company, even after I was gone.

77 | ON SALE

Apart from what I had learned from Chuck, the totality of my knowledge about what happens when companies get acquired came from newspaper articles and movies. Someone would come along and offer a pile of money, you'd sign some contracts, and everyone would be happy, right?

Unsurprisingly, there was a lot more involved in the process. In the case of acquiring a service business like ÄKTA, a lot of it wasn't great news. In fact, the more I learned, the more I asked myself if I had made the biggest mistake of my life in choosing to do this.

The nature of any service business (from consultants to lawyers to public relations) is that it holds somewhere between zero and very little intellectual property or other tangible assets. The value of the business is purely cash flow and profit, generated by human beings who are paid to do a job. Contracts are the only "guarantee" you have for what you may make in the future, so they carry some weight, even though everyone in the game knows they're worth about as much as the paper they're printed on.

Most other businesses can amass a wealth of assets that create intrinsic value outside of the company's growth or cash flow.

Even as Sears was failing as a retail enterprise, the corporation was still worth billions, thanks to all the real estate it had purchased on which to build its stores. Instagram had thirteen employees and no revenue when it was bought for a billion dollars by Facebook for its technology and the future opportunity it promised. (At the time of this writing, Instagram is worth about $130 billion.)

Many other businesses also have this magic thing called residual revenue, meaning they make money even when not putting in a relational, proactive effort to do so. Consider the example of a gym that charges $100 a month for membership. Whether ten members or one hundred members show up on any particular day, the gym makes the same amount of money from its total number of subscriptions. Many businesses operate this way. They have a fixed or low relational operating cost, so as revenue grows, profits follow.

ÄKTA had none of that. We didn't make any of our own technology. We didn't have any guaranteed revenues. We had a one-to-one ratio of effort to revenue. I had to pay Joe $100 an hour to work at ÄKTA. While Joe was on a billable client project, he brought in $300 an hour, grossing me $200. When Joe wasn't on a project, he cost me $100 an hour. When Joe quit, his value ceased immediately. Such factors made the valuation of a service business extremely difficult and, from my side of the table, especially brutal.

In order to determine what amount of money a company would purchase ÄKTA for, we had to first determine what they were actually buying.

They weren't purchasing my team as a long-term asset, as each employee was at-will and could quit or be fired at any time. They weren't buying my contracts, as any contract could be canceled at any time, by either party. They weren't buying future profits, at least not any assurance that things would continue to go as well. Nothing could be guaranteed. There was value in the reach and stature of the brand, but it wasn't as if we were Starbucks. ÄKTA's reach was limited to a very specific business community.

What an acquirer was really buying was this: the team, structured as it was today, building into a vision of tomorrow. They were buying a future result that still must be achieved. If the day after being bought, we all were to quit, the buyer would literally have nothing for its money. But if we continued growing at a breakneck pace and were doing five times revenue in three years, it would be a great purchase.

So, as you can imagine, the valuation becomes completely dependent on fulfilling that goal. See where this is going?

Your service company has been growing and is on pace to make $100 in profit this year. In that case, an argument could be made that the value of the business is, let's say, $500, based on a five times multiplier of EBITDA (a way to look at gross profit). So, someone agrees to buy the company for $500. But! You, the seller, only get $50 up front. Because the buyer wants to be sure its investment pays off—which means the company it purchased continues to grow and operate successfully—it will pay the seller $100 per year, assuming critical goals are reached and employees don't quit, et cetera. After the fourth year, the seller will receive $150, finally getting him to the $500 purchase price, perhaps with an additional kicker or bonus attached.

The case above is an oversimplification, but in essence it's what I had to grapple with. Even in a great-case scenario of being acquired for a big chunk of money, most of it would be held back for a number of years, with the payoff based on very difficult goals. And if any of those goals weren't reached, I wouldn't get my money. So, I'd effectively just be working for someone else, and shifting risk from one place to another.

The only chance I had to sidestep the classic agency-acquired hamster wheel was to find an acquirer who had different priorities than revenue growth and cash flow. A company who wanted us for a different reason.

With all due respect, ÄKTA was a *tiny* company compared with the megacorporations in the tech world, which probably spend more on catering than we made in a year. From their financial viewpoints, we were effectively a rounding error.

That said, we could still have a huge amount of impact, even on a large company. If it was seeking a new internal engine of innovation or to install a design-led culture, our team could make waves, just as we had been for our clients. Likewise, for a company that was doing its own hard-core digital project design and development, having a group like ours internally, instead of having to outsource it, was a dream.

It was my dream, too. In order to earn my freedom, I now had to find a company not only willing to buy us, but to buy us for the exact right reasons.

78 | MAGNUM OPUS

By August 2015 I could see everything heading for a collision course.

The new office was about done. It was *beautiful*. I can't explain the joy and pride I felt walking into that space and watching all my little ÄKTAnauts explore their new home. Millions and millions had been invested to create the most breathtaking office I'd ever seen. We were weeks from officially moving in.

Chuck's structured acquisition process was getting down to the finalists. My executive team had joined me on the road show, doing full-scale, half-day-long management presentations for about the dozen companies that were our most interested buyers. When the travel was finally over, I had taken 150 flights in six months.

The list of prospective purchasers included one of the largest global agency holding companies, a blue-chip $200 billion tech firm, a large British design agency, and a bizarre Chinese holding company.

Chuck had set a hard deadline for bids at midnight on August 31. But we urged that all bids be submitted a week earlier, in order to give us proper time to negotiate. We had hired one of the world's largest law firms to manage the process, and a war room had been assembled on the fortieth floor of their downtown office building. It held what was seemingly the world's longest conference table, lined with phones, documents, printers, and shredders.

Tension was now at an all-time high. The executive team avoided me in the office, the same way a baseball team keeps its distance from a pitcher as he prepares for the ninth inning of a no-hitter. The matter was fully in my hands now. Close the deal, or fail. This was the finish line. We were so close. But advancing from 99 percent to 100 percent wasn't a matter of just an additional 1 percent, but of 100 percent. Everything had to go right, or nothing would matter.

I was wavering perfectly between two mindsets. One was a wildly high level of confidence and determination, like that of a prizefighter entering the ring. The other was a morbid fear that I might have finally pushed us too close to the edge.

One development had made things a lot better: I no longer had any lawsuits to disclose to our suitors. Miraculously, after our little run-in with the police, Tony had agreed to drop his suit, and got Florida

Man to do so as well. One day I am walking around with an anvil above my head, ready to fall and smash me at any moment. Then a quick call from our lawyers, and, *poof*, gone. Like it never happened.

During the lead-up to formal offers, hundreds of deal points are discussed and negotiated up front, so prospective buyers know they are making the most competitive offer they can. Because no one wants to be too high, or too low, on any point, they all poke and prod, vying and jockeying for insight and information that will help them. The bankers and lawyers on my side obviously knew the game, so they played it nimbly, cleverly communicating and pitting buyers against one another, to guarantee that we'd get the best offer.

During this process I more or less lived in that conference room. Because sleeping had become impossible, I'd arrive before dawn, wearing casual clothing. My job was to sit and wait to be told to make a decision, or to sign something.

"John, they're demanding credit on the security deposit of the new office, arguing that this was a sunk cost you took on preacquisition, and they aren't going to cover it. Are you okay with that?"

"John, they're challenging how we are doing revenue recognition for Q3 2014, because one of our contracts was pushed into the next two quarters, affecting our rolling EBIT by 10 percent that quarter, what should we tell them?"

"John, this buyer is proposing a four-year lock-up, with a weighted 30 percent at closing and no performance goals, including a 10 percent kicker based on an eighteen-month escrow, what do you think?"

A volley of such questions hit me for hours at a time. I'd lie on the large windowsill, staring at the drop ceiling of the room, answering them as fast as they were put to me. The background was an unforgettable symphony of muffled conversations, the humming of laser printers, and a flurry of ringing phones. The game was devilish, both sides dealing in half-truths and empty threats. I don't have the words to express the emotional gymnastics that I experienced listening to all of this.

"While we appreciate your offer, I think we are too far apart. Thanks for your time. Yep, take care." *Click.*

Jesus. Did they just kill one of our offers?

"There is no way John will ever agree to that. Please reconsider that in your next offer."

That was our best lead. What if they don't call back?

"We actually have a trip to Southern California already booked for tomorrow. Perhaps John and I can stop into your office then."

We do?

I would close my eyes and try to enter a meditative state to drown out the chaos around me. From time to time I would turn my head and consider the five-hundred-foot drop behind the glass I was leaning against.

79 | THE FINAL DAY

Offer day.

I wore my favorite dark blue suit. Thin lapel, ticket pocket. Appropriate for a wedding, or funeral.

Rather than taking a car service, I walked the two miles to the law office in complete silence. The sun was just cresting Lake Michigan as I took my seat, alone in the war room. Hundreds of pages of documents were neatly piled across the table, my fate sealed in all their legalese.

I considered the expanse of downtown Chicago spread out before me. Cold concrete and stone were starting to soak in the summer sun, breathing life into the hustle taking place below. Today felt like the culmination of my life's work, even though less than five years had passed since we made our first dollar. I knew I'd be dogged by endless reflection in the years to come, one way or another. There was no unconflicted emotion in my body. I felt happy and sad. Forlorn and hopeful. Stoic and apprehensive.

The deal team started to file in. Today there was a much different energy in the room. Things were either going to go very right, or very wrong. No one wanted to set any expectations, so there were no words of encouragement or warnings, just slight nods of the head, coffees poured, and seats taken. At the end of the day we all wanted a great result, but I was the only person in the room whose life was fundamentally changing today. Everyone else would go home to their regular lives and be thinking about their next deal.

I kept my gaze out the window. Not a moment of the proceedings today was in my hands, so I opted to watch the birds flying above the buildings, and the ants marching below. Today I had to relinquish any illusion of control.

At the opening of the business day, phones started ringing and printers started whirring. The sales antics were gone. The team was patiently answering final questions and confirming details. Processes were being laid out and timelines determined.

Lunchtime had been set as the cutoff for all said processes. The bidders now had five hours to submit their written offers.

I felt a pressure building behind my eyes. For some reason, I was very upset. I hadn't spoken a single word all day and didn't intend to start now, so I abruptly left the room, headed to the elevator, and pressed the button for the ground floor. Stepping out onto LaSalle Drive, I was overcome with emotion. I don't know if it was the sight of so many people going about their typical days, or simply the realization that this was in fact the end of the road, or what, but my knees gave out. I stumbled backward against the building, the back of my head banging the wall as I slid to the ground. I felt as if I were going to be sick, or pass out. I gripped my face with my hands, praying my vision didn't go dark. This was not the time to end up back in the hospital.

A warmth washed over me as I realized a hand had been gently wrapped around my wrist. I released my own shaking hands to see an older woman leaning toward me. She hesitated before speaking, as she considered my state, and then lightly pressed on my hand and said, "Everything will be okay, young man."

She held my gaze until I could softly thank her, and then she smiled and squeezed my arm again before continuing down the street. My pulse lowered and my vision began to clear. Somehow, I knew she was right.

80 | FIN

That day, we received formal offers from six companies across three countries.

Two weeks later, the largest tech company in San Francisco, Salesforce, fully acquired ÄKTA. Led by easily the most forward-thinking CEO in the enterprise game, Marc Benioff, Salesforce knew that it would have to lead with design, not solely technology, if it was going to continue its meteoric growth. The Salesforce team had to theorize, ideate, and innovate on behalf of their best clients, not just sell them software. This made ÄKTA (which ultimately became Salesforce Experience Design), along with other similar acquisitions, pivotal to their long-term consulting strategy.

I legally can't say how much money changed hands. But it's a sum that allows me to live any life I choose and enables me to spread my new wealth to things I care about.

Our deal called for me to work as an executive at Salesforce for almost a year. I continued to run ÄKTA inside Salesforce while being an evangelist for innovation and design externally. ÄKTA quickly doubled in size as we gobbled up some of Salesforce's internal consulting practice.

I thought I would be free after the sale. I thought the stress was over, the risk had passed, and I would be able to wake up the next day and feel like a new man. In fact, the opposite happened. My body and mind had become so attuned to the toxic stress and lifestyle that it was weirdly *working* for me and had kept me operating at this insanely high level. But once the risk was gone and the major stress fell away, the problems came rushing to the forefront, and it wasn't pretty. One psychologist called this the Olympian effect: you are so focused on one goal for so long that when it suddenly goes away, your body and mind have no idea how to cope. It's why so many gold medalists melt down after their victories.

After the sale, I was introduced to an incredible doctor, who practiced medical engineering in Chicago, and who guided me through a long process toward wellness, for the better part of a year.

Brain scans showed that my executive functions (working memory, flexible thinking, self-control) were firing off the charts at scary levels, even during rest. Stress and sleep tests revealed dangerous patterns and communication imbalances in my brain. The activity in my head was past redlined, 24/7. My limbic system, which is responsible for emotion, was highly suppressed, and not communicating efficiently with my frontal cortex, which is a recipe for severe depression. I shook when I would try to sit still. I'd have panic attacks walking down the street. I'd awake in the middle of the night, standing in my living room, sweating. I had a relentless sensation of dread. My heart skipped and pounded at an irregular beat.

I tried all sorts of treatments, from psychotherapy to neurofeedback. IVs pumped chelation therapy and high-dose ketamine through my body. Acupuncture, ashtanga, tai chi, chi gung, and yoga helped to center me. I took almost fifty supplements per day, in an attempt to repair my body from the inside out. Small, brightly colored pills were still on hand for when nothing else worked.

Eventually, I started feeling like a human being again. I came back to a level of consciousness, clarity, and calmness that I forgot existed. I was mindful and in tune with my body, and the unique opportunity I had been granted. There are still lingering effects from my years at ÄKTA, including permanent memory damage and post-traumatic stress.

Finding mental balance was the ultimate reward. I had forgotten what a normal emotional range felt like.

By all standard ways of measuring, ÄKTA was a big success.

Especially to outside observers. A lot of people became rich. The staff was well taken care of and ended up on incredible career paths. Everyone was offered jobs at Salesforce and many are still there thriving. Kevin is a happy man and still a close friend, which was one of the most important results for me. I made the down payment on his new house to show my appreciation. Tony got rich via the money I promised him and, unfortunately, still hates me. The rest of us talk from time to time, but for the most part, we said our good-byes and went our separate ways.

I was one of the lucky ones. Not just to win the entrepreneurial game, but to then have the opportunity to repair myself. I was surrounded by an amazing support structure, comprised of friends, who had every right to give up on me, and the greatest family ever, who eventually brought me back to my old self. Now everything is about quality relationships, time with my niece, being a good friend, looking after my family, exploring the world, working to make it a bit better, trying to be the best person I can, and telling my story. These are even sweeter feelings than they ever could have been before, as I can feel something I feared I had lost.

With all of that said, I'm still an entrepreneur, and I doubt that anything will ever completely scratch my entrepreneurial itch. In the five years since selling ÄKTA, I've started or invested in over thirty companies, ranging from luxury real estate to fashion to hospitality. I also began collecting art and producing films, hosting a podcast, and I got serious about practicing martial arts. And I've, obviously, started writing. I stay deeply involved with a number of charities I care about, and often think about revitalizing Digital Hope. Thankfully, these are all hobbies. I know that if I ever try my hand at my next big company, I'll feel infinitely more equipped to manage it and myself more conscientiously, create balance, and, most important, never bet the farm again.

There is a way to operate in and succeed at this game without allowing it to take so damaging a toll on your mind and body, if you are realistic about the challenges and have the support structures to empower you. This is what I hope I can encourage folks like me to speak more freely about.

AFTERWORD

What outsiders rarely see, and what I've tried to detail in these pages, is the all-too-common story of an individual's trying to take on the world when they are woefully underqualified, pressured to double down endlessly on risk, and placed in a do-or-die position, often at a too-tender age.

In the process of writing this book, I read many other accounts of the "dark side" of entrepreneurship, and was routinely shocked at just how grievous and jarring other people's experiences can be. Almost weekly, friends send me news clippings about other entrepreneurs melting down, taking their own lives, or losing their livelihoods to the pressure of this game.

So, how do we address a problem that is likely to only get worse in today's accelerated economy?

To start, we should promote a culture of honesty and vulnerability in entrepreneurship and business. Leaders are human beings with flaws and ongoing struggles. The standards of toxic masculinity that affect both men and women, forcing them to keep quiet, do their jobs, and never let the world know there is a problem, should change. Founders should have channels of support, and be encouraged to seek them out. Leadership should be encouraged to eliminate these modern "Don't Ask, Don't Tell" policies and allow executives to be open about any problems they are experiencing, and to cooperate to address them, rather than suddenly deeming these individuals unfit to lead.

With any movement, we need to shine a light on positive behavior, and rain hell down on suppression. Boards should be scared to death at the idea of firing a CEO because they are struggling personally. The media should be focused on presenting illness and humanity in a positive light when it comes to entrepreneurship and leadership, and show these people for who they often actually are: heroes. Heroes who are trying to take on and change the world—who are human, flawed, loved, and respected. We should honor these attributes, not diminish them. Entrepreneurs should be *proud* to be vulnerable, not ashamed of it. Other industries have achieved this. Actors, musicians, and athletes have begun to pull back the veil over the last decade and thrive in their humanity. Now, it's our turn.

Next, we need to create channels of support that leaders trust. While I was running ÄKTA, despite being surrounded by other "friendtrepreneurs" who were obviously dealing with their own trials and tribulations, I never *once* had an honest conversation with any of them about what any of us was actually going through. We were all too caught up with trying to one-up one another and boast about how thoroughly we were "crushing it." That is as sad as it is ridiculous.

During my journey, I didn't believe there was a single support outlet that would actually have helped me. Obviously, that wasn't true. I had a loving family and friends. I knew therapists were just a phone call away. I could have booked myself into a wellness center.

It wasn't the literal lack of knowledge that these options existed, but rather, my lack of confidence that they could actually be relevant to what I was experiencing and had the ability to treat me the way I needed to be treated. I didn't want merely to be told I had a problem, and I didn't want to be "fixed." What I would have wanted was someone to just sit patiently and listen to me, allowing me to tear myself open and be human for a moment. We have to provide access to some nonintrusive ways to cope, methods that don't attempt to dull our spears or stop what's actually working. If entrepreneurs knew such outlets existed, they'd be used en masse.

The world needs to come to terms with the fact that entrepreneurs and leaders are not invincible and embrace them for showing their true selves. As entertaining as it is to watch yet another Hollywood film manage to make the challenges of a genius billionaire seem oddly enticing, we need to advocate for truth in the media, even if it's tough to watch. And whatever Schadenfreude we might enjoy while watching documentaries about the most epic entrepreneurial train wrecks (Theranos and Fyre Festival are just two recent examples), we should instead take a serious look at the culture that allows and even encourages these disasters to happen.

For the up-and-comers, we have an obligation to create a system that rewards hustle and risk taking but also includes a healthy dose of blunt honesty, so they are truly aware of just what they are signing up for. This may be an unpopular opinion, but I believe business today is riddled with too much false optimism and positivity. We are so fearful of facing the realities of life, and success, that we shield ourselves from them through self-help books and courses and find comfort in superficial motivational quotes. While it might not feel as good, applying some tough love to and sharing some fierce truths with the younger generation will actually be doing them a monumental favor by preparing them for the real journey.

Finally, for those readers who have a friend or parent or child who is an entrepreneur, please, tell them you're proud of them. Give them a hug and tell them you're there if they ever need you, even though it may be difficult to completely understand what they're experiencing.

I don't have all the answers or a master plan of how to bring about the changes I believe must take place. But I'm looking forward to embarking on my own new journey by dedicating my resources to facilitating these necessary conversations, and doing what I can to impart whatever wisdom I and others have gained to help the next generation of doers. I challenge others in my position to do the same.

With love,
John Roa

Acknowledgments

To Mom, who taught me how to be a good man, even though there were times I forgot. Notably, chapters 1, 53, 54, and 66. Hopefully you skipped those like I asked. I love you so much.

To Isabel, thanks for being an amazing older sister and showing me what strength is—and for bringing us Margaux. I am so thankful for the love and connection that beautiful little monster has brought all of us.

To Papi, Andy, Maggie, Bridget, Avocado, Brooke, Blake, Wyatt, Sawyer, Milo, Reina, and the rest of my family, I'm very lucky to have you all.

To my editor, Rick Kot—who foolishly told me I'm a capable writer, so now will never be able to get rid of me—and the team at Viking, Brian Tart, Andrea Schulz, Camille Leblanc, Louise Braverman, Katie Hurley, and Lucia Bernard, thank you for believing in me and my story.

To my agent, Alan Nevins, at Renaissance, who was the first professional who said, *"You've got something here,"* and then proceeded to perform multiple miracles. You and your team have been fantastic.

To Hamza, who read these words as I wrote them, sat with me through endless brainstorms, and pushed me to keep writing when I wanted to quit. And to Hart, who helped build the bridges that allowed this book to happen. If this bombs, I'm blaming you guys.

To Lydia, my long-lost friend whose timing on re-entering my life was serendipitous. Thanks for all your support, love, color, and my red wine PTSD.

ACKNOWLEDGMENTS

To Kevin, you crazy animal. Thanks for being my comrade-in-arms. I can't wait to meet your son. And I can't believe you're a dad. Lincoln is lucky to have you. Hopefully he's a bit more sane than us.

To Drew, Matt, Dean, Jimmy, Chuck, my employees, partners, clients, competitors, and plaintiffs at ÄKTA. My life story doesn't exist without each one of you. This was a complex and delicate puzzle, and I appreciate each and every one of you being a part of it. Even to Tony, the unlikely friend I lost.

Many of you lived in my pressure cooker for years and may not have seen the best version of me at times. I want to apologize for the times I pushed too hard, demanded too much, and lost sight of what should have mattered. I will never forget our lunch 'n' learns, beach parties, ringing the sales bell, silly pranks, lip sync karaoke, endless Ping-Pong battles . . . but most of all, the endless pride I felt every time we shipped amazing work, moved into a new office, or when I got to sit back and admire all the wildly talented people I was lucky to spend time with.

To Alex, Amanda, April, Aris, Arturo, Bender, Blake, Brad, Chris, Courtney, Damian, Danielle, David, Diana, Elle, Farah, Garcia, Greg, Haaris, Hartwell, Hemingway, James, JC, JD, Jenna, Jock, Jordan, Kevin, Kyle, Leah, Leo, Luke, Manos, Mark, McCall, McVay, Michael, Monty, Nick, Parker, Paul, Robert, Sara, Scott, Shaw, Shawn, Skoog, Sylvain, Tina, Todd, Tom, Unna, Veronika, Vince, and Weaver. I think that's everyone who asked, *"Will you put me in your book?!"* Just kidding. If I missed anyone, it wasn't intentional—so many people helped me on this journey. I couldn't ask for better, more supportive friends. Thank you.